YOUR ENGINEERED HOUSE

YOUR ENGINEERED HOUSE

Rex Roberts

M. Evans and Company, Inc.
New York, N.Y. 10017

Let's say that a man wants to build a good house for his wife. The most important step toward success will have been to select the right wife.

Let's say that a man wants to write a book about how to build good houses. He has to know what to say. He finds out by making mistakes, recognizing them, living with them, and going on from there. This process is impossible unless his wife will go along too.

Thanks largely to Gordon, but also to Rudy, Mel, Joe, Peter, and Dick, this book got written. I'm afraid there would have been nothing much to say if the inevitable mistakes had caused trouble at home.

Therefore this book will have to be dedicated solely to Caroline.

M. Evans and Company titles are distributed in
the United States by the J.B. Lippincott Company,
East Washington Square, Philadelphia, Pa. 19105
and in Canada by McClelland & Stewart Ltd.,
25 Hollinger Road, Toronto M4B 3G2, Ontario

Copyright © 1964 by Rex Roberts

All rights reserved under International and
Pan American Conventions

Library of Congress Catalog Card Number 64-20782

ISBN 0-87131-110-0 (cloth)
ISBN 0-87131-154-2 (paper)

Designed by Edward Gorey

Manufactured in the United States of America

9 8 6 7 5 4 3 2 1

CONTENTS

6   Contents

YOUR ENGINEERED HOUSE

CHAPTER ONE

What is your engineered house?

1. It's too good for chickens

Building houses for people to live in is the largest single business in this world. The basic human requirements are food, clothing, shelter, and reproduction. In terms of money, which means effort, shelter heads the list. We spend more of our effort for our shelters, our touchable environment, than for anything else, with shelter cost approaching a third of all human effort.

We spend more for shelter than for food, child-rearing, personal adornment, transportation, government, or guns. The very size of this effort seems to have kept it from critical attention. In terms of getting our money's worth we are least critical of shelter, spending more time worrying about entertainment, the destiny of man, skirt lengths, and internal combustion engines.

This book will examine our expenditures for shelter. I believe that most of us are getting about half as much as we should for every dollar spent. This makes me angry, but I have no one to be angry with except myself.

I believe that few houses are as comfortable, as spacious, as pleasant, as handsome, as economical as they might have been had more thought been put into their creation, but who is to do the thinking? The spectacle of a million new houses a year being either inadequate, or too expensive, or both, is an impressive but impersonal tragedy. A million of anything is beyond my comprehension.

One poorly conceived house is something to grieve over, particularly if it happens to be mine. The place where my concern properly begins is with my house. If my house turns out to be less rewarding than it might have been, or more expensive than it should have been, this is not the fault of a professional builder or architect or banker or real-estate salesman. It is my fault.

This book will tell you how to avoid my mistakes. When you build a house, the professional skills may come from others, but the thinking has to be done by you. Your house is a very personal thing, yet it is an expensive and permanent thing, the largest expenditure you will ever make. It is as intimate as your bathrobe, but it can not be thrown away or sent to the laundry. The mistakes in it are yours to live with or to correct at your expense. The successes in it are yours to enjoy. Your house is worth thinking about before you ever start to build it.

With thought, you can have a house that is distinctively yours. It will be a good house, a fun house, a year-round house, a lifetime house. It will be your shelter, your tool for living, and your statement of belief.

Your house, for the same money, will be bigger and better than an equivalent stereotype. The reason for this is simple. In our enormous expenditure for shelter, we are taking an enormous beating. With this kind of money at stake, cheating is not only inevitable but compulsory. A house is the assembly of many things from many vendors. Assuming that each vendor is honest, he still seeks a larger share of our money for himself. Millions of expensive words are thrown at us to explain what we should buy. No dollars are available from anywhere to explain what we do not need to buy.

Although I will explain to you what you do not need to buy, it is not the purpose of this book to persuade you to spend less money. That would be economic heresy. The purpose of this book is to explain to you how, through thoughtful choice of plan and materials, to get more house for the same money.

If each house consumer can get a better bargain for his money, more houses will be consumed, that is, more people will have houses to live in, more money will have been spent, in total, and the houses themselves will be fit to live in.

At this point I want to tell a story. Some years ago, in West Groton, Dick Bissell was putting up a house. I stopped to look the place over. Dick, a friend and fellow carpenter, rested while I looked.

After a while, when I hadn't managed to find anything very flattering to say, Dick remarked, "You have to admit it's too good for chickens."

I admitted it. He frowned. "But not" he said, "quite big enough for cows."

In that moment I started to write this book. Dick had reminded me that chickens can be persuaded to lay eggs in chicken houses, and cows to give milk in cow houses, but the functions required of houses for humans are more complex. In criticizing his own handiwork, Dick expressed his sorrow that most human houses are less satisfactory than they might and should have been. Somehow, in this largest of human expenditures, we are not getting our money's worth.

The way for you, as one family, to get your money's worth is to decide for yourself, without regard for style, type, sales pressure or advertising, what you want and what you need. In doing this, you will be helped by some knowledge of what it takes to make a house work. This is the function of an engineer, and I propose to help you engineer your house.

There isn't any name or type for your engineered house, no pigeonhole to put it in. For one thing, it most emphatically is not "modern." The first modern architect was a man who looked at his family, his needs, his location, his available materials, his tools, his strength, his resources, then built accordingly. He lived a long while ago.

No one has successfully applied a name to his architectural method. I hope no one ever does. Once a design has been named, the name becomes a style and takes precedence over thought. Having become a style, it stultifies the use of new technology to satisfy old desires. It transforms engineers into draftsmen, and honest carpenters into nail drivers. It inhibits our sense of place, our awareness of the weather, even our knowledge of whether we are comfortable or not. Worst of all, it makes us pay for things we neither need nor want.

The world is strewn with examples of misapplied style. If we like we can call these houses "non-engineered." The fact of non-engineering, that is, the absence of thoughtful appraisal even in such simple matters as location and orientation, is obvious at a glance.

You can't tell an engineered house by looking at it, at least not from the outside. What may be right for one person/place combination may be wrong for the man next door. An engineered house is a subtle thing. You have to live in it to find out.

If engineering sounds like a difficult process, let me explain how you go about it. I was raised in Iowa to be a journalist. The principle of this profession was stated for me in Rudyard Kipling's jingle:

I have six faithful serving men,
They taught me all I knew;
Their names are What and Where and When
And How and Why and Who.

When, in pursuit of regular meals, I switched from newspapering to engineering, I retained Kipling's what-where-when-how-why-who prescription as a good approach to any task requiring decision. It fits the thinking of an engineer, who hopes to be at once disciplined and creative. It approximates the way in which the first architect-builder-craftsman-head-of-the-family reached his decisions. It will help me help you approach the problem of getting a pleasant house at the lowest cost.

Kipling's chapter headings now become:

WHAT Is Your House?
WHERE Shall It Be?
WHEN Shall It Be Built?
HOW Will It Be Built?
WHY Will You Build It?
WHO Are You?

To begin this book, and the day, what does it take to get morning sunshine into the kitchen?

2. East, west, north, south

The sun comes up in the east and goes down in the west. Your engineering must begin with this obvious but all-governing fact. If bacon is to be fried by daylight, the kitchen will look southeast. If shaving is to be by daylight, the bathroom will be close by.

Two vital work areas have been located on your previously blank piece of paper. You spend crucial morning minutes at lavatory and stove, and you have given the southeast sun a chance to make those desperate minutes as warm and cheerful as your own nature may permit. The house, at least, will begin its day pleasantly.

A cry, "The eggs are boiling," can be heard through the bathroom wall. Your house, while pleasant, is also efficient.

Since both kitchen and bathroom run on running water, the closer together they are, the shorter the pipes. Your house, already pleasant and efficient, is on its way to being inexpensive.

As the day progresses, your planning follows the sun. By noon it is high in the sky, dead south. Whether you eat lunch, dinner, feed school children, or swallow arthritis pills, the dining table begs to be in the middle of the south side. Next to the kitchen, of course, and at noon the brightest spot in the place.

The sun moves on, and so do you, westward into the living room for a meeting of the garden club. Your guests remark on how warm and sunny the house is, while you smugly refrain from answering that it was planned that way. When the sun glows pink through the southwest windows, the garden club knows that it is time to go home.

Perhaps it is you who come home, unloading in the carport to the northwest, pausing to admire the sunset. Briefly, though, because from the beautiful but violent west comes the most heat and the most wind and in season the most snow.

In the fading light, the living room is being transformed from a part of the outdoors to a place of shelter. You dine, still on the warmed south, then in early dark the fireplace is waiting.

When, after a while, the children go to bed, it could well be in the northwest corner. They are rugged creatures, better off in the cold, and they like to sleep a little later in the morning. So do guests, if you have guests instead of, or besides, children.

Finally off to bed yourselves. A logical place is the northeast corner, where it is moderately warm, moderately quiet, and where the glancing blow of tomorrow's sun will tell you it is time to get up and start the day.

Wielding a pencil on the now not-so-blank piece of paper, you will find that the sun has provided your first tentative house plan, or rather not so much a plan as an arrangement, laid out east, west, north, and south something like this:

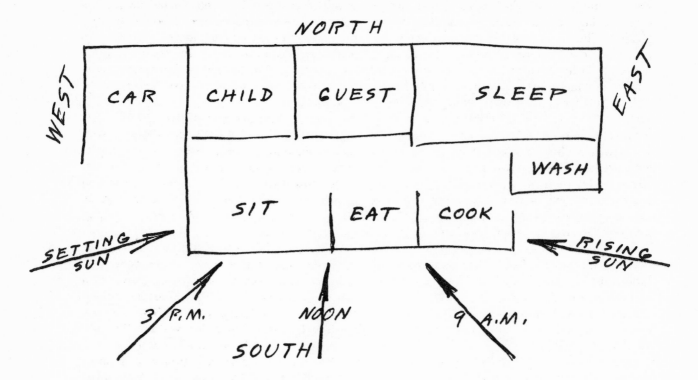

Compass points on the sketch are for the Northern Hemisphere. South of the equator, south and north are reversed, but east and west remain the same.

This rough beginning is based on what the sun does, and you do, from morning to night.

The next consideration is what the sun does from June to December, and what you would like it to do for you in the process. In this sketch, again the compass points are for the Northern Hemisphere.

The difference in angle between winter sun and

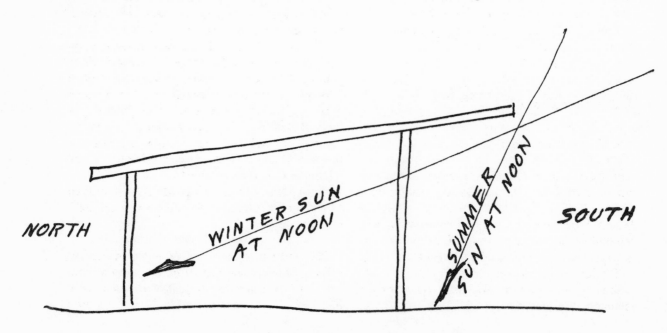

summer sun is a tool which remains unchanged, costs nothing, and can work enormously for your comfort. The amount of difference in angle depends on how far north or south of the equator you live, but for almost all of us there is a useful difference which can be put to work keeping us cool in summer and warm in winter. The angles sketched here are for an average location in a temperate zone—say, Pennsylvania.

There is nothing mysterious, or even clever, about it. In summer we want to keep direct sun out of the house. In winter we want it in. This is exactly what will happen if you put the high side of your roof, and the most glass, facing south in Indiana, and facing north in Peru.

Use of the sun can be checked against an ambitious list of goals. You hope that your house will be warm, dry, light, quiet, clean, useful, spacious, pleasant, and paid for. These goals are points of departure in every decision on what your house shall be.

Some decisions will involve compromise, that is, they will contribute strongly toward one goal but at some expense to another. Use of the sun involves no such compromise. All goals win. No goals lose.

I believe that proper orientation to the sun is the most important of all decisions to be made. It's easy. It helps with everything. It costs nothing. All you need do is observe the sun's behavior and put it to work.

The next step in engineering your house is to see what else you can get for nothing.

3. Uphill and downhill

The behavior of your first bargain, the sun, is predictable. Your next big bargain is scenery, which is whatever you choose to call it and thus not definable. Scenery can be anything from a fine view of the neighbor's wash to a peek at Mount Penobscot. To many people scenery is something they see when away from home. This is expensive scenery. The bargain kind is the stuff which is all around you.

Scenery may include the long view from a mountain top, and then again it may be a tree or a bush or a boulder. From the outside looking in, it can be an arrangement of house and hillside and grape arbor that makes you want to meet the people who live there. From the inside looking out, it can be the window-framed view of a maple tree that makes you happy to be where you are.

Scenery is the aggregate of features that give character to a landscape. As was the case with "non-engineering," scenery can best be appreciated when we see it being destroyed. To observe non-scenery, watch the bulldozers work on a "housing" development. With all features gone, the sense of place is gone, and with it anything definable as scenery.

Dollars have been spent to destroy scenery, as if, having cost nothing, it was of no value. The bulldozer is a wonderful tool in the hands of a master craftsman. But to get valuable scenery at no cost, we will keep what we have, disturbing it as little as possible. We will use the bulldozer to build roads, not destroy scenery.

Scenery is two-directional: from outside looking in and from inside looking out. Since even the hardiest of us spend more time inside than out, the inside-looking-out scenery is the more important.

In saying this, I have said that you will worry first about how the world looks to you, then later about how you look to the world. This tells you where to put your scenery, or rather, where to put yourself in relation to the scenery which was there before you came.

If there is scenery all around you to look at, that's wonderful, but if there is only one thing you want to see, let it be outside the kitchen windows. If there is a second thing of pleasant aspect, let it be seen from the living room; if a third thing, from the sewing room, and so on, bearing in mind that the function of scenery is for the visual delight of your waking hours, wherever they may be spent.

If there are things you positively don't want to look at, you can always hide them behind the carport.

Like the sun, scenery can be put to work, but whereas sun-use emerges from known and constant facts, scenery-use benefits from your own imagination. No two desirable house locations are exactly alike, and certainly no two families are alike. Given a beloved site which does not conform to the ideal assumptions of this book, scenery may influence your plan more than anything else except the sun.

You will begin by thinking about scenery from the inside of your house, looking out. Which parts of the environment do you prefer, and which do you want to see at different times of the day? For instance, one decision which everyone must make is what to do about the sunset. It can be a gorgeous part of the scenery, and you get it for nothing. It happens at family time. But it happens in the hot, cold, windy and snowy west. One way out of this dilemma is to create a sunset place, which will let you take the west when it is wonderful, or leave it alone when it is dangerous.

Trees are bound to influence your house plan and its location. They take a lifetime to grow or a fortune to move. With your pencil poised over a second sheet of paper, it is easier to move yourself. Here are some of the things you might be thinking about as you locate yourself among the existing trees.

No shade wanted in the morning, just trees to look at. A graceful tree to filter the ten o'clock sunlight. No trees obstructing the long view. Solid shade against the mid-afternoon hot time. A gap through which the sunset can be seen, then windbreak trees to the northwest. Since in your dreams you can have anything you want, let there be some really big trees in the background, just to bring everything down to size.

A sketch of this situation would work out something like:

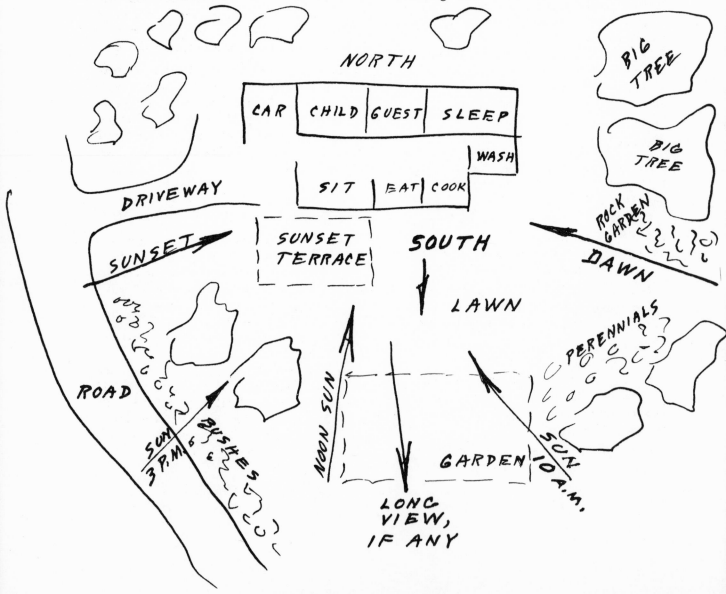

This is a dream, to be sure, but dreams are lying around everywhere, waiting to be realized. Starting with this particular batch of scenery, the house located itself. There is full sun on the terrace for morning coffee. Full sun again at eleven o'clock, the best sunbathing time. Shade is available against the afternoon heat, and naturally there is a breeze from the west. The arriving guest at sunset time quickly feels at home.

If you are gregarious, you have the reassuring nearness of the road. If you are retiring, you have a screen of shrubs. If indolent, you have at least three good places for a hammock, and if athletic, there is a lawn and a croquet set. If you are hungry, the kitchen is handy, and for those who just can't stand it anywhere very long, there is a waiting automobile.

Scenery is what you see from where you live. If your scenery is to cost you nothing, you will leave it where it is, and if that scenery already has character, you will make only minor modifications. You will move yourself around, move the house around, but you will not move the scenery around until you have lived with it for a while as it is.

4. Goals

You hope that your house will be warm, dry, light, quiet, clean, useful, spacious, pleasant, and paid for.

Warm means that you can control temperature rather than put up with it. Warm when and where you want it warm and cool when and where you want it cool.

Dry means not only that the roof doesn't leak, but the floor doesn't either. It means that condensation will not be destructive. It means that your house will take the trouble out of wet weather and leave only the fun of it.

Light means the enjoyment of dawn, daylight, dusk, and darkness, as they occur. It means maximum use of natural light and effective control of artificial light.

Quiet means freedom from irritating noise. It means that assorted noisemakers may live to-gether in peace, and that desired sounds may be well heard.

Clean means freedom from undesired clutter and unwanted foreign material. It means relative ease in keeping your house that way.

Useful means that you, the occupant, will be more important than the house; that you will be able to work and play as the owner rather than the servant of the building.

Spacious means that the controlled portion of the world which is your own shall be somewhat larger in proportion to your dimensions than a bird's nest is to the bird, or a fox's den to a fox. It shall seem less crowded with occupants than a chicken house is with chickens, or a barn with cows.

Pleasant means that the joint can jump with jive or dream with Debussy, that it will be so nice to come home to, that it will have warmth beyond function, and satisfaction beyond reason.

Paid for means that the realization of these goals has not imposed a crippling sacrifice upon you, such as staying too long away from home in order to get home paid for. It means that you will get your money's worth, and that the initial cost of your estate will be low enough to let you begin to build it now.

Here we have specified what the structure is required to be and do. In designing a machine, I begin with a "specification," which is nothing more than a set of goals. Frequently the goals contradict each other, with one goal saying that the machine's base be heavy and another goal saying that it be light. These contradictions result in compromise.

Successful house planning also involves some compromises, but most of your goals will aid rather than defeat each other, provided you do not try to force them into a preconceived architectural style. To show how goals may aid each other, here is a sketch drawn with just about as few lines as possible.

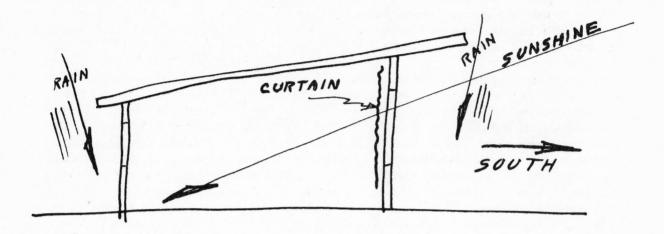

If you had to live in one room, nothing much simpler than this could be devised. The basic structure includes a high wall and windows to the south, a single roof plane that slopes upward, again to the south, a low wall with smaller windows to the north, two end walls, and heavy curtains which may be drawn across the southern windows.

Several goals have been met already. Your house is warm when you need warmth; cool when you want it to be cool. When rain falls, it is pleasantly outside your windows. In any season, available sunlight is used or not, as you please. Because of its shape, your house, or rather, your room, is acoustically excellent. That's four goals down and five to go.

To make the house clean and useful, further work may be required, but nothing in the design so far has done these goals harm. The room, in any size, has a built-in feeling of spaciousness. Night-closed or day-lit, winter or summer, the room is pleasant. As for the last goal, because the structure is simple, it will be easy to pay for.

Perhaps if you were a hermit, the design of your house would be complete right now. Since your requirements are probably more compli-

cated than those of a hermit, more decisions must be made. As your decisions become specific, one goal may be satisfied but others harmed. You may be forced to retreat from a decision which in the beginning seemed brilliant.

It saves time to test each decision against all goals at once, rather than work first toward one, then another. However, a start must be made somewhere. I choose to begin thinking about the hard facts of the structure itself, in this order:

5. Upstairs and downstairs
6. Arrangement for use
7. Shape
8. Heat
9. Light
10. Air
11. Noise
12. The inside
13. The outside
14. Flexibility
15. Efficiency
16. Pleasure
17. Where do you go from here?

5. Upstairs and downstairs

How many floors is your house going to have? Before you give your answer, let me remind you that the simplest answer to any such question is inevitably one. If your answer is to be any number other than one, there will have to be a reason.

A decision to have more than one floor can be reached for any one of several reasons, but the number of such reasons is shrinking. About all the reasons left are site use, orientation, special family needs, special hobby needs, special emotional needs, or the plain statement that you want it that way, if you honestly know your own mind, is as good a reason as any.

Unfortunately, the how-many-floors-question is so fraught with built-in notions that in the argument, reason gets left behind. Architects lose their clients, and clients their architects, in heated debate over the difference between reason and prejudice, or rather, who is doing the thinking and who is just sitting there.

What is a floor? The usual choices for domestic structures, one, two, three or more floors, are called different names in different countries. So that we may communicate with each other, I will lay down some definitions.

A "ground floor" will be taken to mean any floor level which gives access directly to or immediately above ground level. By this definition, a house built on a hillside might have two or even three ground floors, depending on the steepness of the hill.

An "upper floor" will be any floor level reached by one or more flights of stairs from a ground floor, that is, any floor where in case of fire you have to jump out a window to reach ground. The phrases first floor, second floor and so on are variously interpreted and will only confuse us.

A "basement," or, to be specific I should say a "full basement," is located in a hole dug in the ground, from which stairs must be climbed to reach ground level. Most of a basement's vertical dimension is below ground, though it can admit light by the device of raising the "ground" floor somewhat.

A "semi-basement" is a type of ground floor which has an earth-retaining wall on one side, but appears at ground level on the other. The definitive difference is that water which runs into a semi-basement will run out again, but water which runs into a full basement will not.

An "attic" is the interior space created by the combination of a steep roof and a flat ceiling below it.

So much for the definitions. Your next concern is how much space you need on each of these floors, if there are to be more than one. I have tried this for myself. Estimating space requirements for all activities of the day and year, and listing the most efficient location for each, I find that everything has gone into the ground floor. In terms of most convenient use, all other floors are blank.

If you will make a list for yourself, I think you will find that anything you want to do can be done more efficiently on a ground floor. Therefore, moving anything off the ground floor will involve compromise between goals. Thus a square foot of space on the ground floor can be called standard, or value one, and a square foot on any other floor is sub-standard, or value less than one. To repeat, if your house is to have more than one floor, there will have to be a good reason.

Depending on circumstance, there can be lots of good reasons. An obvious reason is a building site so small that multiple floors are required to make enough room. This reason applies only to urban centers where land prices are staggering.

A second good reason involves a site where the view is improved by placing the viewer nine feet higher up. In this case the daytime rooms probably belong on the upper floor, a fact which may or may not represent compromise.

Another reason is the conviction that a high house carries more prestige value than a low one, and thus more satisfaction to the owner. This is purely a feeling and is not debatable. The feeling comes with interesting variations. A friend of mine, clergyman by trade, told me that he enjoys living and working on an upper floor, because it lets him look out over the rooftops of his neighbors. I myself enjoy looking out of my office windows into the tops of trees, which is quite a different emotion, especially since ground level is on the other side. I believe that the best answer to these height wishes is to put the house on rising ground.

The most common reason for an upper floor is an emotional need to walk upstairs to bed. There are people who have no trouble in a ground-floor motel but find it difficult to sleep "downstairs" at home. The structural reasons for placing bedrooms "upstairs" are historical and have all vanished. All the remaining reasons, such as fire safety, to mention only one, indicate that if there are to be multiple floors, the bedrooms should be on the lowest floor.

Fire does not approach the automobile as a taker of life, but it remains a good sound thoughtful and emotional reason for sleeping downstairs. Firewise, if you must have multiple floors, put the waking hour rooms upstairs. It is a journalistic convention to say that the fire victims were "trapped by flames." The words have a dramatic ring. In most cases, let's say nineteen out of twenty, that isn't what happened. What happened was that the victims were suffocated by smoke before they woke up. Smoke rises, and the higher up you are sleeping, whether in hotel, mansion, or tenement, the smokier it gets. Flames burn upward too, but the smoke they make gets there a lot quicker.

With all reason telling us that bedrooms should be downstairs, emotion remains a hard fact. We spend a third of our lives in bed, though asleep most of that time. I know a man who worked out his own compromise. He admits the validity of all this reasoning, then walks up four steps to his bedroom level, and is content.

Small departures from a single floor level are useful in many ways. Three steps up to an office or two steps down to a living room contribute much to the desired mood. They represent compromise in moving pianos and wheel chairs, but otherwise not much harm is done. An area broken by minor changes in level remains, by my definition, a single floor.

The multiple-floor house is one in which one usable floor is built directly above another. At best this is a compromise, involving extra work in building it and extra work in living there. There has to be a reason. In my opinion the best reason of all is to take advantage of terrain. Here is an attractive and not uncommon example:

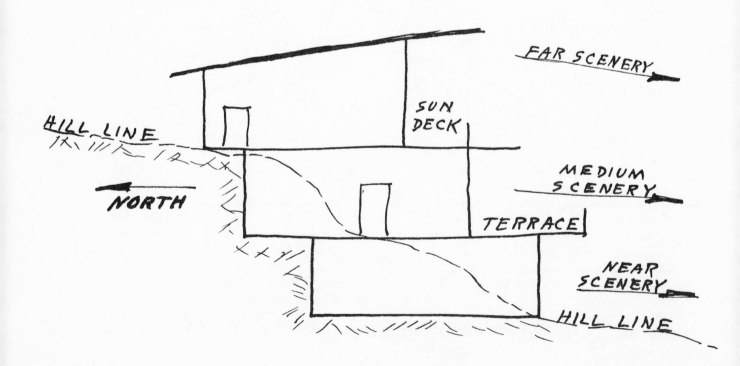

An abrupt hillside has been put to work, providing three ground-level floors. If the garage is to the right, or south, the public entrance is on the lowest floor. Two stairways later, the world has been well lost. If the road and garage are to the north, the situation may be even better, with all floors well lost, and stairs for the tired homecomer to walk down instead of up. Either situa-tion can be delightful, with the choice depending on terrain, road location, and the preferred scenery.

The so-called split-level house, a combination of two ground floors and one upper floor, when properly sited makes use of a gentle slope, like this:

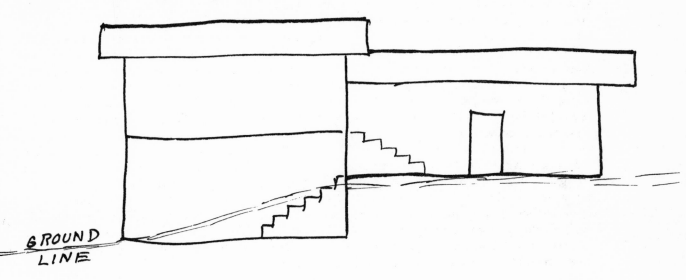

The design of this house is suited only to a small, sloping lot. Regrettably, the design became a style. Millions of split-levels have been forced upon level ground, where the arrangement makes no sense at all.

A medium slope suggests an inherently simpler and more useful design with two ground floors.

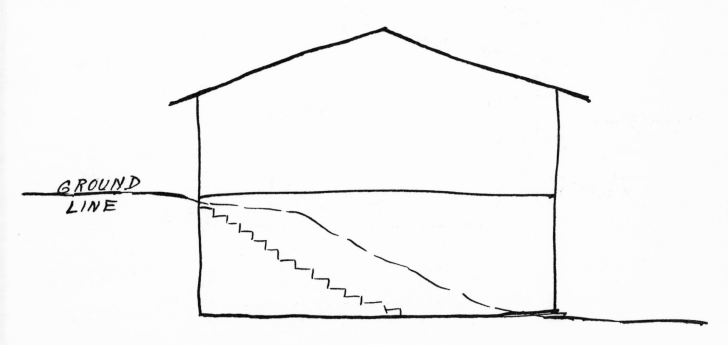

If the road is on the left, the passerby sees a single-floor house, and if on the right, multiple floors. The living room can be on either floor, according to mood, scenery, compass directions, and the occupants' desire for privacy. There is a house next door to me, built in 1735, which has two living rooms, one up, one down, one north, one south, both exactly at ground level, and the happy owner can take his choice.

In each of these three multiple-level sketches, use of a hillside, steep or gentle, has been the motivating reason. Each sketch shows the ground dug away to some extent, though later on I will suggest that no digging need have been done.

Having explored some reasons for multiple levels, let's take a look at non-reason. The full-basement house, built on level ground, looks like this:

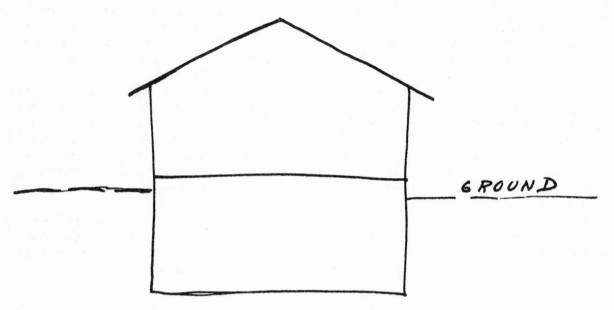

You are looking at the most common of all multiple-level designs, and the one for which I can find no reason whatever. I have stared at this design from every angle. I have tried to find some justification for it—structural, technical, useful, cultural, emotional, or economic. Why anyone, nowadays, should dig a big hole in the ground and then put a house in it escapes me completely.

I know what the reasons used to be, but the historical and technical reasons for basements have long since disappeared. There is not one single thing on my list of day-round and year-round activities that I would put in a basement unless the basement were already there. To be sure, you can use a basement if it's yours and you're stuck with it. Once the potato bin, coal bin, and jam shelves have quit working, it's better to fix up a basement for something else than to let the rats move in. But it's expensive. I

wouldn't do it again if I had the whole job to do over.

The full basement violates every one of our goals. Only with effort and expense can it be kept anywhere near as warm, dry, light, quiet, clean, useful and pleasant as the same amount of space on a ground floor can be for less money.

The cost of a basement keeps adding up in many ways. First the builder has to dig a hole, overturning gravel and rock which were better left undisturbed. He casts that material aside, covering good topsoil and making a mess of everything, then comes back later and wonders where to put it.

The builder then has to line the hole with earth-retaining walls, which to be of equal quality are more expensive than walls above ground. Having dug a well, the builder now hopes that the walls of his well will keep water out. He also has to figure a way to get light, air, and people in, and such furniture and equipment as the basement is supposed to contain.

He winds up with space which is sub-sub-standard, or value far below one, yet it has cost more, all told and by the time it has become usable at all, than equal room above ground. I'm stumped. The emotional need to get onto an upper floor I can understand, but when it comes to basements, I can't even think of an emotional reason.

The visible evidence seems to point toward a house which is all or mostly ground floor, possibly an upper floor, and certainly no basement, but I'm still not quite satisfied. It is not safe to abandon any widespread practice without trying to understand how it got to be that way.

The history of upper floors and how they acquired their present inertia is easy to understand. The first houses were set high on tree trunks or posts, for safety. When man learned to build fence, he could make a larger area safe from tigers, and his house came down to the ground. More convenient that way.

Some time thereafter man started building his houses higher in a race for prestige. Prestige-hunting has been around a long while, and a castle is higher than a hut. Though castles attract the enemy, they make nice places to watch for his approach.

At various times upper floors have also been used for methods of defense, such as shooting arrows, throwing rocks, and pouring boiling water. In fact, the hot water method of discouraging unwelcome visitors was the origin of the second floor overhang which persists in many houses. I still get an uneasy feeling down the back of my neck when standing before one of these places. The dropping of garbage from an upper window was another popular method of indicating disapproval.

In these gentler times, with defense no longer an object, many people continue to refer to the first upper floor as the "first" (meaning important) floor. The owners live there, in genteel inaccessibility. The servants live on the lower floor, where the kitchen is, and it is the servants, where there are any left, who do most of the stair climbing.

This situation became exaggerated back when well-to-do men lived in cities, where they chose to stay as close as possible to others of the well-to-do. They built like this:

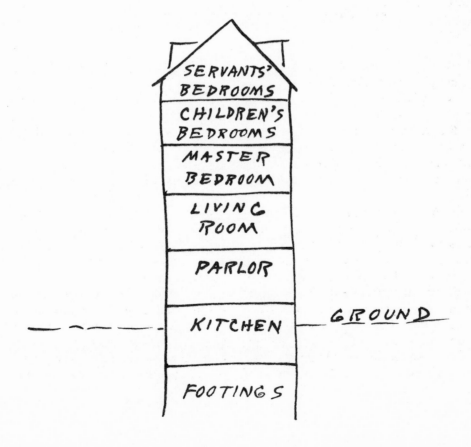

Here the servants cooked in the basement, lugged the food up two flights to the boss's dining room, and from the kitchen, late at night, climbed five flights to their well-earned rest. Roughly a third of the volume inside the house was devoted to stairways. Another third was devoted to servants, all of whom had bulging leg muscles.

Unable to tolerate the airlessness, lightlessness, and general discomfort· of his town house for long at a time, the well-to-do man fled to the country. Taking his habits with him, he continued to build high houses. A common rule of behavior is that in "getting away from it all," a man finds or creates an environment as much as possible like the one he seeks to escape.

Another man of prestige, the working sailor turned shipowner, built his house high for a view of the ocean on which he spent most of his life. There was even a special room at the top from which his wife, and after retirement he himself, could watch for the vessels' safe return. Thus began still another architectural style which was lifted out of context and carried far inland.

Generally speaking, men of prestige have built high houses for one reason or another. Perhaps the universal reason was that they could afford to do so and didn't mind having other people know it. Though this attitude has become less fashionable, it is not surprising that prestige and height are firmly associated in the minds of many people.

Men of less prestige also built high houses, for a more practical reason. They wanted to keep warm. A tall house, roughly cubical in shape, exposes less of its surface per unit volume than any other form. This fact was important when no thermal insulation was available, and fuel to be had only with axe or pick.

It was nice to build a cooking fire in the kitchen, which was the only room used much in winter, and have it take a bit of the chill off the room above. There is a popular notion to the effect that "heat rises." Heat doesn't rise, it goes in all directions, but warm air rises, and a hole in the ceiling will let a little warm air through from the stove below. Notice in passing why the bedroom came to be upstairs. There was just enough heat up there to let you get safely under the covers.

With technology and availability of manufactured materials, practical reasons for height have vanished. Prestige remains, if you think so, and the desire to create landmarks, or perhaps simply to reach for the sky.

Historical reasons for wanting to go underground are somewhat harder to trace. When man first discovered that he possessed the technology and tools to emerge from his cave, he was probably glad to get out of it, though I imagine many felt homesick for water dripping from the roof. In any event, the cave man had not dug his cave. It was there, he found it, and its entrance was in the side of a hill. It would not have occurred to him to dig a hole in level ground and live in it.

Possibly the first basement was designed as a dungeon for the purpose of storing political prisoners where their shrieks could not be heard. Succeeding generations, running short of political prisoners, found the old dungeons a fine place to store wine, where it was protected against theft and against sudden temperature changes. In the meantime the wineless and prisoner-less peasant got along fine without a basement.

With more people and thus more crime, basements acquired purpose—for the criminal to hide or plot in with no light showing, for the honest man to hide either his valuables or himself when outnumbered by criminals, for the general purpose of doing anything which for some reason it were better that other people didn't know about. Notice, please, that all basements so far have been completely below ground and the farther the better. The basement with windows defeats any point one might have for being underground.

North America, with its potatoes, may have provided the first practical reason for a poor but honest man to have a basement. The fairly constant low temperature which never goes below freezing, the high humidity which keeps the spuds from drying out, the dim light (one tiny window is permissible) which deters them from sprouting—all are exactly right for the storage of potatoes, whose earliest charm was that they could be kept all winter and still leave something to eat next spring.

The potato cellar began modestly, with a hole dug inside one corner of the house's foundation. These conditions were not right for smoked meat, which could stand freezing and was left in the smokehouse, but when the science of preserving fresh vegetables and fruit came along, the potato cellar had another occupant. Under pressure from hundreds of glass jars containing a winter's balanced diet, the cellar began to grow, and now there had to be a stairway in order to get there conveniently from the kitchen.

The idea back of central heating was to have one stove to tend instead of many. In the absence of any means of circulation except the fact that warm air or water will rise and cool air or water will fall, that one stove, now called a furnace, had to be down below. Once again the potato cellar was enlarged, becoming less suitable for potatoes, in order to make room for the furnace. Some of the early furnaces burned wood, which had to be carried downstairs from the woodshed, but coal keeps all right underground, so the coal bin was added, then later a mechanical stoker to feed coal into the furnace. Petroleum fuel took care of that rather quickly, with the oil tank sitting beside the now unused coal bin.

With all of this machinery to be serviced, you need more light in the basement to see your way around, and you need room to add pipes from the furnace, so you keep digging and add some windows to the dungeon. Presently to everyone's delight the washing machine arrives, but with no place to put it upstairs, the laundry sits incongruously between oil tank, furnace, coal bin, a few leftover potatoes, and the now empty jam shelves.

Then along came forced circulation of heat. The principal function of the basement had been to put the stove below us, but with forced circulation you can put it anywhere you like. Grocery stores already have left the jam shelves and the potato bin to gather dust, and the basement has lost any function it ever may have had. My personal conviction is that the basement never had a particularly good reason, but sort of grew on us with one thing leading to another.

In any event, as of now I no longer store a year's supply of potatoes. I have not yet had to defend myself from attacking savages. My natural eagerness for prestige is not affected by distance above ground. I do not depend on one stove to keep me warm. I do have an attractive hillside, but there will be more on that subject later.

For the moment, I commend one floor to your attention as the right number with which to begin planning your house, though more may be added as we go along. For the sake of simplicity our thinking and sketching will continue with one floor as the point of departure.

6. Arrangement for use

This is the horizontal arrangement department, or which-end-is-which. With one floor to deal with, you can visualize what goes next to what on one piece of paper. How can your house be useful to you, as well as warm, dry, light, quiet, clean, spacious, pleasant, and paid for? Briefly, what is your house supposed to do?

We are not yet looking for a precise floor plan showing dimensions of walls and partitions. What we want now is an arrangement of uses. The number of uses to which your house may at one time or another be put is unpredictably large. The number of possible arrangements of these uses is infinite, but that's all right because all you need is one good one. To find it, you begin with the predictable uses, emphasizing those which you believe most important, and arrange them in a pattern where their relationship will be agreeable to you.

Your problem is exactly opposite to that of the architect who is hired to produce, for mass consumption, a house plan suited to the average family. He is inhibited by his knowledge that the average family, even as the average man, is a statistic. It doesn't exist. The living family engages through its life and growth in an enormous number of activities, with no two families ever being more than very superficially alike.

The number of requirements placed upon houses has grown so much that no one house can possibly include them all. Fortunately, neither you nor anyone else wants them all, but what you do want, you want all the way. You want it to be good. You can afford to have it good if you're willing to decide between the uses you want and the ones you can do without.

It will help us to remember uses if we look at where they came from and how they developed. What happened to houses, not in terms of how they look, but in terms of what they are used for, was this: The one-room hut, cabin, or tepee had one function, shelter from the weather. Within this shelter the family cooked, ate, sat, and slept. The outdoors was used for everything else.

As it grew, the cabin was divided into four use areas called kitchen, dining room, living room, and bedroom. The four-room, four-use house was established as a basic pattern. All other functions were met either by the outdoors or an assortment of outbuildings. With each new function arrived a new outbuilding, specifically designed for its task, until the standard four-use house was tiny beside the barn and its growing brood of useful shelters.

Then several things happened to increase the importance, size, and use-density of the house. Water under pressure, plumbing, and the flush toilet created the bathroom. Here vanished one outbuilding which, though inconvenient, had served as a useful retreat.

Later a dramatic shift from farm to factory as a way of earning a living destroyed the barn and most of the other outbuildings, leaving no place for the host of side activities which they had sheltered. The demise of the barn served to overcrowd the house, with all part-time activities from carpentry to trumpet practice being attempted first in the kitchen, from where they were forced into the ever growing basement. The obvious solution of adding a low cost, barn-style utility wing to the house had trouble getting started, possibly because it looked "countrified," or because while people had to walk to the factory, urban lot sizes were much too small.

Central heating brought even more tasks inside the house, where they could be performed close to the furnace, not to mention away from the neighbors' curiosity. The mass move from country to town had eliminated even the outdoors as a useful place, until the automobile rolled people out of the jammed city, increased lot sizes and brought the outdoors back to feeble life.

The house, once required to provide only areas for cooking, eating, sitting, and sleeping, must now provide suitable quarters for almost everything we feel like doing. In an attempt to define more use-areas, architects call them playroom, mud room, workshop, hobby room, rumpus room, family room, studio. All of these names are epitaphs on the tombstone of the barn. Many of these uses are now jammed most inconveniently into existing attics and basements. I contend that the use of attics and basements for these purposes is a device of improvisation; that they get used not because they are suitable, but because they are there.

Not only are the old needs still with us; more have been added. For one thing, since we now live by numbers, made out in triplicate, an office is required. Sound by electronics has made it difficult for the family to sit together in the living room, therefore a noise room is advisable. The world's love affair with the automobile has led many people to believe, though I do not, that the auto need be housed in greater luxury than the horse ever was. Hence the built-in garage. Last, a machine room is needed for convenient housing of all the pumps, motors, burners and blowers that make the house run.

The obvious conclusion is that houses aren't big enough. Where most houses have shrunk in floor area, they should have grown in order to accommodate the demands placed upon them. Therefore your house must be designed so that you can have plenty of use room at a price you can afford.

The how of that will be explored later, but the basic idea has already been suggested. We are in the habit of discussing building costs in terms of dollars per square foot. This ignores the fact that some of the square feet in your house will be very expensive; many others can be very cheap. The trick is to get more room by holding down the expensive footage while splurging on the low-dollar areas.

Let me now pretend to be the head of an average family, which I have already said doesn't exist, and try to arrange a house for myself. I would prefer the exploratory mistakes to be mine, rather than yours. The eventual successes of your own special arrangement will be yours.

To see how much room may be required, I will try a simple arrangement of obvious uses. By the rules of the game, this is pure speculation.

I do not know where the road is or the scenery is. The only thing my sketch can relate to for sure is south. I know where south is. It's always at the bottom of the page, with north at the top, the way maps are drawn.

The first lines do not represent walls. They indicate family movement and relationship of function. Beginning with kitchen to the south, the first try turns out to be a sort of rough oval, like this:

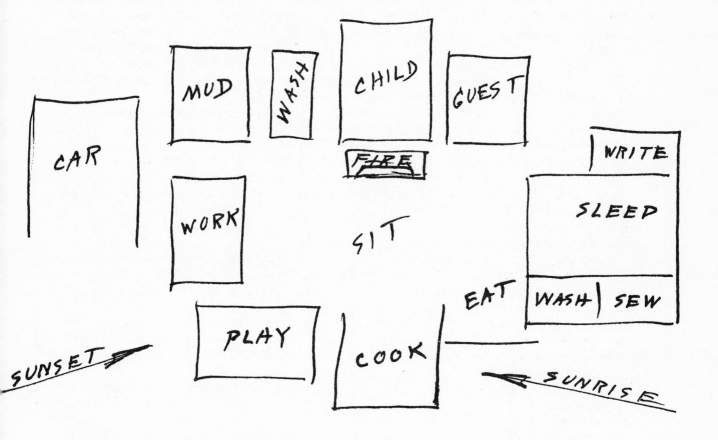

Stepping back to take a look, I notice that every function seems to want at least a corner sticking into the sunlight, and at least the possibility of an outside door. This left a hole in the middle, where the living room, which I had forgotten, became a hallway between other functions. Going round the oval, the sequence of uses is fair for a starter, but only fair.

One thing looks good. The kitchen is the command post, the pilot's cabin, with sunshine all day long. Even so, it may be too far from the carport, for lugging groceries. Much else is wrong. Eat is in the wrong place, because it separates cook and wash. Play doesn't need that choice afternoon area. Move it where work is now and

move work to where it can touch both car and mud. I forgot the machine room, which wants to be somewhere not too far from the plumbing. Sleeping areas are too close together for my taste. Plumbing areas are too far apart. If the road is to the west, where is the front door? Pretty bad, now that we look at it.

From studying this not too successful sketch, what did I learn about my own feeling for arrangement? I learned that the barn functions (vehicle storage, outdoor clothes and gear, physical work, physical play) tend to group themselves, as if they belonged in a separate or semiseparate building.

I found that the word bedroom is too limiting.

What my pencil keeps wanting to draw could better be called private room, a sort of apartment, whether large or small, in which the comparative privacy desired for resting the mind in sleep can be extended to using it in work.

Pursuing the private room idea, I found that to be effective it must be repeated for each generation to be housed. Assuming the presence of either children or parents, I will love them more if their private rooms are some distance away from mine.

I learned that if too many activities abut my living room, it becomes overflow space, a hallway, a battleground rather than a meeting ground. With the privacy function and the play function removed to separate apartments, the living room can stand comfortably between, getting back to its proper social function, a pleasant place for people to sit and enjoy each other.

I now realize that the name living room has not been helpful. We live all over the place. Let's call it social room. Now that I know what this area is for, what other functions can be left in close relationship?

The most social thing we do is eat. From campfire through banquet hall and back to breakfast nook this one fact of society has never changed. The social status of the cook, however, has had its ups and downs. Now it's up, possibly up to stay. With no servants left for most of us, and with cooking regarded as a social art rather than a menial task, it is difficult to draw hard lines between the functions of cook, eat, and sit. In terms of dividing the house into use groups, we're back to the big stove-warmed kitchen, where it seems they had the right idea after all.

I'll try a sketch of how the use groups shape up now.

From this sketch I have learned that what I really want is four houses, or semi-houses, with the four probably, although not necessarily, in contact with each other. I observe that the social house is the old basic house, less outbuildings, and with bedrooms enlarged into semi-houses of their own.

I also observe that all four houses enjoy both north and south exposure, and that no house seems particularly willing to give up either. For a moment I am convinced that the arrangement I seek will run east and west, a hundred yards long and one room wide. It might come to that, but for now I will elect to favor the social house with both north and south exposure, then see what I can do with the others.

In order to pull the four houses back into one, some compromises will be needed. I'll give up my rights to the physical playroom, letting the children own it. I will undertake to carry groceries to the kitchen, and I will then walk back to my own workshop, with the resulting arrangement something like this:

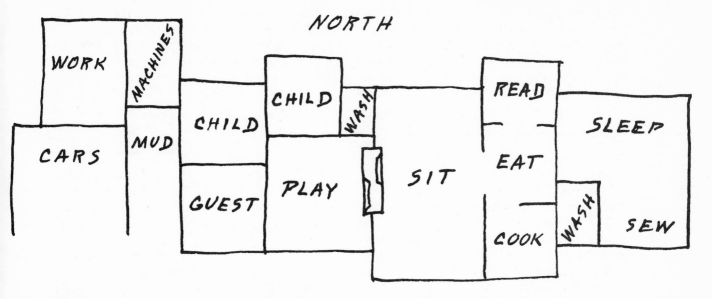

Here the four houses have been joined almost without alteration. I moved the playroom from the barn into private house Two, and I compromised by calling my own office the library. Placing the forgotten function of read next to eat is not a bad idea. I know one family that combined the two, placing four walls of books around the dining table so that points under discussion could be settled almost without getting up.

Though it isn't fair to show detail this early in the game, I couldn't resist sketching back-to-back fireplaces in social room and playroom. The opportunity was too good to miss. Obviously the playroom now becomes a junior grade social room, not too far from the food supply, and is available in case of an overflow crowd.

The machine room's noisemakers are handy for servicing, but I don't like the expensively spread out plumbing. Also I'm not too happy about my own workshop being on the extreme northwest corner. I do have some question about placing the adult section farther from the road than the non-adult section.

Leaving the road to the west, reversing private houses One and Two, and juggling a little, I come up with this suggestion:

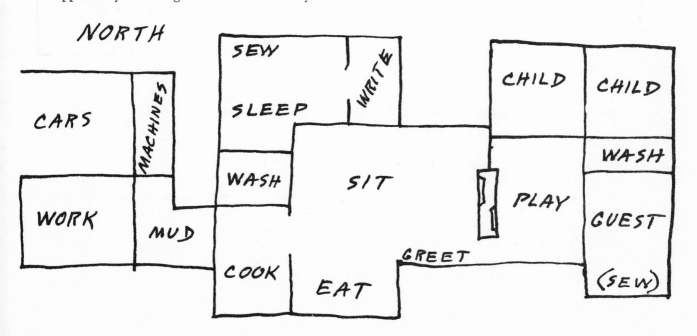

Not too bad. Hot water now gets to the kitchen quicker than before. Night traffic doesn't disturb the children. The cook can see who's coming to the front door. However, by being cramped back to the social house, private house One has lost most of its charm and character. Sewing, for instance, has to be done in the coldest corner, or moved completely to the guest room.

Now I'll try one of the tricks of the game. If, without changing a line, I move the road from west to east and turn the whole thing mirror image end for end, here is what happens:

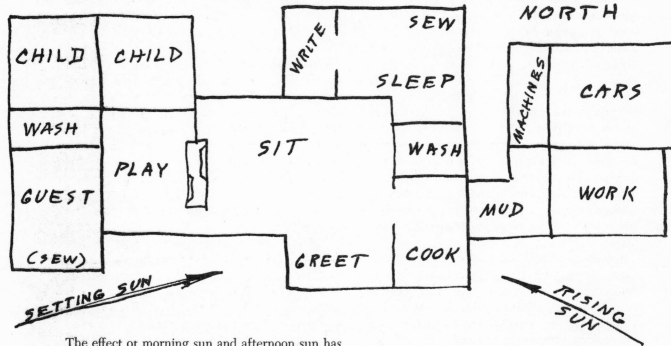

The effect or morning sun and afternoon sun has been reversed, to the benefit of many uses. Kitchen on the southeast, children northwest, social room at its best in the afternoon. Carport gets morning sun. Private house One is only a little improved. It continues to suffer by the loss of southern exposure.

Leaving the road to the east, I'll try once more. This time I'll grab the good spots for myself, assuming that I want to be next the road, have the most sunshine and the most room to work. It might turn out this way:

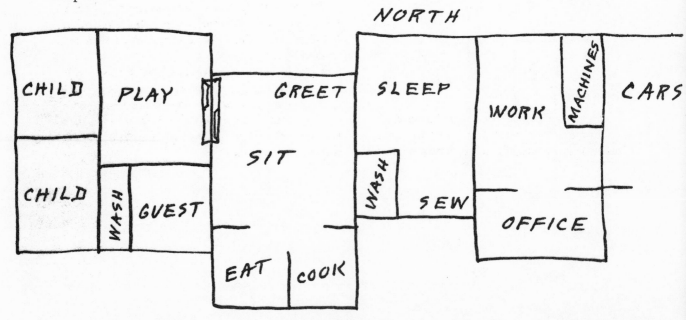

There are use arrangements here that I rather like. What I did was put my own office in the barn, where it has room to grow and is well removed from the social house, yet convenient for fixing teeth or selling insurance.

The general symmetry of this layout has its advantages too. I can move the road back to the west, turn the house end for end, with nothing much changed as long as north and south are not disturbed. Thus far it would seem that a clear division between the four use houses works out well.

These exercises in arrangement could go on and on, but to no point, because the sketches here all assume the same non-existent average family and the same set of obvious uses. All these arrangements result in houses of about the same size and shape. The game begins to get interesting when the house being arranged is specifically yours, with you supplying your own special use list.

Special uses have so far been omitted: the music rooms, sun decks, greenhouses, studios, dark rooms, which make your life something more than a matter of survival. If you think so, a special use can be more important than cook-eat-sit-sleep, causing your planning to begin with a different set of assumptions. We will look next at some of the ways in which special uses might affect your house.

7. Shape

I believe that the shape of your house will best be determined by what you want to do in it. Please do not arbitrarily select an exterior style,

then force your family into it like butter into a crock. I have little patience with those who begin a house plan anywhere other than from the inside.

I have even less patience with the opposite extreme, which is the business of doing something unusual for the sake of being different. This practice is bound to be expensive, and because it didn't start with a pattern of uses, it accomplishes nothing.

Design from use treads most of the time down the middle of the road. It is neither conformity nor non-conformity. It ignores both. In this frame of mind, you are willing to undergo the risk of being different only if it is going to get you more for your money. If you admit to a special interest, here is a solid reason for shaping your house accordingly. If the desired shape remains essentially buildable, your house will cost no more, yet it will be more useful to you and therefore worth more.

For what do you live? You might be an outdoor gardener, orchid grower, interpretive dancer, gourmet, party-giver, musician, photographer, or painter in oils. You might be gymnast, woodcarver, bibliophile, botanist, butterfly collector, or the best billiards player in town.

In the interest of earning a living at home, you might be a lawyer, accountant, optometrist, real-estate salesman, or manufacturer of special-purpose ball bearings. As a sideline, you might cut semi-precious stones, cast dentures, make and sell horse-radish, assemble audio amplifiers, or deal in tropical fish.

You probably prefer to eat and sleep at home, yet you want to do something else there too. The list of special things you might want to do is remarkably long.

To take a non-strenuous example, let's say you are an addicted sunbather. You're in a fairly cool climate where the family sometimes needs protection from wind, and you prefer to sunbathe unobserved by the general public. Your house might work out like this:

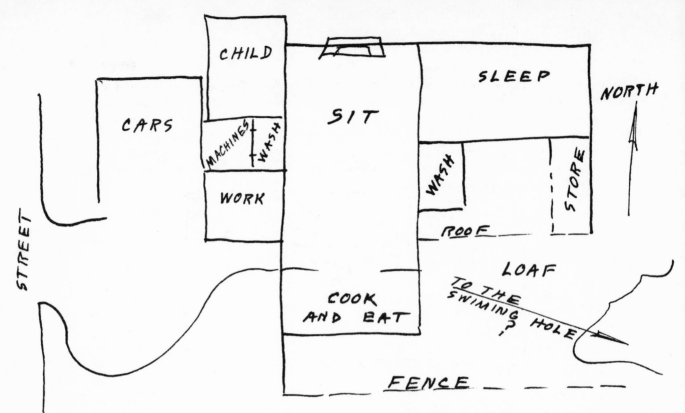

It's a small house and hasn't cost much, yet its shape lets you indulge your favorite pastime in comfort and privacy. Granted suitable terrain and a water supply, you can have a swimming hole too, but that subject comes later.

Here is another small house. In this instance you are semi-retired, with children long gone. Your two reasons for staying alive are gardening and entertaining.

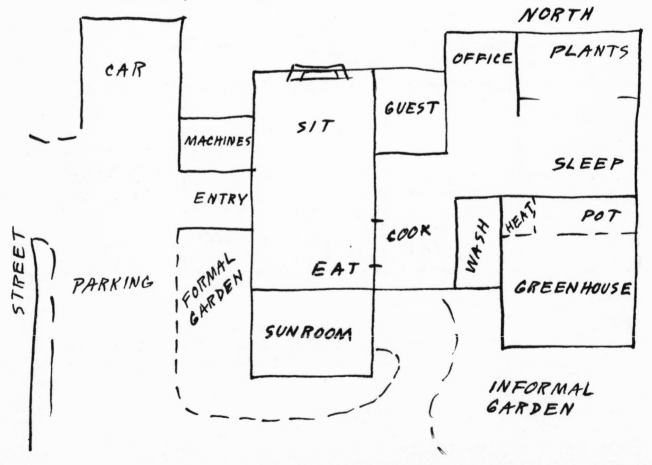

When you started out forty years ago, with less money than you have now, you put some plumbing and glass in an old workshop, like this:

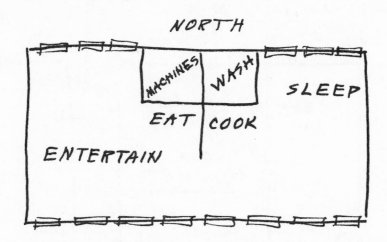

You had north light and south light, used according to what the plants needed. You ate and entertained in the middle of your greenhouse, then slept after the company went home. You have a little more room now, but your domestic inclinations haven't changed much.

If at the same age and the same state of poverty you had been artists, working at it, you might have arranged the same building like this:

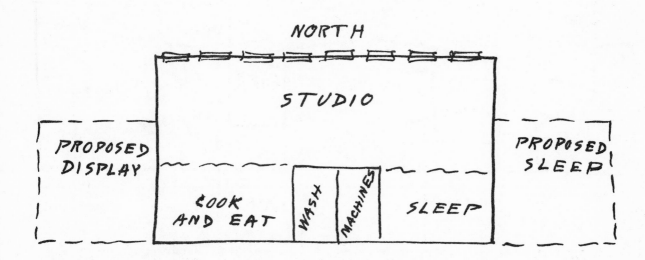

Your ingenuity paid off, you've made a little money, and you're still working. What you have now is:

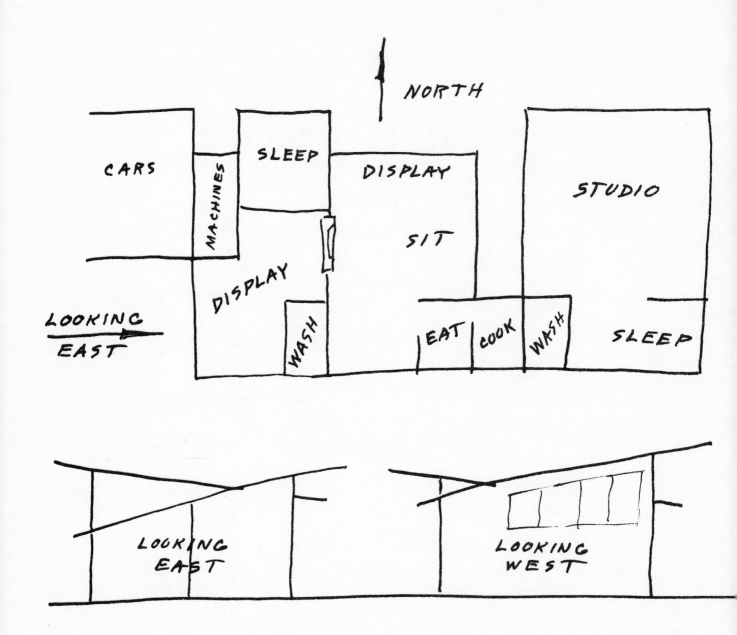

You had to do a bit of thinking on this one. In building your house, you made the studio almost a separate structure. That let your studio roof lift to the north, a professional requirement, and your house roof to the south, a comfort requirement. Better light was provided for both uses, while your painting and living habits remained about the same.

Not everything has to run east and west. Here is what you might build if you were an insurance agent with eight children. You're a good family man, you're crowding the dollar, you want to have your office at home, and you can't have the kids around bothering the customers.

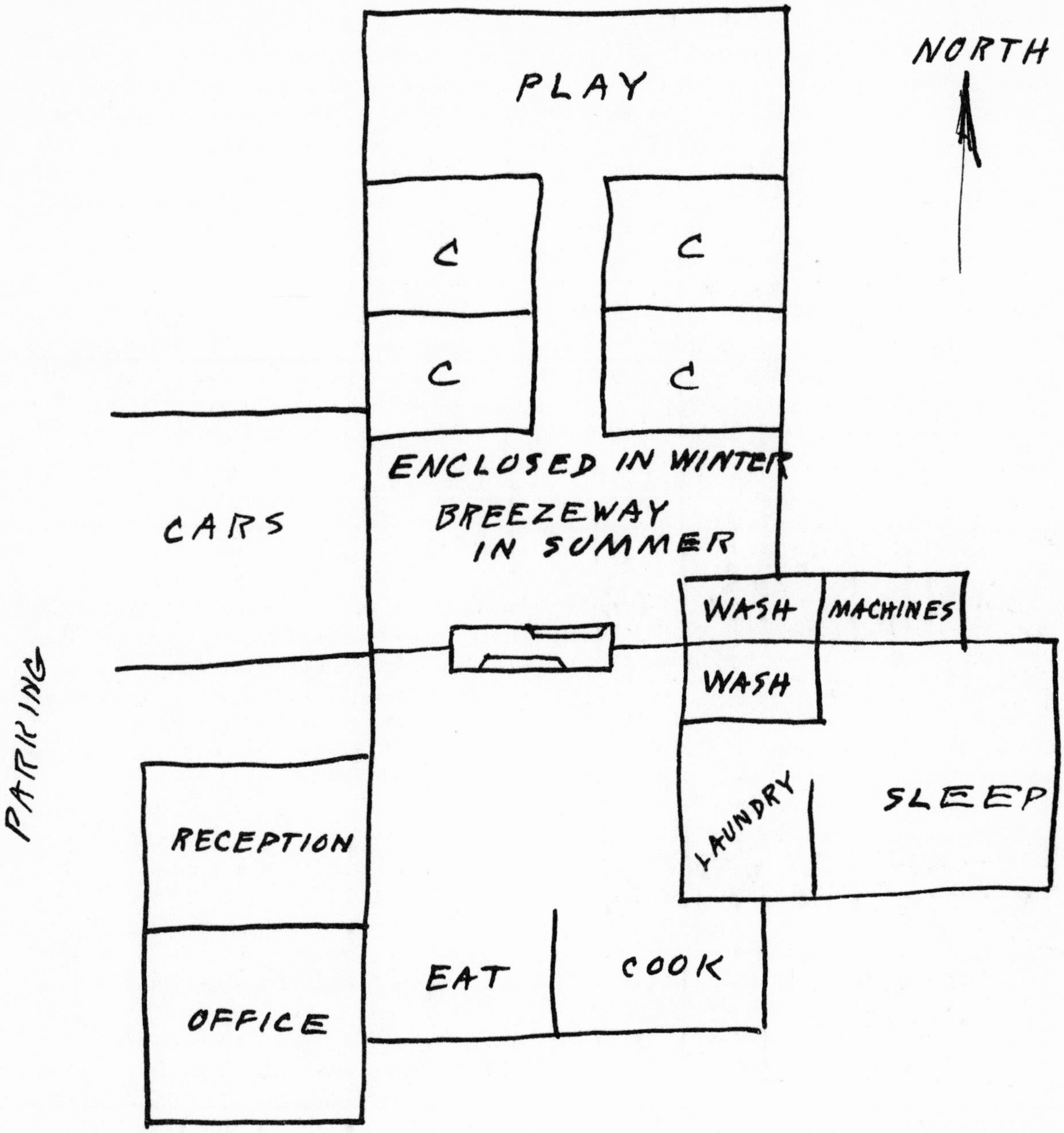

NORTH

PLAY

C   C

C   C

ENCLOSED IN WINTER

BREEZEWAY
IN SUMMER

CARS

PARKING

WASH | MACHINES

WASH

LAUNDRY   SLEEP

RECEPTION

OFFICE   EAT   COOK

You do a lot of work here, and you have a lot of fun. Often there are two parties going at once, but with back-to-back fireplaces and back-to-back bathrooms your big, useful house didn't cost nearly as much as your customers think it did.

I know a movie enthusiast who has his own projection room, and a member of the theatre group who has his own rehearsal stage. There is a small arms expert who built his own indoor firing range. There is a musician who likes to record jam sessions in his own sound studio. I know a man who just likes to watch people have a good time, so he built the only room in town big enough to throw a dance.

In talking about shape, arrangement for use cannot be forgotten. All of the easy-to-say tag names, Colonial, Garrison, Modern, Ranch, Early American, Split, Rambler, or whatever else the advertisements happen to be currently misusing, attempt to impose a preconceived shape upon what happens inside your house. If you plan from the inside out, you can have what you want, yet the result need not look very much different from the house next door.

Whatever shape you build, you can be sure that someone will hang a tag name on it and tell you what it is. A master carpenter friend of mine, under whose gentle supervision I learned the trade, had the right answer for this one.

We're laying boards on a roof, saws and hammers working away. In comes the curious driver, who always says, "Hey Frank, what'r'ya buildin'?"

Boss Frank, anxious to get on with it, always says, "Started out to be an eight-holer, but we're licked. Can't find a big enough board."

8. Heat

The subject of heat comes early on our list of what to build, because heat is expensive. Heating equipment is expensive. Fuel is expensive. Whenever there is money to be spent, other people—manufacturers, advertisers, salesmen, installers—are understandably anxious to advise us how to spend it. Whatever is expensive thus becomes controversial, with strong men coming almost to blows over this or that method of heating a house, not realizing that most of their arguments are unrelated to heat itself, which is where the discussion should have started in the first place.

Heat is a rather complex subject technically, but that need not worry us here. The principles of heat flow are simple, and do not change. There is a lot of money to be saved by ignoring controversy and looking instead at the principles.

In a house, what do we want to heat? "Heating a house" is not quite the correct statement. What we want to heat is ourselves, or more correctly, to keep ourselves losing heat at the desirable rate.

We are all food-burning stoves. Our built-in thermostats keep our insides warmed to 98.6° Fahrenheit, or thereabouts, with almost any variation therefrom causing discomfort.

To keep the thermostat in control, we lose heat constantly through our outsides. This constant loss is essential to a feeling of well-being. We all want our outside to be cooler than our inside, but how much cooler depends on many things. Choices as to desirable skin temperature can range all the way from 50 to 80, or even wider under special conditions. The choice of the moment depends on our disposition, mood, physical make-up such as depth of capillaries and amount of fatty layer beneath the skin, contents of the stomach, and probably most important of all, amount of physical exertion.

With all these variables, if one person says he feels too warm while right beside him another is feeling cool, they may both be correct. Another complicating factor is that many people don't really know whether they are warm or cold. That will be discussed later. This section is concerned with what it takes to keep our bodies losing heat at the desired rate, whatever that may be.

There are four and only four ways of keeping a human body desirably warm. The first is clothing, which serves to slow down the loss of the body's own heat. The second is to place it in contact with warmed objects, such as going to bed with a hot water bottle. This is called conduction, and is not practical for those who want to keep moving about. The third is to surround the body with warmed air. This is called convection, which reduces the rate at which the body loses heat by conduction to the air which touches it. The fourth method is the most common of all. That is to environ ourselves within warm solids such as walls, or else stand in the sun, which amounts to the same thing. This reduces the heat loss from the body by radiation, since the human body, being warm, radiates heat constantly to all surrounding bodies which are cooler than it is.

What complicates the discussion is that all of these factors—heat retention by clothing, convection through air, radiation to solids, and to a small degree conduction—are going on all the time. What saves money is to arrange the house so that it has more or less of one or the other, according to taste.

Obviously the cheapest way to keep our skin at the desired temperature is to put on or remove clothing. This method controls heat loss at the source. In public places, social convention frequently limits us in this regard, but at home we can make effective use of dressing for comfort.

Since the addition or removal of clothing has its reasonable limits, some heat control has to be added to the house. There are just two ways a house can help keep us warm; by convection and by radiation. Every house ever built uses both of them in some combination. They are both going on all the time, although in varying proportions.

Most heating equipment offered for sale is somewhat misnamed. For instance, a "radiator" is not primarily a radiator, or source of radiant heat. It is mostly a convector, or means of warming air. Most of its heat reaches us by air movement and not by radiation. For another example, the often repeated arguments between "hot air" and "hot water" heating systems are frivolous. Both systems refer simply to the manner of conveying heat from a single furnace to remote locations. The end result of both systems is to fill a room with warm air. Thus they are both convection systems and you can take your choice.

Having filled a room with warm air, the walls and ceiling get warm eventually, and the radiation loss from our bodies to the surrounding enclosure is diminished. It takes time to heat up a cold house because air is a very poor conductor of heat. If the sun is shining, however, we are instantly warm, because there is no time lag in radiant heat. You feel it right now, just as you can tell with your eyes shut whether your hand is in shadow or in sun.

Heating a house, and by heating the house, heating you, always involves some combination of convection and radiation. Indoors, neither can exist in pure form without starting up the other. The difference lies in which happens first, and most.

Convection begins by heating air. Radiation begins by heating solids. Emphasis on the latter method is more comfortable to the human body, which exists in a state of well-being if the air around it is cooler than it is, the surrounding solids slightly warmer.

Unfortunately, the equipment for heating the solid part of your house costs more than the equipment for heating the air inside it. Artificial radiant heat is comfortable but expensive. The radiant heat which comes to us from the sun, if and when the sun is shining, costs nothing.

All of this has a direct bearing on the shape of a house, as well as the method of heating it. I mentioned earlier that at one point in time and technology houses were built in cube shapes to cut down on heat loss. With technology, manufactured materials, and machines to keep a slow fire burning all night, we can go back to some earlier methods of keeping warm.

For thousands of years the sun was man's only source of warmth. It cost nothing then, it costs nothing now. I've already sketched a way to take advantage of this bargain. Here it is again:

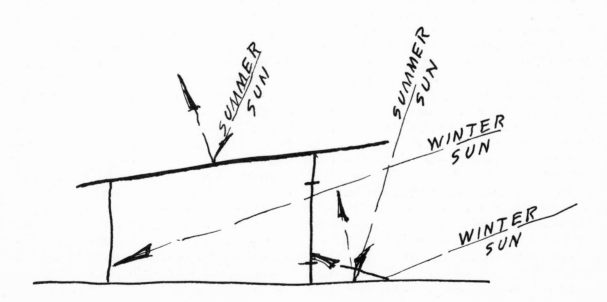

This shape of house lets the sun warm us in winter; avoids its heat in summer. A longish structure, facing south, picks up a lot more free heat than a cube-shaped house. Granted this fact, our next problem is to keep the place warm when the sun isn't shining.

Primitive man preferred his cave or hut to face toward the sun, for both light and heat. His wife complained that those shady-side caves were damp and gloomy. Man became somewhat less primitive the night he learned how to build a fire. Not only did it scare off the tigers; it maintained warmth built up during the day before.

In the cave he slept close to the fire, keeping a warmed stone wall behind him and thus getting a little radiant heat from both directions. If the cave wasn't too drafty, he got a bit of convected heat from warm air. Some time later, in the country store, he put his feet on the stove rail, roasted on one side and froze on the other, emulating the King of England, who once wore furs on his back, while exposing his noble chest to the radiant heat in front of him.

People who wanted to use several rooms built a fire in each room, a simple scheme but not very warming because almost all the heat went up the chimney. Very recently, someone got tired of building and tending fires in every room. He invented central heating, which was a great timesaver in that one fire took care of everything. As long as fires had to be fed with solid fuel, central heating was demanded because of this one advantage. With the coming of fuels which could be piped or wired, central heating lost this advantage and has been hanging on ever since through habit.

What are the disadvantages of central heating? The first is expense; it is costly to install a furnace and costly to provide the pipes and ducts to distribute the heat throughout the house. It is obviously much easier and cheaper to pipe fuel than to pipe heat. The second major disadvantage of central heating is that unless elaborate control equipment is installed, adding still more to the expense, the house will probably be heated to one constant temperature.

For many reasons this uniform temperature is not a good idea, the most obvious being that how warm we want to be, or how cool, depends on what we're doing. Central heating does not adapt itself quickly to the variety or location of our activity. There is no reason for a room to be kept expensively warm if no one's in it. It seems obvious to me that to live, move, work and play in a variety of temperatures is natural, healthful, stimulating, and psychologically and economically correct. Constant temperature for everything is both stultifying and expensive.

Further technical development has let us go back to area heating, back, if you like, to the stove in each room, except that now the "stoves" take care of themselves and do our bidding. This system is much less expensive to install and to operate.

Area heating means that in one way or another we control the temperature of the various parts of our house, up or down, to fit the occupants, what they are doing, how they are clothed, and what time of day it is. For example, let's take the insurance salesman's house and put some numbers on it.

He works at home, makes average money, has eight children, wants the family to have all the fun they can afford. In this fairly big house they do many different things, and get maximum comfort at the minimum expense for heat. The temperature figures on the sketch are not intended to be exact. They indicate a possible range which one family might elect.

First the reception room. It is a winter's day, temperature below freezing. Customers arrive in heavy coats, which they by habit do not remove until invited to do so. Anything above 60° in this room is a discourtesy, and the colder the day, the lower the temperature should be.

In his office, the agent is all dressed up in jacket and vest. His mind and personal comfort are both at their best below 70°, and he shades his own preferences toward the low side, remembering that the customer has just come in from the cold.

Going on around the house, the family eats at 70°. Food in the stomach makes us feel a trifle cooler on the outside. The kitchen, however, wants to start out much cooler. Not only is there physical activity, but local radiant heat from oven and stove. The after-dinner drowse on the sofa wants to be conducted in the warmest temperature of all.

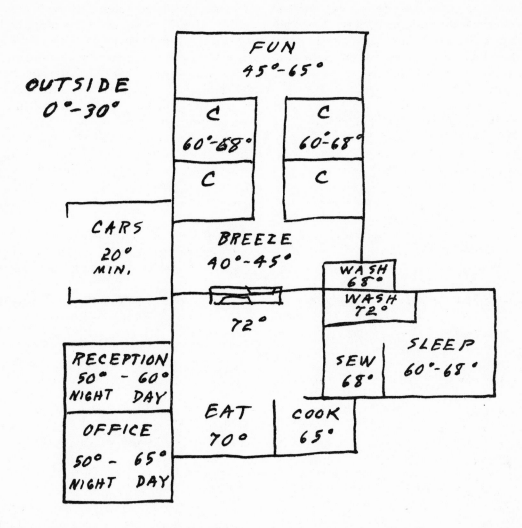

If the bedroom becomes a sewing room during the day, 68°, to keep the mind clear but the fingers nimble, is about right. Sleeping temperature is a matter of individual choice and I won't argue, except to point out to the habitual window-openers that the body requires less ventilation when it is asleep than when it is awake.

In the enclosed breezeway, where the kids are having a winter-time cookout, it will be warm enough to keep their breath from showing.

Children's bedrooms, vary to taste. Study is best at around 65° for most youngsters, but since I am not a youngster, my own office is held a little lower. The old bean, or the young one, begins to slow up at anything over 70°. Sleeping temperature, once again to taste, and let the kids fight it out.

Fun room, for ping-pong, 50° Wrestling or gymnastics, 45°. Darts, 60°. Bridge party, 65° and be careful. Remember that as soon as a room gets full of people the temperature will overshoot even with all heat turned off. And don't forget to turn the fun room way down at night.

Last, the automobile. You have noticed by now that I never sketch doors on a garage, preferring to spend my own money on other things. I depend on the morning sun coming into my south-facing carport to help me get the car started. If, as in this sketch, my garage faced west, or if my profession required me to go traveling in the middle of the night, I would put doors on, leave plenty of ventilation, and set the temperature at 20°. If the car won't start at 20°, it needs fixing anyway.

Why is all this important? Because artificial heat is expensive. Getting more for your money is the principal reason for this book. Having paid for artificial heat, you would like to keep it around.

Heat loss through a barrier speeds up as the square of the difference in temperature from one side to the other, as shown here:

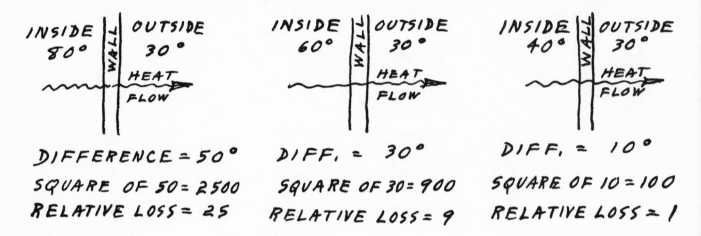

This diagram says that with the outside temperature at 30°, the cost of heating any given enclosure to 80° is about three times the cost of heating it to 60°, and twenty-five times the cost of heating it to 40°.

A well-insulated structure changes the dollar amounts but not the relative amounts. The rate of heat flow, that is the pennies per minute per square foot going from the warm side to the cold side, gets less as the insulation is improved.

For any given building, large or small, poorly or well insulated, if the outside temperature were assumed to stay at 30°, and it cost you a hundred dollars a month to heat it to 80°, it would cost you thirty-six dollars a month to heat it to 60°, and two dollars and fifty cents to heat it to 40° during that month you spent away from home.

A discussion of heating methods comes later. The merits of gas, oil, coal, electricity for fuels; the convenience of area versus central fuel consumers; the benefits of automatic as opposed to manual control; these things are matters of how, not what. They are fascinatingly debatable details, more fun to argue about than whether to use steel or aluminum nails in the siding.

Further, a discussion of the psychology of heat-ing, that is, definitions of conduction, convection, radiation, and what they mean to your comfort and pocketbook, will be found in the *Notebook* section at the back of the book. Technology is a great money-saver. The farther we go the more important it gets. For the moment, I want to show you the relation between what we call heat and what we call light.

9. Light

All non-nuclear energy used on this or any other planet arrives here now, or arrived some time before now, from the sun. All of this energy is heat.

It arrives by a process which we do not as yet clearly understand. We call it radiant energy. The only thing we know for sure about radiant energy is the speed of its arrival, which is a hundred eighty-six thousand and some odd miles per second. We believe that the energy arrives in a fashion which for convenience we choose to call "waves." It now becomes convenient to describe the speed with which these waves travel, divided by the number of waves arriving per second, as the wave length, and the number of waves per second as the frequency.

It is in frequency that you, the potential housebuilder, are interested. The arriving heat, or energy, covers a very wide range of frequencies. A narrow range of frequency is visible to the human eye, and we call this light. The range of frequencies included in light is about one octave. An octave means double at one end what it was at the other end, which is to say that the waves at the blue side of the rainbow are half as long and are arriving twice as often as the waves at the red side.

Beyond the blue side of the visible octave are still higher frequencies and thus shorter waves which we call ultraviolet. These stretch out over many octaves. Most of this high frequency energy is absorbed by the air and does not get through to us. Coming down in frequency from the red side of the visible octave are many more octaves which for convenience we split up into various bands called by various names. The frequencies just below red, which are most successful in penetrating the air and bringing us useful heat, we call infrared.

As you lie on the beach, wearing sunglasses against the visible light, it is largely the infrared which is making you feel warm, and largely the ultraviolet which is making your skin turn brown. If instead of going to the beach, you relax behind glass on a sun porch, you will feel almost as warm as if you were outside, but you will not get a tan.

The reason is that the things we call transparent—glass, clear plastic, air, thin clouds—are more transparent to low frequencies than to high ones. To put it the other way around, more of the high frequency and thus short-wave stuff is absorbed. That barrier which is transparent to a low frequency may not be transparent to a high one, and that's why the sun looks red in the late afternoon.

The significant difference between light and the rest of the heat spectrum is that light, which by definition is for seeing, cannot be stored to be seen with later. Once its energy has been converted and then reproduced outside the light octave, we can no longer use it to see by.

On its first arrival from the sun, light is free. As we did with heat, let's being by investigating how much we can get, if and when it is wanted. Once again the best solution seems to work out like this:

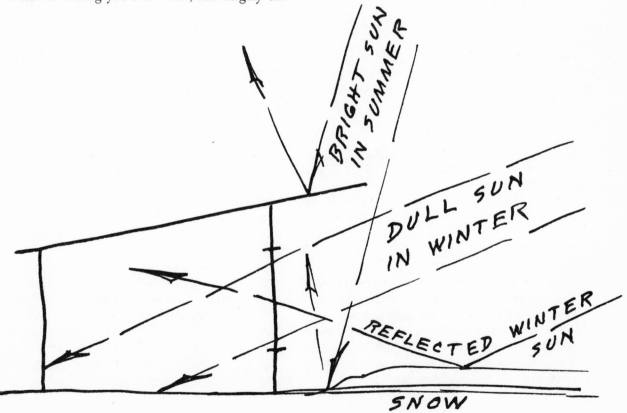

In summer we want to keep out the heat, because there's too much, and also that part of the heat which we call light, because it's too bright. In winter we welcome both. The sunlight, having come through more miles of air, has lost its high frequency side. We welcome what brightness it can manage.

To get the most light for nothing, we want a house which is all south side and very little else. In the case of heat, we had to decide between a longish structure, which will pick up more natural heat, and a squarish one, which will retain artificial heat better. In the case of light, there is no argument. The long house wins.

We can retain heat with insulation, but light is either on or off. We can not insulate against light loss. Therefore we try to get all the light we can while the getting is good. As a house nears cube shape, it has less light admission. Parts of it are farther away from a window than we would like. By stretching out the shape of the house, we move ourselves closer to a window.

For an at-hand example, here is where my typewriter and I are sitting at this moment:

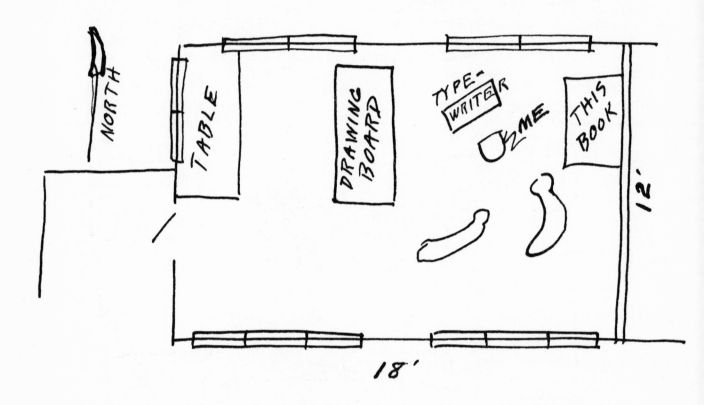

The room is twelve feet wide and eighteen feet long. The triple lines indicate windows. You can see that no point in the room is more than six feet away from at least two sources of natural light, from north and south. The drawing board and reference table have west light as well. It's difficult to cast a bothersome shadow.

The two lozenge-shaped objects behind me are two Saint Bernards who have decided they like it here too. That makes three of us.

The most natural light for a given area is to be had in a slender house shape, such as this:

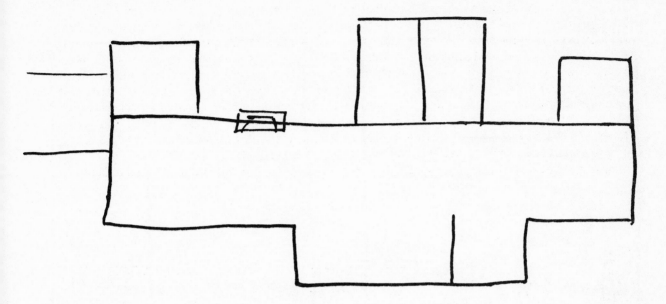

Or perhaps better still, if you prefer the court-
yard shape, this:

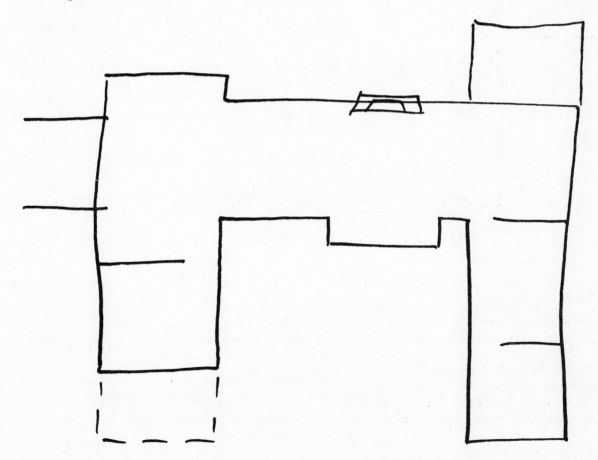

Whereas what retains heat the best is this:

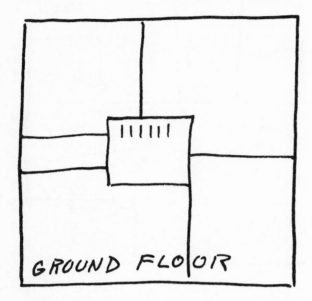

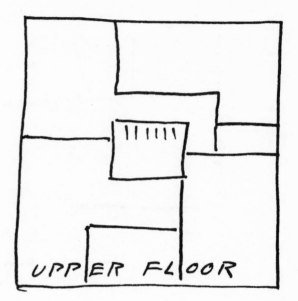

Many people compromise the issue by stretching out a little:

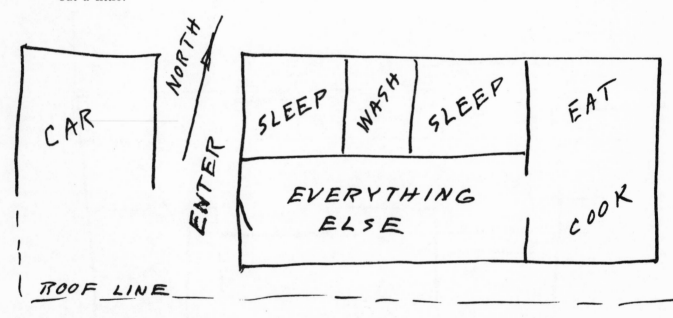

This compromise has been built a good many millions of times, varied by placing the car at either east or west end. It lets in quite a bit of light for its size, and as a starter, a good buy for limited dollars, I can't quarrel with it much.

But here I am talking about shape and economy, when the subject was supposed to have been light. It would seem that no one subject in house design can be completely separated from all the rest.

There is day, and there is night. Back in the days of the cave, artificial light came from the fire, thus:

Much later came the Coleman lantern, which we put on the kitchen table and had this:

Then Mr. Edison's lamp arrived, which we at first used, without changing our habits, this way:

Naturally it was quite a wrench when some brave soul suggested that the source of artificial light should be put back over our shoulders, sun-wise, like this:

The improvement is apparent. Two light sources enable us to work or play with efficiency and comfort. We can use the whole room rather than a little bit of it in the middle.

As long as artificial light involved fire, whether the fire were from pine knots, candles, whale oil, kerosene, or gas, we had to be careful where we put it. Electric light is more tractable, permitting us to locate multiple light sources where they will best imitate daylight.

The cave would have been a better place in which to skin tigers if it had been equipped with indirect light. Having moved out of the cave, we wish to retain the option of cave illusion. Notice that the candles on the table need not be lit until the roast is done, the dog combed, the last stitch drawn, the homework put away. Then we switch off our artificial daylight and return to the inefficient cave, which is not unpleasant.

10. Air

The subject of ventilation is tied to that of light only because for many years we have used the same hole in the wall for both purposes.

When—according to how rich or energetic I was, and also according to what materials were handy—the walls of my house were made of mud, or sod, or stone, it was troublesome to put holes in them. A hole left in the wall for the admission of light also used to let in air.

The problem of how to let in light without air was eventually solved with pieces of glass, which we put in frames, hanging the frames on hinges or slides so that the glass could be pushed aside. Anyone who has tried to open a swollen sash in wet weather knows this solution to be of dubious merit.

Recently we started objecting to flies and mosquitoes, and we put screen cloth over the holes. The screen kept out the mosquitoes. It also kept out a third of the light.

When you stop to think about it, the best place for admitting and releasing air is almost never the best place for admitting light. Air and light are not governed by the same laws.

Light, traveling in straight lines, will go along those lines as far as we let it go. When light strikes something it can't get through, some of it bounces off, the amount and direction of the bounce depending on whether the surface is black or white, rough or smooth.

When there is no wind blowing, air is sluggish stuff. It won't move at all until something pushes it. When the wind is blowing, we generally want less ventilation, not more. In winter we go around plugging cracks to get less ventilation.

That's one kind of ventilation, but the kind we were talking about is what there isn't enough of on a summer day when we wish a breeze would stir up. Before you start buying electric fans, let's see how much breeze there is to be had for nothing.

Breezes are caused by differences in air pressure. That is to say, air weight. And *that* is to say, air temperature, because warm air is lighter than cold air, and when it rises, starts a whole sequence of motion.

Starting with the basic shape, and thinking about warm and cold air, I can sketch a simple way to stir up a breeze.

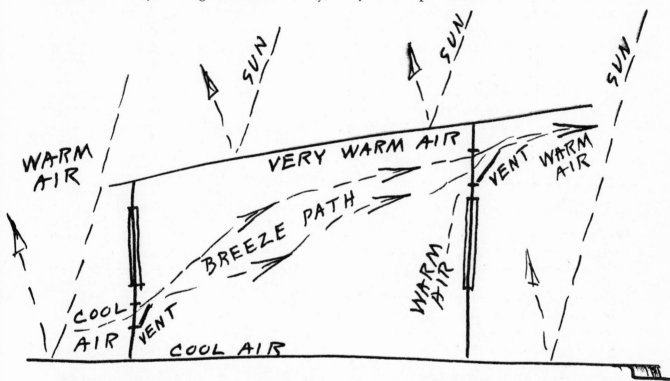

The idea is to open a hole above the windows, as high as possible on the warm side, and open another as low as possible on the cool side. In neither case would there normally have been a window where these holes are located.

If the house is oriented so that it has a warm side and a cool side, you will get a surprising amount of free breeze for a given area of ventilator doors.

If, for some reason, you had to depart from the ideal arrangement to some extent, you can still get plenty of breeze by adding more ventilator doors.

If some other factor makes it impossible to come even close to the correct orientation, you can help the cause along with two power fans, one at the highest point, pushing out, and another at the lowest point, pushing in. You will, of course, always try to draw in from shade and push out to sun.

So far no windows have been opened. The screens which keep the mosquitoes out—and if they are over the windows also keep out about a third of the light and heat—are now over the ventilators instead. And they can be left there, too, in winter and summer.

The reason we haven't opened any windows is that they are fixed in place. If you have trouble digesting the idea of a window that won't open, I may be able to help you by talking about money some more. We all want lots and lots of windows in our houses. They have become, in most cases rightly, the symbol of a pleasant place to live. But the cost of a manufactured window frightens us, and we wind up including fewer than we would like, or else doing without something else.

It is expensive to put glass in a frame, put that frame in another frame in such a way that it will open, supply and fit complex hardware, weatherstrip the whole thing so it won't leak too badly, make and fit removable screens, pack it carefully so the glass won't break, and ship it. At the house, our carpenter has already built still another frame—that makes three frames in all—into which he fits the store-bought window and seals the joints, inside and out.

I'm not criticizing the window manufacturers. It's amazing they do as well as they do. As a machine designer, I say that when we treat the window as a machine, asking it to perform multiple functions—admit light, admit air, or exclude it according to the weather, keep out bugs in summer, never mind the bugs in winter—and do all this at the twist of a crank without leaking or sticking—the window is bound to become expensive.

If we give the window one function and one only, to admit light, we can have all the windows we want at no extra charge. It is inexpensive to fix panes of glass permanently in place. Any smart carpenter can build a wall of glass about as quickly as he can build a wall of anything else.

As for the ventilator, it's a wooden door on the simplest of hinges, rigid, unbreakable, easy to weatherstrip, easy to screen. One frame does the whole job.

If we keep windows and ventilators separate, we wind up with more light, better ventilation, less trouble, less maintenance, and lower cost.

I found in my own house that I had provided for more ventilation than I needed. Many of the vents included in the original plan will never be built. Some parts of a house need less ventilation than others, and under normal family use, all

parts need less than most people think. Given a moderate family density of, let's say, one person to a room, a breeze in your face is a source of pleasure, a psychological rather than a physical necessity.

Imagine a domestic structure, comprising perhaps 15,000 cubic feet of air enclosed by twenty windows, three doors, and 1,400 square feet of far from airtight wall, all permitting air flow whether we like it or not. In this building put five people, one dog, two cats and a canary. You can see that it would be expensive and difficult to make this house tight enough to discomfort its normal residents. We open up mainly to feel the wind in our hair.

If, however, we plan to put twenty people in one room, the volume of air flow required for their physical comfort goes up by a factor of twenty-plus. Normal air leakage into one room will by no means keep that many people happy.

The factor becomes more than twenty because you also have cooling to consider. You would like the room to be warm enough so that the first guest to arrive will not feel chilly. Then as you add nineteen more people, each one a little furnace giving off heat, your problem is not heating but cooling. Once again we see that the problems of a domestic structure can not be considered separately. The meeting of the bridge club, with no joke intended, needs some air.

Some special problems around the house also deserve an airing. Cooking odors are stimulating, but too much can be too much. Kitchen ventilation is to be had for nothing. You notice that all sketches thus far have put the kitchen on the south side.

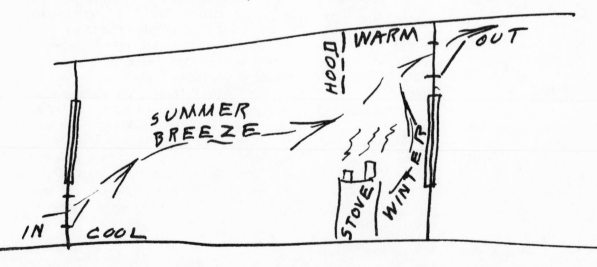

The situation shown here provides ideal ventilation. Warm air rising from the stove goes up and out, with no fan required. If the arrangement were less than ideal with respect to warm side and cool side, a screen can be dropped from the roof to trap a pocket of warm air above the stove. From here it will flow out, winter or summer, when the ventilator is opened.

By now we have seen that the living room, with its possible concentration of heat and scent-producing people, and the kitchen, with its broiling mackerel, need extra ventilation. There are other problems. The woodworking shop with its sanding dust needs an extra blast. The party room needs a way for the smoke to escape. The mud room, where wet clothes and bathing suits hang, feels damp without ventilation.

Even without added moisture, any room which is allowed to remain much cooler than the outside temperature is, if not ventilated, subject to condensation and will get uncomfortably wet. Air in contact with a cooler solid invariably deposits some of its moisture thereon. For example, if your unventilated workshop remains cooler than the outside temperature, your tools will get damp and rusty. Any such room needs to be ventilated.

Take, for another example, an automobile sitting in a closed garage. As the air warms up outside in the morning, all metal parts of the car, not to mention the steering wheel and upholstery, get wet. Any closed garage should have a ventilator open near the top. Lack of air flowing past a shut up automobile is unpleasant, dangerous, and an invitation to suicide. Worse, it makes the car hard to start.

On the other hand, there are areas which we are inclined to ventilate excessively. The lower our level of physical activity, the less air we need. In all conscience I am compelled to point out that two people asleep in a bedroom require less air than they do at any other time.

11. Noise

Most things work together to produce a pleasant house, but sometimes what is right for one reason may not be right for another. Hence we compromise.

One of our goals requires no compromise. The house design which is right in all other respects will keep your ears comfortable.

We all have a sound level which is comfortable to us. That level, as with heat and light, varies with mood and with the time of day. The dime-in-the-slot juke box is carefully engineered to make as loud and disagreeable a noise as, in the opinion of the engineer, people want to hear inside the corner tavern. Not for a moment does the engineer imagine that his people would put up with the same racket at home.

Absolute quiet can be as disturbing as absolute darkness. Excessive noise and excessive light are equally disturbing. The quiet house, or rather the one which is comfortably alive but free from irritating noise, costs you less than the worst noisebox ever put up. Ear comfort can be built into the original design for nothing.

After your house is built, it is too late to correct the damage. Ear comfort comes from the shape of the boxes within which you have housed yourself. Once the wrong shapes have been built, the cost of correcting them acoustically, of changing shapes so that they dissipate rather than amplify noise, is prohibitive.

It just could be that the sound of a house does not seem important to you. If so, you may not realize what is causing those headaches. Light you can see and warmth you can feel. Warm, dry, light, clean. We like those words and we're willing to work to get them. Yet we often fail to do much about sound, the one inescapable phenomenon.

If you're cold, put some clothes on. If too warm, take them off. If the house is too light, drop the curtains, and if too dark, turn on the lights. Close your eyes, pull up the covers. Everything has vanished except sound. The ear remains open and receptive, light or dark, cold or warm, awake or asleep.

We undertake to survive, comfortably, in an environment which is usually too warm, too cold, too dark, too dirty, too wet or too dry. It would seem that all nature is against us. The natural environment of sound is almost always pleasant. Man-made sound is all too frequently unpleasant. To take a mild example, compare the sleep inducing effect of surf or waterfall with the wakeful irritation of a dripping faucet. As the examples become more violent, we can compare taxi horns with wind, and gunfire with distant thunder, although I admit that any of these can become an acquired taste.

Though it is hard to acquire a taste for radio announcers, we have wind in trees, bird song, rain on the roof, all easy on the ulcers. We make most of the irritating noises ourselves, with our gregariousness, our communications devices, and our machines. Most irritating noises are made inside the house.

It is very simple to minimize the unhappy impact of our own noises. The first rule is to avoid squareness of room shape and of angle. Here is why.

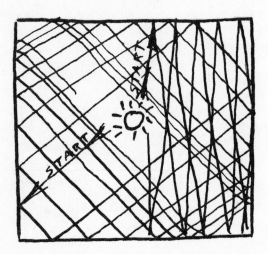
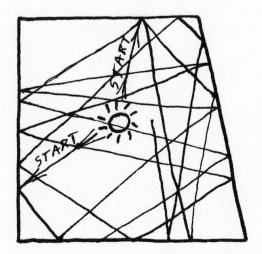

At the left we have exploded a firecracker or beat on a drum, or uttered an angry word, inside a square box. At the right the same thing happened inside an odd-shaped box. The lines in each case trace just two out of many possible sound paths as they bounce back from the walls of the box.

What makes a sound irritating is not so much its original occurrence as its persistence, that is, the number of times it comes back to your ear before it dies away. Some persistence is desirable. Too much is irritating. People who sing in shower stalls may sound wonderful to themselves, but not so wonderful to other people.

In the sketch at the left, the square room, you will see that the sound pattern keeps repeating itself. Whether a sound is desired or undesired, its excessive repetition is always unpleasant. In the non-square sketch at right, you can find no place where the repeated sound keeps beating at you without mercy.

The next time you find yourself in a new house, square and true, walls all parallel and smoothly plastered, vertical windows, hard-finished ceiling and floor, try an experiment. Walk to the middle of the room and snap your fingers. If nothing happens, move six inches and try again. Pretty soon a little man will say snick snick snick snick in your ear for two or three seconds after the first finger snap. You have located a "standing wave" which is caused by the finger snap reinforcing itself every time it comes around.

Then try your finger snap in a room with an irregular shape, one with halls, openings, corner cupboard, beams, bookshelves.

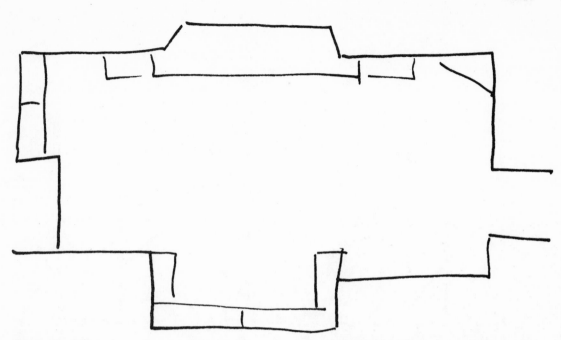

I think you will not be able to find a snick snick snick anywhere.

I'm sure the builders of this room were not worried about acoustics. They built what they felt like building. As a no-cost by-product, their ears were kept happy.

All of the sketches so far have been in plan view, looking down. Tip your acoustics up on edge, and there has been no change. The preferred basic shape, which I keep sketching over and over on almost every subject, turns out to be a splendid noise de-irritator. It is nothing more than the out-of-square box shown above, except that the roof is used as the one out-of-square side.

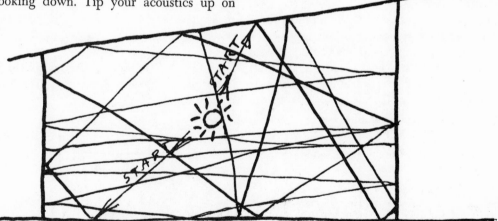

If you take a pencil and keep following those two lines around, you will find they take a long while to come back on themselves, by which time the noise is too weak to matter.

The noisiest house you can live is has been carefully built by a master carpenter, straight and true. Ceiling and floor, opposing walls and windows, all are square and parallel. Nothing, says the master carpenter proudly, is a quarter inch out of line.

Furthermore, the walls are plastered, the carefully leveled ceiling is plastered, the floor is of carefully laid hardwood. At worst, each room approaches a cube in shape, as high as wide as long. I can't help calling this kind of thing an acoustical prison cell.

In the acoustic sense, squareness, the demon to avoid, means perfect symmetry of almost any kind. The so-called cathedral ceiling has acoustic problems which in some respects are even worse than the cubes.

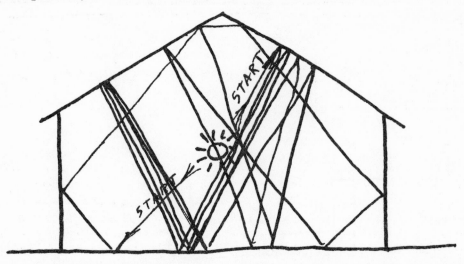

Built with the roof dead center, it's worse than a flat ceiling. As you can see from the sketch, there are in this shape three concentrations of noise, a big one right in the middle, slightly smaller ones about a third of the way out on either side.

The remedy is simple. If the walls are almost unnoticeably off-center with the vee of the roof, or if one wall is built two or three degrees out of parallel, the joint will quiet right down.

The nicest sounding room you could live in would, in theory, have no two of its six sides parallel with each other. Fortunately, there is no need to go that far. Throwing any one of the six sides out of parallel will be a wonderful improvement. Failing that, any departure from the square, the flat, the symmetrical, is, for any given volume of noise, easy on the ears.

I have not as yet mentioned specific dimensions, or talked much about the effect of materials. That comes toward the back of the book.

Also we have been talking more about how to make noise tolerable, than about how to reduce it.

The only free-for-nothing sound-reducer I know of is distance. Here is a sketch of three noisemakers:

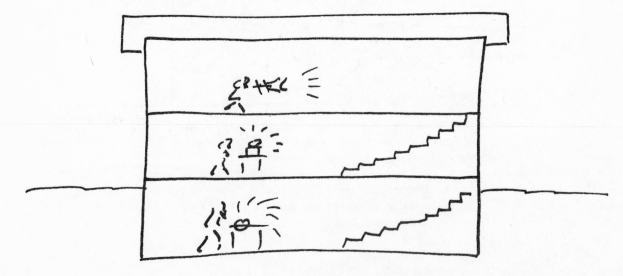

The trumpet upstairs, the mixer in the kitchen, the power saw in the basement, are forty feet apart as the walker walks—and I'm throwing in vertical feet at no extra charge—but eight feet apart as sound travels.

Now let's rearrange:

Using a reasonable translation of the interior spaces shown above, the noisemakers are now twenty-four feet apart as the walker walks, or a sociable sixteen feet closer together, but are also twenty-four feet apart as the sound flies, or three times as far as they were in the other house.

Since, with all other things being equal, sound volume reduces by the square of the distance, the noise reaching one from the other is one-ninth what it was before. Here is one more good reason for the single-level house.

12. The inside

Every domestic structure, no matter how it is built, creates an enclosed space. That space is its reason for being. The enclosure inevitably has an inside and an outside. The appearance of the inside and the appearance of the outside depend largely on how the structure is put together.

A structure reveals itself whether you like it or not. Attempts to conceal structure are always expensive, often aesthetically absurd, and usually fail because they wind up fooling almost no one.

In deciding upon the appearance of the inside of your house, then later of the outside, it will help to begin with structure. Here is what the first one may have been:

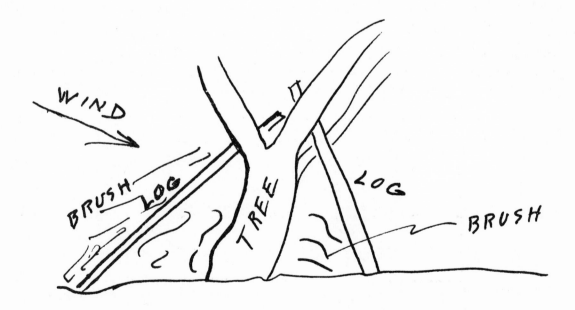

Two or three such logs propped against a tree would hold up branches to keep out the wind.

Much later a genius propped three or more logs together, thus creating more room inside.

To make still more room, his twentieth great-grandson created the first post-and-beam structure.

Durable roof and walls were probably the next concern, with the elements of domestic structure evolving into these parts:

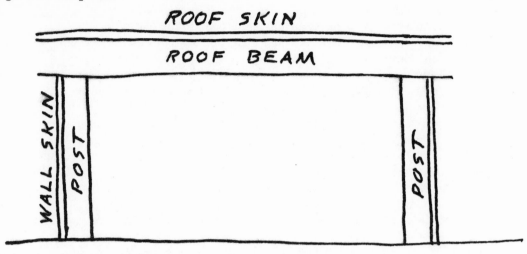

The builder then discovered that a roof beam which is heavy enough not to break in the middle is too heavy to lift into place. To increase the size of his house, he began to put together pieces of wood which were small enough for him to handle. He invented the superbly logical A-frame,

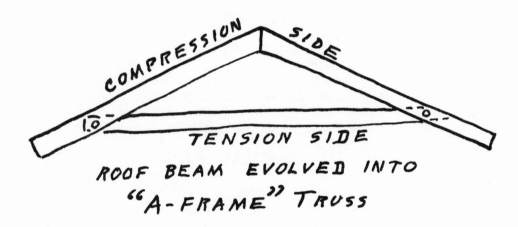

using two pieces in compression and one in tension. He doubled the size of his house, fortunately, but unfortunately for later technology he established the idea that if the roof doesn't slope two ways it isn't a house.

The architect has been working from hut to mansion with these same basic parts, and struggling with this same problem, ever since.

You will notice that as the structures became larger, they became more difficult to erect, more permanent in nature, more difficult to destroy or to leave behind. This might be read as a description of home, a place to come back to.

In most times and most places, people have felt that being able to see its structure makes a house more home-like. In time of danger, or more often just plain bad weather, it is comforting to be at home and see the post holding up the beam, the beam supporting the roof, the wall keeping out the wind, and, for refinement, the floor lifting us out of the mud. Most people have found comfort and beauty in creating handsome structures of obvious strength, and they didn't try to cover up sturdy working parts.

Unfortunately, for a hundred years or so we have been struggling with a style concept called decoration, which teaches us to build an obviously inelegant framework, then hide it behind non-structural skins. This is a very expensive way to go about building a house.

It has been fashionable, though I hope decreasingly so, to separate the tasks of mason and carpenter from the task of decorator. In this procedure we first ask the carpenter to build a box, the function of the box being to keep out wind and rain. Then the carpenter goes away and the decorators arrive; plasterer, paperer, and painter. Last the "finish" carpenter comes back to square up all the frayed edges and lay "finish" floors which could not be put down until the "decorators" were through. Before these artisans leave you alone, the cost of the place is more than double what it was when they arrived.

It is not the fault of the decorators. If we ask them to do expensive things, they are willing to comply, for hire. The fact remains that in the frame-then-decorate method of building, more than half of the cost is in decoration.

The decorators may have made you happier, if you think so, but they have not made your house any stronger, or more durable, or significantly warmer. They have not made it any lighter, dryer, quieter, or more spacious. Granted that you started out with a fixed ceiling on the total amount of money to be spent, the decorators, at your behest, have shrunk your house to half the size it might have been.

The non-decoration concept begins with the selection of structural materials which are in themselves decorative, that is, good to look at. Once they are in place, you have paid once, and you pay no more. The materials we think of as purely decorative do no useful work other than to cover up something we didn't want to see. Some of these materials can be used, in limited quantity, with great success, but they are expensive. Use them where you will, always with caution, and never on the assumption that their use is unavoidable.

Here are some comparative costs to illustrate my point. The weather surface roofing on a house is an important part of structure. If it fails, you're miserable. The cost of a square foot of laid roofing is about one-third the cost of a square foot of lath and plaster. Add two coats of paint to the plaster, or one layer of paper, and its square foot cost has become four times the cost of the roof.

What makes it worse is that the surfaces inside a house add up to an incredible number of square feet. Let's go over in one corner and build a conventional closet. Never mind the cost of the walls, let's just figure the cost of covering the inside of the closet, which no one ever sees, with the cheapest possible plaster and one coat of paint. Assuming that the closet is 6 feet long, 3 deep and 8 high, the inside surfaces come to about 160 square feet. Then, if we peg costs at 55 cents per square foot for plaster and one coat of paint, the price tag comes to about $90. Personally I would rather spend the money for an overcoat and struggle along without painted plaster inside the closet.

As one more example of the cost of interior surface coverings, let's look at tile walls in the bathroom. I admit that in this case the tile has merit, whereas the plaster inside the closet had none. You can see tile; it's a symbol of luxury; it looks reassuringly waterproof (though why this point is important I don't know); and it is easy to clean. The catch is it's expensive, about ten times the square-foot-cost of a roof.

You have to decide for yourself. If your bathroom is to be 10 by 12 feet, tiled floor and walls to a height of 5 feet, that comes to about 360 square feet. Without specifying the quality of tile, we can figure about $2 a square foot, or $720, which sum would equip you with both automatic washer and dryer. If you don't do your own laundry, one bathroom temporarily deprived of tile will buy you a fairly decent fur coat. Three bathrooms so deprived will put a second car in your garage. The choices are yours to make.

The structural purpose of a floor is to hold us up. Softwood boards will hold us up and are pleasant to walk on, at an undecorated cost of about twice the cost of the roof, or two-thirds the cost of a plastered wall. If you want to save money, stop right there. If you want a decorated floor, the possible materials include hardwood, which adds some structural stiffness at 60 cents a square foot, asphalt tile, a bargain at 30 cents, rubber tile at 50 cents and vinyl tile, the most durable of all, at anything from a dollar up. Carpeting starts at a dollar and goes up as far as you like. Paint and varnish, which contribute nothing to the quality of your floor, are down at the bottom at 20 cents a square foot, or about the cost of the roof.

Having looked at the cost of non-structural decoration, we can now look for the alternatives. What do you want to see on the inside of your house? This is an aesthetic question, difficult to answer, impossible to debate. Is a stone wall beautiful? Certainly, unless you happen to be a prisoner sitting inside four of the darn things.

Four walls all made of anything—plaster, brick, or wood—can be just as confining to the mind, if not to the body. One wall should be different, suggesting escape. At the other extreme, if all four walls are different, escape becomes compulsory.

The recommended middle of the road solution is to use some variation in materials, with accents of color and texture against a dominant theme. Properly selected, all of these materials can be structural, with none being purely decorative. A great many structural materials are pleasant to look at if used in moderation and erected with skill.

Within any given enclosure, one material should dominate, but not too much. I have always chosen wood as my dominant material. It makes a good post, a reassuring beam, an excellent skin. It mellows, unfinished, to warm colors. Visually it presents a soft and graded texture even though it is smooth to the touch and thus easy to clean. Wood doesn't need much cleaning because it is good at not showing dirt. Because of its low heat conductivity—about the lowest of any truly structural material—it contributes to insulation. Because wood surfaces are seldom exactly in plane, it is not bad acoustically. Wood is hard to break but easy to change. It lends itself to modification and to repair. If well-ventilated, it requires no other maintenance. Pound for pound, wood is more expensive than many other strucutral materials, but a pound

goes farther. If you avoid exotic and expensive veneers, wood will build you a structure about as cheaply as anything else.

As the dominant material, wood pleasantly accepts accents of almost anything—of stone, glass, fabric, plaster, paper, pictures, bookshelves, display cabinets, brick, or cinder block.

In my own social room, I have used accents against dominant materials to the point where the accents dominate and the base material becomes background. Each of the six surrounding surfaces has its theme, with little feeling left of any finite room boundary. One wall, the south of course, seems to be all glass, although it isn't. With the curtains closed on a winter night, this wall converts and now seems to be all fabric, although it isn't. An adjacent wall is dominated by a massive block of masonry which houses back-to-back fireplaces. It is broken by a heavy mantlepiece, accented by a beautiful oil, and pleasantly littered with colorful objects of no particular artistic merit. The effect is one of warmth.

The north wall is dominated by high windows, never curtained, which look out upon greenery. In daytime the windowed hillside is all you see. At night the working tools below come into view —books, desk, piano, bull fiddle. A harp would look nice if I had one. The actual wall is effectively invisible.

The remaining wall isn't a wall at all, but a complex of things: bar, cabinets, doorways without doors, and the shoulder-high view through distant windows. The dominant impression is simply one of distance.

The floor is of random width pine boards, all fairly wide. To keep the floor from becoming too much of a conversation piece, and to break the effect of parallel lines, there is a scattering of large and small rugs. The rugs dominate, and also vary the picture. After each housecleaning they seem always to appear in somewhat different places.

The sixth enclosing surface, the roof, is made entirely of wood, but is actually the most varied surface of all. There are many reasons why this is correct, from aesthetic, technical, and practical considerations. The roof, seen from the inside, exhibits its structure of beam, sub-beam, and skin. The variation lies in shape, color, light and shade. Technically, acoustic considerations, which demand variety in shape, are completely satisfied. Practically, in another plane this variation in shape would present an intolerable number of dust catchers, but an overhead surface doesn't catch much dust. Aesthetically, at eye level these shapes would seem inexcusably restless. Well above eye level, they are in peripheral vision where the light and shade patterns are restful.

Several goals have been achieved. Reading around this room as described I find surfaces which speak of light, warmth, work, and distance. If I want to change my mood, I don't have to move to another room, I just turn around. Though the room contains a vast number of tools for living, it does not seem cluttered, simply because it is big. It is big because it can afford to be big. I built the area for four dollars a square foot, or about one-quarter of the conventional cost. It can afford to be big because there is not one ounce of material anywhere which could be said to have been put there for the purpose of decoration.

The room is decorated with structural materials and useful things. They try to tell me my house is "modern." I deny it. My house is the exact opposite of the well-known magazine picture showing one coffee table glittering in the middle of an acre of polished terrazo, with the last spot of dust having been mopped up just before the picture was taken. For living efficiency, my house is a much closer relative to the widely admired colonial kitchen, with its big and little skillets hanging in a neat row on the wall.

I grant that you may not want to go quite as far as I in eliminating formal decoration entirely. Before leaving the subject, I would like to make some specific points.

The decorative value of a material bears no relation to its cost. For instance, the masonry end of my living room is made of cinder block, the cheapest of masonries. All of this masonry, including three chimneys, two big fireplaces with heat ducts, and two sit-on-able hearths, cost eight hundred dollars. Built with the conventional fireplace brick, the cost would have been three times as much. A few observant people have noticed the absence of brick and asked why. The answer is sixteen hundred dollars. Most people just don't notice. The thing is massively but unobtrusively there, and it works. Who cares what it's made of?

Textured materials are almost always pleasanter and easier to maintain than shiny ones: more pleasant because they diffuse light rather than reflect it; easier to maintain because they don't show dirt. Many housekeepers make work for themselves by insisting on status-slick materials from which dust can be easily wiped. I prefer materials, textured either in color or in surface, which don't have to be wiped at all. If I were compelled to use a purely decorative material on a wall, my first choice would be colored burlap. Though not cheap in first cost, it comes in any color you like, meets all of our goals well, and lasts forever.

As of this writing, the plastics industry is beginning to think about molded chemical products for interior decoration. These materials, offering any color you like, any texture you like, a growing range of physical characteristics, opacity or translucence as you like, reluctance to support combustion, total unattractiveness to insects, no affinity for either oxygen or dirt, willingness to be formed into almost any shape whether plane or convoluted, may soon take care of much of our interior décor. As of this writing, they're on the way.

My last reminder is, don't forget about the roof. A flat, plastered ceiling does everything wrong. The underside of a working roof, exhibiting its structure, does everything right. Not walked on, comparatively dust-free, half-consciously seen, eloquent as to its own strength, the underside of your roof is the easiest place to make home a little better than what other people have.

13. The outside

Interior decoration may have begun with pictures drawn on the wall of a cave. Mr. and Mrs. Cro Magnon, burnt sticks in hand, were fixing up the place.

A long time later their descendants became concerned about what houses looked like on the outside. Their first concern was to remain as inconspicuous as possible, so as not to attract the attention of the enemy.

Still later a conspicuous house became desirable. The local landlord built his house at the very top of a hill, so that everyone could see how important he was, then hired as many bodyguards as he could afford, to keep someone even more important from knocking him off.

A house on top of a mountain is expensive, and so are bodyguards. Nowadays we prefer a location about halfway up the hill, striking a delicate balance between being visible to our friends and invisible to tax assessors, bill collectors, and encyclopedia salesmen.

The exterior appearance of houses has always shown what their builders believed themselves to be. From the castle on the hill to the hut in the valley, the external appearance of these structures has spoken not only of the occupants' economic status, but more eloquently of their social intentions.

We want our houses to look the way we ourselves would like to be. In building them we have a slowed-down opportunity to make a statement about ourselves. Most of us do not wish to appear in public as flamboyantly big, bright, colorful, tall, wise, handsome, and successful.

We wish instead that our acquaintances will peek around the veil of our becoming modesty, and through their own powers of observation perceive us to be big, bright, colorful, tall, wise, handsome, and successful.

Your prestige no longer depends on the apparent size of your mansion. You want your house to be big and useful on the inside, yet look deceptively small on the outside. You want your house to show that you are successful but modest about it. Solvent but not loaded. Hardworking but fun-loving. Friendly but reserved. Original, of course, and different in a nice way, but with no intention of giving offense.

These contradictions add up to quite a large order, impossible for any one person to convey while walking down the street. A house can be made to speak for you, untiringly, day and night, to the passerby as well as the friend. Boards and stones and trees can present almost any impression you wish. Even while walking away, you yourself can look back and say, there now,

that's the way I want to be. This is the best reason I can think of for worrying about what a house looks like on the outside.

How do you accomplish this marvelous compromise between beauty and invisibility? An ideal exterior will be visible from the road, allowing your friends to find you, but not so visible as to block the view. Your house will not present its longest dimension to be seen easily. Its bulk will be away from, not parallel to, the road. The arriving guest, entering through a convenient front door, will discover your house, bit by bit, and find out for himself that you are big, bright, handsome, colorful, and so on.

Your house will ornament the landscape but not obscure it. Your house will arouse envy in the breast of the passerby, but an envy that makes him want to know you for his own betterment, rather than harm you for his own satisfaction. This delicate balance between ostentation and humility can not be lived by a human being, but your house can say it for you with no trouble at all.

There are two principles. The first is orientation to the road, from which an attractive portion, but only a portion, of your house should be discreetly, but only discreetly, visible.

The second principle involves economy of purpose. From the outside looking in, economy of purpose is difficult to describe. It involves what you don't do at least as much as what you do do. Never put up a board without making it do work. If your stone wall keeps horses in the pasture, the passerby approves. If it serves no purpose except to keep him out, he questions your motives.

The passerby enjoys a glimpse of a big house that looks usable. He dislikes the sight of a big house fronted with useless ornamentation. He also dislikes a little house which has spawned some useless boards in an attempt to look big.

The passerby dislikes gateposts without any gate. Fences which go nowhere and keep nothing in or out. Grape arbors without grapes. Terrace coverings that obviously don't keep out the rain. Shutters which obviously can not be closed to cover the windows they hang alongside. Stone pillars which hold up nothing, and balconies with nothing holding them up. Doors with no footway leading to them, and tiny patches of lawn on which no one has ever trod.

The passerby is important· because he sees the outside of your house oftener than you do. You don't really care what the outside of your house looks like. By the time you have come home three times you hardly see it any more, but you do care what the passerby thinks, and you want to please him.

I believe that if the inside of a house fits the needs of a going family, if the skin surrounding the inside is honestly and economically built, and if the business of building the house seems not to have disturbed its setting, the result can hardly escape being quietly approved by the passerby.

The outside appearance of a house is subject to infinite variation. Without knowing either you or your house site, I can not presume to tell you what it should look like. What I can do is suggest some dollar savers to help you with your own planning.

Just about the biggest dollar saver of all, both in first cost and maintenance, is to dispense with paint. If you don't want to dispense with paint entirely, at least know why you are using it.

Paint on wood is a cosmetic, not a preservative. Paint is pure decoration. Its only purpose is to make something a different color from what it was before. Paint does not extend the life of any building material I can think of except steel. Paint does slow down the rusting of steel, because the oxiding (rusting) of steel has to begin at the surface.

Paint is most emphatically not a preservative for wood. If anything, paint probably speeds up such rotting as may occur, because it slows down ventilation. If the piece of wood is poorly ventilated, rot can begin anywhere, front, back, or in the middle. Paint a red brick yellow, and you have done no harm to the brick, except that you have to keep on painting it.

Once you have painted something, the endless process of maintaining that paint job has begun. Removing paint is more expensive than putting it on in the first place. Therefore, if in doubt about painting, don't. For the outside of your house, save yourself a lot of money, now and later, by choosing materials you think are handsome in the raw.

If you later decide you want to make a black

thing white or a yellow thing blue, go ahead. Paint used as a decorative accent can be most effective, but keep the painted areas small. Don't in any case start slapping paint around under the impression that if your house isn't painted, it will fall apart next week.

My second big dollar saver, again both in first cost and maintenance, concerns shingles. Shingles are ghosts from the past. The cabin builder, working with the materials at hand, split pieces of wood and put them side by side on his roof. He staggered each succeeding row to cover the cracks in the row below. It was an improvement over pine boughs or grass.

The small size of his wooden shingle had created a pattern of horizontal lines crossed by staggered vertical lines. Many people came to believe that if this pattern were not exhibited, it wasn't a roof. To satisfy this belief, manufacturers take perfectly good roofing material, cut it up into little pieces, then cut slots in the little pieces so that the end result will look like little pieces of wood. It doesn't, but they've done the best they could.

The imitation shingle, with holes cut in it, has used twice as much material, burdened your structure with twice as much weight, taken twice as long to lay, cost twice as much, and will require earlier maintenance. This is a heavy price to pay for an imitation.

The general rule is that any attempt to make one material imitate the appearance of another material is expensive. The imitation shingle is only one example of good material, misused.

Expensive misuse of materials gets into our building habits for several reasons. Three major causes are:

1. Misapprehension
2. Anachronism
3. Accident

Misapprehension can be illustrated with paint. When our very great grandfolks fit back the Indians and built their first barn, it housed a cow. From her milk they made butter, and had some skim milk left over. Skim milk is casein. Casein is a fine paint.

They also had bricks, cheap ones, as will be seen later, hence brick dust, which generally came in red. They mixed the brick dust with the skim milk, and painted the barn, creating the dearly beloved dusty red barn of American history. Very great grandmaw thought it real pretty, and so it was, because the sight of it made her different from the Indians, who painted their faces, not their barns.

Naturally there came a paint manufacturer, eager to turn a fast shilling. He observed that if you leave a piece of wood lying on the ground, it will rot. He quietly kept his mouth shut about the fact that if you put the same piece of wood up in the air, not in contact with ground or masonry, it will not rot. He sold paint. There arose the misapprehension that paint is essential to the preservation of wood.

Wood in contact with masonry or subject to insect damage requires a chemical preservative. We have fine preservatives and should by all means use them. They have no effect on the looks of a house, only on its longevity.

If you want your house painted blue, or mauve, or shocking pink, that is your privilege. If you think it has to be painted to keep it from falling apart, you are under a misapprehension.

An anachronism is an error in time. Our ancestors covered their roofs with whatever was handy—evergreen branches, bundles of straw, pieces of slate, mud, sod, tile, anything that would shed water.

The American colonial settler had to get rid of trees anyway, so he split the best trunks up thin and made shingles. The arrival of many kinds of manufactured roofing has made the shingle an anachronism, an error in time, and an expensive one, at that. It seems to take anywhere from one to ten generations for a building anachronism to die out. It would appear that the imitation shingle, a piece of roofing paper cut up to look like shingles, is slowly vanishing. Soon we may quit trying to copy the roof picture created by great grandpaw who was, many years ago, only doing the best he could with what he had.

It was an accident of history which gave great grandpaw his brick dust with which to paint the barn. The big operator of American colonial days was the shipowner who hauled grain to England and brought back manufactured goods.

Since a thousand dollars worth of manufactured goods weighed less than a thousand dollars worth of grain, he looked around for something to ballast his ship on the return trip. Something more profitable than rocks.

England had little wood but plenty of clay. Poor folks were building their houses out of bricks, the only material they could afford. So bricks became the ballast of choice and the ships sailed home, full of bricks and calico. When the shipowner wanted to build a house, he used bricks. I would have done the same. When other folks saw that the richest man in town lived in a brick house, they wanted to live in brick houses too.

The brick became a symbol of wealth, stability, permanence. It got written into bedtime stories, with the third little pig laughing at the wolf from inside his house of bricks. Worse, the one-time humble brick got written into municipal building codes as being desirable and in some cases compulsory.

The symbolism of brick for the well-to-do persisted as brick walls became more expensive. Higher cost led to the so-called brick veneer, a structural nightmare consisting of one layer of brick against a wooden frame. Some folks built just one brick wall, that facing the street. Finally came the ultimate travesty—bricks printed on paper.

There is delicious humor in all these events stemming from the historical accident of a shipowner's ballast. The joke is that for any structural purpose I ever heard of, brick is not one of the better building materials and never has been.

14. Flexibility

What are you going to build? The many decisions which must be made in answering this question seem desperately final, unchangeable, unfixable, so permanently wrong if they are wrong.

Yes, you're going to build your dream house. Once built, for a little while it may remain just that. Then your dreams change. They change because you change. Your family changes. Your income, your physical strength, your interests, your friends, all change.

Do you stay the same, think the same, do, act, behave, want and plan for the same things now and forever? Of course not. The house is to fit the family, I have said, but what family, and for how long?

In addition to meeting all of your goals for the moment, your house should be built so that it can be made to meet them as your interpretation of need changes. Unless you plan for change, the business of pulling nails and rebuilding your house can be very expensive.

I suggest three economical ways to prepare for inevitable change; choosing an arrangement with possible change in mind; using a construction technique adapted to change; and building in installments.

If you were a pair of hard-up but working artists, you might have begun with the arrangement shown in the solid lines. Some years later both eugenics and economics have smiled upon you. Two additions later your minimum arrangement of studio, kitchen and sleeping alcove has grown to hold four children, two baths, two cars, an office, and a display room.

The arrangement is not ideal. It is not what you would have built had you started it today, but the growth was without backward steps. No money was spent in removing something which was there already. Outside doors have remained

on their hinges to become inside doors. Windows stayed where they were. When a new room was built, the old outside wall was left undisturbed. With the north light a necessity, the children's rooms went south. The plumbing needed to be extended only a few feet from where it was before.

Fortunately, you decided to start out in a longish house. Between long-type houses and square-type houses, the long house is easier to modify. Here is what happens when you try to enlarge a square house.

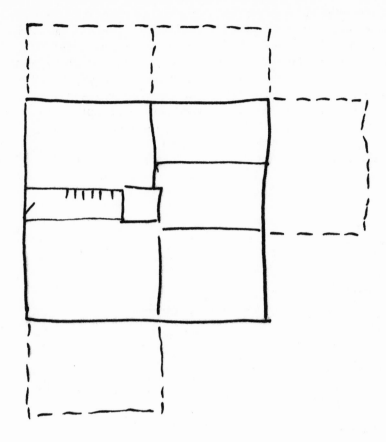

Everything you add covers up something else. Room areas, already too far inside, become more so. It would have been better to leave the original building alone and start over, like this:

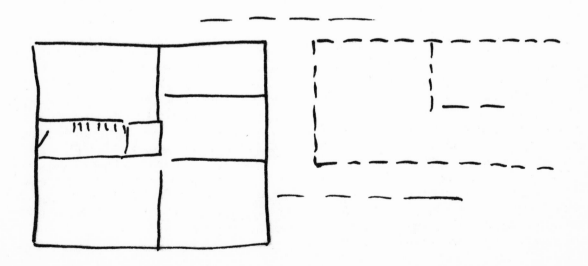

Having stretched out, perhaps to the eastward, you will find that you have engineered yourself into a long house after all. I recommend the long house as being easier to build, easier to change, and the type you will probably wind up with in any case.

Whatever you do, the important consideration in making additions is to spend as little as possible in backing up and tearing away. If a room is too small by four feet, don't tear down the wall and rebuild it four feet away. Change the purpose of the old room, and build another which this time is big enough.

If your old roof is all right, don't touch it. Don't even try to add to it. Keep the new roof headed in the same direction, but higher or lower, and leave the old roof alone. In making any physical change to your house, add but don't subtract. Don't pull one nail or remove one board that isn't standing in the way of what you want to do.

The construction technique best adapted to change is "post-and-beam." In one form it comes out like this:

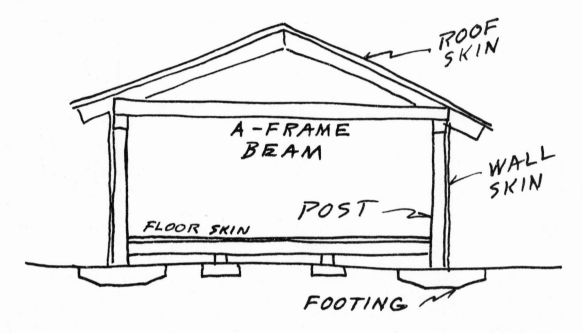

Here are footings, posts, and a roof structure supported thereon. The roof skin goes on first, then wall skin and floor skin can be finished at your leisure, rain or shine.

The wall skin keeps out the wind, but does not hold up the roof. Neither do such partitions as you may choose to have inside. With the walls and partitions holding up nothing, they are easy to move. This architectural concept is possibly the beginning of building by reason: the idea that you could stand up some posts, put a roof on them, and add to the structure in the same manner as your family grew. It predates history. I don't know when the idea was invented, but it was old when Solomon ordered cedars from Lebanon.

The technique of building walls and partitions to hold up a roof is wrong for many reasons, the first of which is that a house built that way is not adaptable to change. In a domestic structure, never build a wall that you can't move if you decide you want to.

The most flexible house of all is the one which will grow as you would want it to grow, and are able to make it grow. I choose to call this, in the current idiom, installment building. It is the oldest technique of all, to build what you can and add as you need. Many people use it now through economic necessity. Assuming that you are strong, eager, and adaptable, the story goes like this:

You are poor but honest, willing to work and

impelled to dream. You would like to own your own house, a beautiful, different, exciting home. Mr. Roe, at the bank where you apply for a construction mortgage, is a thoroughly nice fellow, but he doesn't see eye to eye with you at all. Your ideas sound like opium-smoking to him. Besides, Mr. Roe will get fired if he fails to worry about resale. He wants you to spend thousands of his loaned dollars for things you don't think you need.

In fairness to the many alert and imaginative bankers, I must say that the stodgy Mr. Roes are slowly dying out. However, even the most helpful banker still isn't you, and he still has to charge interest. There is a way to bypass mortgage and interest charges entirely. That is, if you are willing to camp out for a while. It sounds tough. It might be the happiest time of your life.

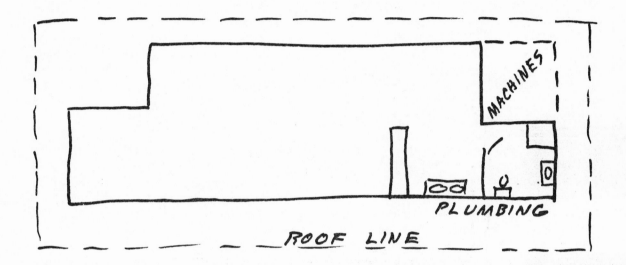

This sketch is the shell of a house. It has a lot of roof, a minimum of wall, some running water, and not much of anything else. Its shape represents, at best, an accurate prediction of the future; at worst, an educated guess. You don't know for sure what the final arrangement is going to be.

The conventional financier insists that a house be completed. He also insists that you have some amount of money of your own before you start. With that same amount of money you can put up a building shell which is plenty good enough for a couple in love to call home.

With that amount of money the original needs can be met in a not too primitive manner. Your requirements will include one roof, one floor, one wall skin, one heat supply, one water supply, one kitchen stove and sink, and one bathroom with a door on it if you insist. Otherwise, skip the bathroom door.

As soon as there is light to see by and water to drink, move in. The moment you stop paying rent somewhere else your first saving begins. Now if you are handy and so inclined, you can take this king-sized love nest from there, building the kitchen counter while your other half hangs muslin curtains to arrange rooms at will.

If you are not handy or not so inclined, and can earn more money in the same time doing something else, don't try to find out which end of a hammer gets hot. Hire a well-adjusted carpenter, off hours, a little at a time. He'll build your love nest faster than you can, while you earn the money to pay him.

With either of these plans going for you, not only do you duck the mortgage and have fun doing it, you are living in a state of maximum flexibility. You see where the sun comes up on a June morning, and on a December morning. You find out which corner is going to feel right for company, which for your own bedroom. You learn which direction most of the rain comes from, where the snow drifts are deep, and where the bird-feeder should be located.

Best of all, you learn what to do without. Starting with no partitions, a partition is built only when its need has become pressing. Most of them never will be built. Since you have to find the money to pay for each new door, no door will get hung until you positively can't do without it. Most of them will never happen, and for the price of the doors that never got hung, you can hang a painting or build a workshop.

Your family habits will form patterns within the enclosure. Use areas will locate themselves. Shelves and movable closets will become room dividers. Artificial light will be located where you find you need it. The dining table will inevitably come to rest in the most desirable location.

When the need for more structure arrives, it will not be imagined, but real to you. By then you will know exactly where to put it. This is the best way I know to keep a house flexible, the best way to design a house from the inside out. By way of bonus, you will come to know yourselves, to find out what you really like and need, as individuals and as a team.

Though you embarked upon this plan from necessity, the end result will contain surprisingly few compromises. You will wind up with a better house than you could possibly have planned in the beginning, and it will have cost you a lot less money.

15. Efficiency

I know a woman who spends her life taking care of a four-room apartment. Every morning except Sunday she begins at the beginning, washes everything, straightens everything. By nightfall she is gratifyingly exhausted. The problem of finding books and papers never arises, because there aren't any books and papers to find. The one concession she makes to dust is to let it sit there all day Sunday.

I know another woman who spends her life collecting books and papers. Every day a fresh layer goes on top, thus keeping the ones under-

neath from collecting that day's layer of dust. With the accumulation covering every horizontal surface, stair treads, mantel, chairs and floor, she keeps room enough on one corner of the kitchen table to rest a doughnut and a glass of milk.

These women happen to be sisters. Most of us fall somewhere between the two extremes. A little time spent taking care of your house is fun. Too much is too much. The breakover point between fun and too much depends on who you are. Wherever that point may be, the work or fun involved is called housekeeping.

The time used for housekeeping varies widely from one housekeeper to the next. All use much the same words to describe their tasks. All housekeepers do three things. They remove dirt, they restore order, they cause the house to function efficiently.

Now try to define dirt, order, and efficiency. These meanings are subjective. For example, you feel that there is dirt on your floor. Take a broom and sweep. Open the door and sweep dirt out. Do you at that moment cease to think of it as dirt? Or does it not cease to be dirt until you have swept it off the flagstones outside?

Contemplate your kitchen counter full of "dirty" dishes. The party ran a little late and spoons, cups, glasses, anchovy cans are stacked up every which way. If you stack all the used spoons in one place and the used glasses in another, do you feel sufficiently orderly to go to bed with a clear conscience? Do you wash the dishes and leave them in the rack? Or do you put them all away and then go to bed?

If you walk a mile through the woods to get water, naturally you will bring back two buckets rather than one. Easier to carry and twice as efficient. Efficiency becomes subjective when the problem concerns the number of steps required to reach the kitchen faucet. Do you insist on one step only, or are you willing to take three? Do you think that a mixer faucet is easier to manipulate than separate faucets for hot and cold? Efficiency is entirely a matter of what seems easiest to you.

Dirt, to begin with, is the housekeeper's generic swear word for anything undesirable, such as a pair of clean socks left lying in the wrong place. In a discussion of how to keep your house "clean," we had better exclude philosophy and define dirt as the presence of foreign bodies you did not invite and which to you are undesirable.

One man's dirt is another man's patina. If a table has dust on it, as all tables do, it's dirty or not depending on whether or not you can see the dust. Let the light shine in such a way as to make the dust visible and the table is dirty. We can all agree to that. Now mix the dust with furniture polish, rub in well, and presently you have patina, which everyone agrees is very nice. How quickly you can convert dust to patina depends on how much dust you have and how often you rub it in.

Almost all of the dirt with which the housekeeper deals was once airborne. Six children stamping their muddy overshoes on the kitchen floor bring in only a small fraction of the dirt poundage delivered by a good brisk breeze. The dirt deposited by the children on the kitchen floor annoys you more because you can see it, but it is easier to deal with because you can sweep it out. Airborne dirt, arriving in greater quantity, creates a subtler but more widespread annoyance.

Airborne dirt has one thing in its favor. It makes better patina. Much depends on dirt particle size. If the breeze is gentle, it can carry only small particles, not big ones. Small particles are harder to see, harder to feel, and they rub in nicely. A violent sandstorm brings in large, unusable dirt particles which are pure annoyance and no good to anyone.

Airborne dirt also differs in quality. The particles resulting from fuel combustion, while small enough, are in most cases greasy. Though not seriously objectionable in creating patina on horizontal surfaces, greasy dirt is difficult to remove from clothing, wallpaper, and paint.

To recapitulate; almost all of the dirt with which the housekeeper deals has been air-delivered. When the air movement slows down, the dirt settles out, larger particles first, then smaller ones. It collects on top of horizontal surfaces, with much less sticking to vertical surfaces and minute amounts on the underside of anything.

Still recapitulating; to be housekeeper-style dirt, the foreign bodies must be undesirable. If the dirt does not make its presence known, that is, if it can be neither seen nor felt, it isn't dirt at all, because you don't know it's there.

We have arrived at two housebuilding rules for dealing with dirt. First, avoid unnecessary horizontal surfaces. Second, use materials which don't show dirt.

Here are some of the horizontal dirt-catchers, necessary and unnecessary:

Many of them are unavoidable, of course. The horizontals you need to stand on, sit on, put things on, also catch dirt. The horizontals you can get rid of are those built into decoration. The wall and door panelings are serious offenders, because they present their accumulation of dirt at or just below eye level. If the decorating horizontal is above eye level, you don't care how much dirt is on it.

Window sills, with light falling on them, are particularly bad. Here is a way to get rid of window sills:

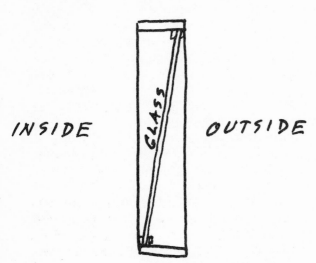

INSIDE   GLASS   OUTSIDE

We have moved the window sill outside the house, where dirt ceases to be dirt.

Getting rid of dirt on the baseboard is easy. Don't have any baseboard. That board was put there in the first place because dirt accumulates in a wall to floor corner, where the board made it both easier to remove and harder to see if not removed. The obvious solution is to make the whole wall, at least up to window level, of a single damage-free and dirt-camouflaging material.

Try as you will, most of the horizontal square feet in your house can not be eliminated. So the second rule, keeping dirt invisible, becomes the more important of the two because it can be applied in some degree to any surface.

It may be difficult for you to accept this idea if you have been brought up to believe that smooth, shiny, uniform surfaces are symbols of quality, and are therefore to be preferred to sur-faces which are textured in either color or smoothness. The linking of shinyness with prestige dates from the time when rich folks could afford enough servants to keep their glossy surfaces looking clean.

The servantless housekeeper finds that texture makes life easier, provided thought has been given to the degree and kind of texture on any given surface. A sub-rule for dirt control can be stated this way: a horizontal surface should be smooth to the touch but textured in appearance; a vertical surface can be textured to touch, to the eye, or both; an overhead surface can be just about anything you like.

For example, a table top, unavoidably touchable, should be smooth, both for touching and for wiping, therefore it has to be textured in appearance so as not to show the unavoidable dirt. A floor is slightly different. It need not be smooth to the touch. If anything, it should be slightly rough to keep you from slipping, yet not rough enough to impede the sweeping away of dirt. As with the table top, it must not be shiny or uniform in color, but textured in appearance, to keep the unavoidable dirt from showing.

Walls do not collect muddy footprints, and they need not be smooth to the touch. They do collect finger prints, but not much airborne dirt. Insofar as you want your wall to be light in color, you need a more heavily textured surface in order not to show dirt. A light-colored, surface-textured wall also makes an excellent diffuser of illumination.

As with walls, overhead surfaces diffuse illumination well if they are light-colored and rough, the rougher the better. There are no footprints, no fingerprints, and very little airborne deposit. A rough-textured overhead surface has defeated dirt. So has an overhead surface made of wood, preferably unfinished, but it doesn't diffuse light as well. Here is an example of compromise between material, cost, and function.

Fortunately for housekeeping, the appreciation of textured materials is growing, a trend brought about by the demise of the domestic servant. Once the owner and the housekeeper become the same person, the housekeeper begins to get smart. The trend is followed closely by materials manufacturers, who are offering an excellent variety of textures. Their advertising states, in this case correctly, that the materials are made that way in order not to show dirt.

Even the periodicals dealing with domestic architecture, which normally follow rather than lead their advertisers, for once are out in front. I was astonished to read in one such magazine that the easiest wall surface to take care of is unfinished wood, a statement which, though offensive to almost all of that magazine's advertisers, is exactly correct.

Orderliness is even more subjective than cleanliness. Dirt is largely a natural phenomenon. Clutter is entirely man-made. Having created our own clutter, it is up to us to sort it out, or to live with it. Here are some characteristics of clutter:

A certain amount of clutter—and you must decide how much that is—is both more efficient and more home-like than complete orderliness.

We all are less annoyed by our own clutter than by someone else's. I can clear up, or at least push around, my own junk. I don't know what to do with your junk.

Clutter being personal, it can be reduced but not eliminated by mechanical aids such as shelves, desks, cupboards, filing cabinets and closets. Such repositories become nothing more than clutter containers, if this is your habit. My own filing cabinet is full of roughage. The important papers are out in the open where I can find them.

Most of us work best at our own clutter quotient, which I will call One Cee, then proceed to create about twice as much as we like, or Two Cee. It is only to bring Two Cee down somewhat closer to One Cee that we worry about clutter control.

A house can help you by classifying clutter in designated rooms or areas. You keep your overshoes in the mud room, your used clothing in the laundry, your ping-pong balls in the playroom, your unanswered correspondence in the office, your unread magazines in the library, your cherished dry goods in the sewing room, and your screwdrivers in the shop.

This system of clutter classification allows the kitchen to be happily cluttered with nothing more than food, the dining room with dishes, the sitting room with chairs, and the bedroom with shoes. By classifying clutter areas, there is a place for every kind of clutter.

With enough clutter areas, you can safely go ahead with the desired quantity of closet, cupboard, shelf, and storage space. Though this system does not guarantee that shirts will be found in the clothes closet, bank statements in the office, condensed milk in the kitchen, and hammers on the tool rack, at least it's a step in the right direction.

The best way of all to live with your own clutter is to have plenty of room for it. If your own clutter quotient is One Cee, and you consistently surround yourself with Two Cee, try working in a room twice as big as before. Though you still have Two Cee clutter, the clutter density will have dropped back to One Cee Dee. This is still another plea to save money where you can, then spend it on bigger rooms and a bigger house. A little house is harder to keep looking clutter-free than a big one.

Dirt removal and clutter control are subheadings under the topic of making a house efficient. Your life is full of many things which, though part of living, are not particularly pleasant, take up your time, and produce nothing.

Bugs, for instance. The housefly got his name because he likes to come in the house. The architectural trend which eliminated the screened porch made life much easier for the housefly, and all the other flying undesirables.

The screened porch has many virtues, the greatest of them being bug control. The porch has only one door, but the bugs don't know that. They sit around all over, thus lowering their population density. The screen door opens out, and the bugs don't know that either. The porch light, properly located, is not at the door, adding to bug confusion. These devices make the human smarter than the bug, enabling the human to enter without bringing swarms of insects with him.

The screened porch is wonderfully efficient. It is a welcoming roof over the head of the arriving guest. It keeps the rain from dripping down his neck as he stands at your front door. It gives him a place to scrape his feet, take off his overshoes and stash his umbrella. If necessary, the screened porch can double as mud room, play room, summer night bedroom. It provides a semi-hospitable place for those doorway conversations where you don't feel like inviting the other guy all the way in.

A relative of the screened porch, simply many square feet of roof over some part of the outdoors, is another efficient device. A roofed area is better for some purposes than complete enclosure and just as good for many others. Yet it costs a fifth as much for its size.

A roof is the basic requisite of shelter. It offers quick hospitality. It breaks the transition from completely unsheltered outdoors to fully sheltered indoors. It gives you a place to stamp your physical and mental feet. It shelters those things which can stay outdoors without harm, yet need to be available for use indoors.

Take firewood, for instance. It makes an attractive fence at the back of the breezeway.

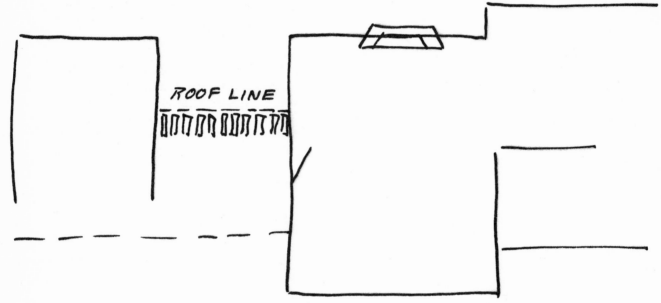

A cord or two of fireplace wood is a low-key, modest symbol of wealth, warmth, and friendliness. Why use enclosed space to hide your firewood? Let your guests enter past a neat woodpile, and perhaps they'll feel inclined to carry in a stick or two.

Washing textiles and washing people are related functions. Both are made easy by soap, drains, and running water. In the absence of domestic servants to do the wash for you, the bathroom and laundry belong together.

Appliance	Hot water	Cold water	Drain to soil pipe	Vent	Electric power
1. Sink	#	#	#		
1.5 Grinder		#	#		#
2. Dish-washer	#		#		#
3. Washing Machine	#		#		#
4. Dryer				#	#
5. Water closet		#	#	#	
6. Lavatory	#	#	#		
7. Shower	#	#	#		
8. Bath	#	#	#		
Totals	6	6	8	2	4

Here is the equivalent of great-grandma's bucket, dipper, stove, washpan, tub, and clothesline. She worked harder at home, but we work harder somewhere else to pay for the replacement.

I have to tell a true story while it's fresh in my mind. Last night at town meeting, the moderator was explaining a proposed ordinance concerning the payment of plumbing inspection fees.

He said there was to be a fee for each house, plus a small additional charge for each plumbing appliance. Enumerating these, he found the water closet, the lavatory, the bathtub, the kitchen sink, even the rich man's dishwasher. "Oh yes," he said, "I forgot the washing machine in the basement."

Though habit is strong upon us, Caroline found the courage to place her washing machine and dryer within arm's reach of the dirty towels. The plumbing inspector was not in the least disturbed.

Having eliminated running up and down stairs to the laundry, let us also eliminate snow shoveling. Whether you run your own snowplow or hire someone else to do it, here is the way to let the plow get rid of it all:

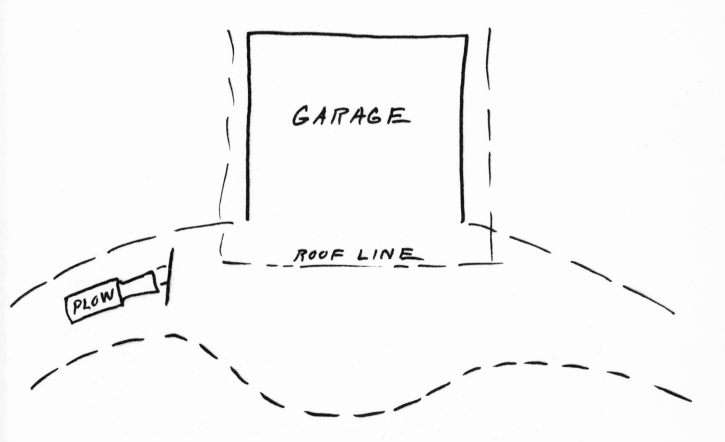

The plow goes right on by the garage without pushing up a dead end for you to shovel away.

Then if the garage roof has a big overhang, like this:

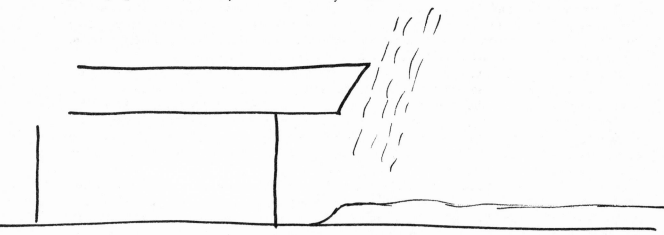

the plow leaves nothing behind. You have already arranged to walk from garage to house under continuous roof. All outside doors are protected by roof overhang. Even blowing snow has been kept away by screened porches. You have abolished snow shoveling. You might live to see your grandchildren get married.

One thing bothers me. In order to want to live that long, you'd better leave yourself a little bit of snow to be shoveled as a token; a few knives to be sharpened, to show you know how; some underwear to be carried to the bedroom, for domesticity; and some fires to be lit, for fun. Don't make the place too darned efficient. It might not seem like home.

16. Pleasure

What good is all this talk about efficiency and arrangement and plumbing and heat control if it isn't fun to be there? Some things you have for no reason except the best reason of all—you want them.

Feeding the psyche is as important a function as feeding the body. A favorite picture isn't making any money as it hangs there. It isn't doing the cooking or sweeping the floor, but if it is helping you cook and sweep, there's function enough.

Prime example of a lovely though unjustifiable monster is the fireplace. Woefully inefficient as a source of heat, splendid as a source of dirt, expensive to build and possibly troublesome to maintain, the good old drafty fireplace stays right in there as the focal point of our sit-down leisure. Personally I wouldn't dream of being without one, and a good big one at that.

If you are thinking of a fireplace not for pleasure but for prestige, as something which all good houses are required to have, as decoration, as something to be ornamented with two yellow andirons and three white birch logs, as something never to be lit because it might put spots on the wall, then leave it out. Skip the expensive monster and spend the money on something you do want.

Spend the money on something in your house which is absurdly and wonderfully non-productive of anything but your pleasure. If you like to make your own music, have a music corner, and a clear area with plenty of room for dancing. The money you saved on rugs can go toward a better piano.

If, instead of making music, you are addicted listeners, the room layout should be built around the location of phonograph, speaker, and you. Further, if you really know and are concerned about high fidelity, you will want your speakers built in, located in the right acoustic places, not the right decorating places.

Perhaps flowers are the big thing with you. Knock off on something else and have your own greenhouse. It needn't be hidden out back, either. Have it right up front, and live in it.

The serious craftsman and the serious seamstress, both taking pleasure in their work, deserve equally good accommodations. The seamstress needs good light, storage space, dozens of drawers, a six-foot table on which to spread her work, an ironing board, and wall sockets for iron, sewing machine, and close-up illumination.

The craftsman also needs good light, storage spaces big and little, heavy duty wiring, room to swing a twelve-foot board end for end, and a set of double doors for bringing lumber in and taking the boat out. The craftsman, especially if his craft produces bulky things, wants to work at ground level. Fortunately his pleasant ground-level shop costs no more than the same space anywhere else.

If instead of boat building, your craft is photography, you would sooner do without a bathroom than a dark room. The requirements for a dark room are special, but imperative to your pleasure. Plan your dark-room sink on the other side of the bathroom wall, using the same water pipes and drain, and you can have both without noticing the difference in dollars.

The reader has his books available. While they sit waiting for him, they look good too. The gunner has his guns in gun racks, where he can admire them. Perhaps his shell-loading bench is also on display. The fletcher's work table, where bright feathers are fitted into arrows, is something to behold, as are the paraphernalia required to tie trout flies. The good cook's kitchen is ablaze with vari-colored spice shelf, pewter bowls, black skillets and ruddy copperware. The pianist never closes the lid on his ever ready keyboard. The cellist never puts his instrument away.

In planning your home, do not be ashamed to admit that the people who live there do something besides grow old.

Your house is a safe, irreproachable place to loosen your mental corset. The juiciest pleasure of all is the pleasure of having something different.

Conformity in dress, in speech and manner, in expressed thoughts, in the shape and size of automobiles, in the right time to work and the right time to play; these conformities are important to most of us, convenient to all of us. Conformity keeps us comfortable away from home. But when you say, "Drop by my house some evening, I'd like to have you look it over," the unspoken translation is, come by and find out what I'm really like.

Conformity can be ignored at home. Not rebelled against, just ignored. There are few of us who do not cherish the dream of a house distinctly and purely our own. Most people are afraid to pursue this dream because they have been told that anything different will cost too much.

Some differences cost more, others save money. Begin with the money-saving differences, which are the things you find you can leave out. To suggest a few: fancy light fixtures, plate glass, trim boards on rafter ends, vertical footings, garage doors, hardwood flooring, varnish, moldings and mill-worked interior trim, wall tile where it does no good, paint, shingles, wallpaper, plaster, false ceilings, brick fireplace facing.

By now about half the cost of a conventional house lies in the wastebasket. You have found a lot of money to "waste" on differences in which you find pleasure, such as that dark room, and more windows, and a greenhouse.

But with all that money in hand waiting to be spent, proceed with caution. There are two kinds of differences, difference in detail and difference in plan.

Striving for difference in detail can be expensive. Be careful about the unusual in non-structural things, store-bought items such as faucets, bathtubs, doorknobs, hinges, ceramic tile. These are small things, making little difference in the over-all impression. Spend your money, if need be, on big differences.

Difference in plan—that is, in structure—can usually be had for nothing. You can be impressively and pleasurably different in locating and shaping your house. Provided the roof lines are kept simple, structural components can be put together to produce any one shape just about as cheaply as another.

This allows you to plan what you want on the inside of your house. The outside will design itself from what goes on inside. Build what you really want, and the result will be different from other houses because you are different from other people. Do not attempt to be different for the sake of being different. The result will please no one, not even you.

If you don't put anything in there you don't need, the result can hardly help but be pleasurable, both inside and out, both to you and other people.

The money you saved by omissions may now be burning a hole in your pocket. If so, build bigger rooms and a bigger house. Here is a real difference which is bound to bring pleasure. With little elbow room left elsewhere, at least you can enjoy the difference of having elbow room at home.

I am not so much interested in helping you get the same house for half the money, as in helping you get twice the house for the same money, or stopping wherever you like in between. Most houses are too small. Whatever else you do, engineer yours to be big enough.

17. Where do you go from here?

The subject of this first chapter has been WHAT you are going to build. I have not told you exactly what. I can't. At this distance, no one else can. Even to try, in detail, might mess up everything. I have tried to help you decide what to build. You're on the scene of action and it's up to you.

What I don't want you to build is any shape, size, style, color, type or location of house because you imagine that society forces it upon you. I don't want you to use any details or materials because you imagine that society requires them.

I am trying to suggest ways of thinking about what you want and need and can afford. Along the way, I hope to disabuse you of some widely held fallacies which not only would cost you unnecessary money, but may be standing between you and what you would like to have. I hope to convey a few technical facts which will help you, not only to have a better house, but to be more comfortable at home.

The meat of this chapter is, in one sentence: What a house should be cannot be decided on any terms other than who is going to live in it, and where it is going to be. No architect should attempt his first sketch for you, and you shouldn't ask him to try, until he knows your family and stands on your proposed site. That is why the discussion part of this book cannot and will not include specific, detailed house plans. I don't know you as a person, I haven't met your family, I have never stood on your site.

The discussion will include specific structural details which are of use anywhere. I have built these details with my own hands. I have refined them through my own mistakes, paid for with my own money. They work. Some of these pet notions have crept into the discussion already. Two of them are important enough to explain now.

First, the built-in, slightly slanted windowpanes. I don't mean the heavily slanted windows used by some architects in an attempt to be different. For years I've been building all my glass with the top leaning out at an angle of about one inch in twenty. I've never happened to run across this detail in any other house, or in a book or magazine. Yet at one look the benefits of this detail are there to see.

The glare is strikingly less than from a vertical pane. This is the first thing you notice.

The glass stays clean longer on the outside, which collects more dirt and is less convenient to clean. The dirt it does have, either inside or out, is less noticeable.

The acoustic improvement is tremendous.

Tipping the panes slightly, not in itself noticeable unless your attention is called to it, removes what some people feel is the glacial unfriendliness of large expanses of glass.

Second, and very very important, are the manifold virtues of a single-slope roof with its long dimension and high side toward the south, or ideally, south by southeast. This one structural detail contributes to more of our housing goals than any other single thing I can think of.

It invites heat in winter, keeps it out in summer.

It invites winter light, controls summer light.

It provides a roofed, sunny outside area at no extra charge.

Its acoustics are superb. No charge.

Ventilation works perfectly without further effort or expense.

It confines the water run-off problem to one side only, the least useful side, at that.

It contributes to a feeling of spaciousness, but

the actual cubic content to be heated is the same as with an A-frame, or a little less.

Its interior shape is friendly, varied, inviting, pleasantly unsymmetrical.

Its outside weather surface is cheap to build and easy to maintain. All parts of its roof structure involve a minimum of cutting and fitting.

The only structural drawback is that the main roof beams have to use more material, or else be more skillfully designed than an A-frame for a house of the same size.

The single-slope roof has been attacked on aesthetic grounds. Though I refuse to argue aesthetics, I believe the attackers just haven't gotten used to it yet, or else may be referring to a single slope aimed in some direction other than south. To me the single slope, properly used, speaks so clearly and naturally of its purpose that it can not help but be beautiful.

CHAPTER TWO

Where shall it be?

18. A large world

When Caroline and I had to pick out a place to live, our first problem was to beat down the conviction that somewhere, if we looked long enough, we would find perfection. Not having infinite time in which to look, we decided that no single place could fill all possible requirements.

We wrote down everything we could think of to want, knowing that many desires would be mutually contradictory. The list started out something as follows:

Ocean; sight, sound, smell, proximity.
Salt-water swimming, warm enough in season.
Rocks, and perhaps a mountain.
A good beach at the kitchen door.
Absolute command of privacy.
A shopping center ten minutes away.
Wide choice of engineering employment within
    one hour's drive.
—and so on, including having everything at half
    price.

By the time our list became two or three pages long, we knew for sure that something had to give. The mountain top didn't seem to fit too well with a salt-water beach at the kitchen door, or with a wide choice of employment just around the corner.

We realized that with judicious crossing off of some of the requirements, there were lots and lots of living places that would satisfy the rest.

It is indeed a wide world. As of this writing, there is still a choice left to most of us, if we go looking for it, and don't take too many years in the looking. The purpose of this section is to offer a few hints on the technique of going about it.

WHERE is the most important single factor about your house. In many circumstances it can be as important as all other factors put together.

Home is of course where the heart is, but some homes are harder on the heart than others. I realize that the right people will have a good home no matter where they are, but the same right people might have a better home somewhere else.

Here we are talking about your house, which is the visible shell of your home. Where, more than anything else, determines how much money you will spend on this visible shell, and your satisfaction with the result.

Your choice of place to live is very broad. Just because you were born in Pickering Junction or West 159th Street doesn't mean you have to live out your days in Pickering Junction or West 159th Street. Most of us are at liberty, within reason, to move to a different hemisphere, country, state, county, or town.

The place you live may be more important to you than the way you make a living. You can with ease nowadays change employers. They're looking for good men all over. With more effort you can change professions if need be. You can change jobs, or get the same job in a different place.

However, let's begin with a fixed area, two hour's drive in diameter. Let's assume you regard yourself as tied professionally to the vicinity of Nemo City. You like your job and want to keep it. You can work in Nemo City and still take your choice from any one of these four homesite categories:

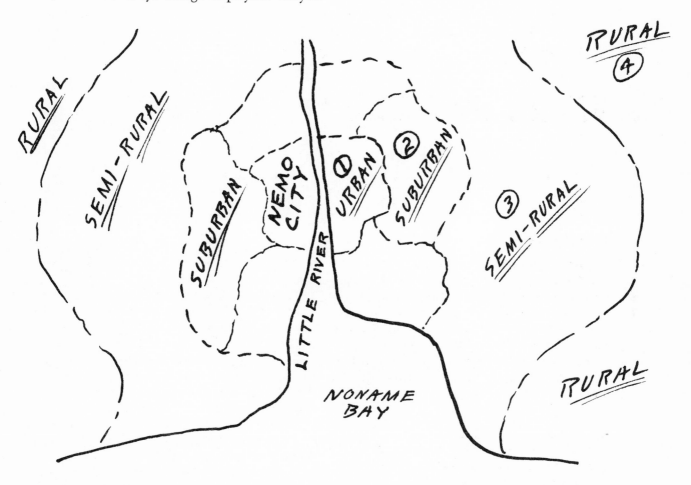

The lines are surprisingly well-defined between the urban site, suburban, semi-rural, and rural. What defines them is money.

URBAN: space sold by the square foot, limited architectural range, high building costs, high taxes, high space rental. Close to work. Transportation by foot, bus, or taxi.

SUBURBAN: space sold by the front foot, architectural type and orientation somewhat limited, fairly high building costs and taxes. Public transportation or automobile.

SEMI-RURAL: space sold by the acre but at living-space premium prices above productive value, architectural type and orientation unlimited, moderate to low building costs, moderate taxes based to some extent on quality of public services. Transportation mostly by automobile.

RURAL: acreage without living-space premium, architecture unlimited, low building costs, low taxes but fewer public services, natural resources available. Automobile transport only.

Some of the money factors work one way, some the other. The emotional factors are another story. If I had to choose on a straight dollar basis of getting the most for my money, the nod would go to semi-rural, that area which feels and looks like country but isn't, because the fire truck and the police car are only three minutes away. Next in order of economy would come rural, after that, urban, and last of all, suburban, that area which feels like city, but isn't, and which tries to look like country, but doesn't.

To begin making a category choice, draw a map, with your place of employment at the center. Around that, draw lines indicating a rough approximation of travel time to work: half an hour, forty-five minutes, one hour.

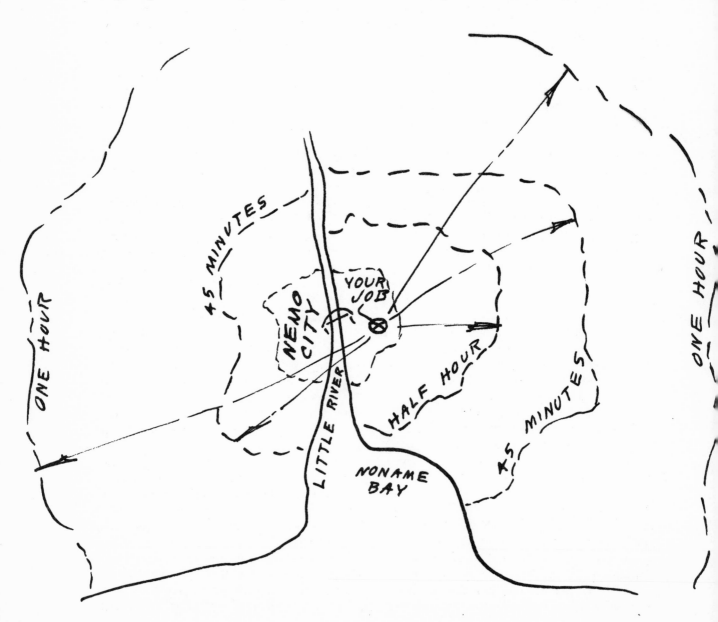

Figure these travel times on the basis of honest door-to-door elapsed time, and you will discover that around most cities an hour represents five times the distance that a half hour does. Five times the distance equals twenty-five times the area to choose from, and possibly one hundredth of the price per square foot or acre of living room.

A mark on your map, representing the irregular outline of an hour's travel time, will around most cities include an area of two to three thousand square miles. That's a lot of landscape to choose from. It is so very much space that you, who work in the city, will wonder which direction you would prefer to call homeward.

Naturally you begin with your convictions, tastes, emotions, family, friends, loyalties, and the areas you know best. These may prompt you to prefer west or north or southeast. If, however, you think you've been seeing too much of mother, try living on the other side of town. Whatever your inclinations, in most cases there are fine spots all around.

You have gathered that my own inclination is to travel five minutes longer in search of elbow room. I think it is cheaper and more exciting. It is my own admitted prejudice that human beings can live gracefully either in skyscraper apartment buildings, or on something more than five acres of their own land.

My prejudice in the matter is that the less space you have around your dwelling, the more money you will spend in unproductive conformity with your neighbors, the more comfort you will sacrifice through improper siting and orientation, the more beauty you will lose that might have been yours for nothing.

Having voiced my prejudice, which is as open to attack as any other, I do not say you are wrong if your own taste runs the other way. If everyone wanted to live in the country, there wouldn't be any.

There are still more places to live, though not within one hour's drive of Nemo City. Let's change the plot and say you don't work in the city. Millions of folks don't. You are a farmer, living on your farm. You can laugh at our two thousand square miles and our description of urban, suburban, semi-rural and rural. You can call your living space—

WORKING RURAL. You the farmer are available to work the clock around, twice if necessary. You chose your place to live when you chose your farm. Within the boundaries of your kingdom, you can build your house wherever you choose. Your privacy, your personal freedom from everything but work, is built in to the nature of your business.

There are other millions of folks whose labor is not confined by geography, who work by mail. Let us call their area—

LONG GONE. Such is the variety of human taste that some of the long-goners wind up living in a penthouse on Fifth Avenue; others on an island in the Indies, East or West. As opposed to you the farmer, astride your large but immobile kingdom, the kingdom of you the novelist may be small, but your choice of its location lies anywhere.

Finally, there are many people who cannot or will not find a solution to their conflicting demands for a homesite. Let us use still another phrase—

DOUBLE-SITING. If you are a general-practice doctor, working twenty-three hours a day, you want your office on Main Street, your bedroom not over forty feet distant. You also want a refuge when you can't stand the pace. You are quite understandably a double-siter. Your home-from-home may be only five miles or five minutes away, but the telephone number is unlisted.

Harder for me to understand are the people who double-site because they think it is fashionable. They have two houses, one close to the office, either urban or suburban, in which the office-worker dwells the year round. The second is long-gone located, some four to sixteen driving hours away, in order to get some part of the family "away from it all."

Dipping into my own prejudice again, this seems to me a clumsy and inefficient arrangement, involving twice as many houses as you need, days of wasted travel time, and the sacrifice of having everything you might want right where you want it.

If your family genuinely wants to double-site, and can afford the effort, that's all right with me. If you are doing it because the neighbors all do it, that's not a good reason. Explore the possibility of a semi-rural compromise between your office and fresh air for the children, get out your map and start looking.

It is indeed a large world. You might find excitement in any bit of it, from skyscraper to hill. Surely somewhere in all these thousands of square miles there will be a place to please you.

19. How far is far?

In this discussion I am trying to help you find a good site. Fortunately, as in picking a wife, there are no standards that will fit everybody. If there were, in the one case all the men would be wooing the same woman; in the other case all site-hunters would be bidding for the same piece of ground. It's a good thing we're not all the same.

Our varying tastes do make it hard to communicate. If, for instance, I write "far away," you might read me to mean five feet, which is farther than four feet, or fifty miles, which is farther than forty.

I might find myself talking to a happy apartment-dweller whose only regret is that the wall of the next building is only five feet away. Move him to a place where the next building is ten feet away and all is well. Another fellow reading the same sentence might find his closest neighbor a cozy twenty miles over the horizon. Let him hear that an interloper is settling only ten miles away and he feels crowded.

When I talk about near and far, lots of room, high hills, wide valleys, big streams, I do it knowing that one man's lake is another man's puddle. Put any dimensions which feel right into these words. They are intended as qualities, not quantities.

How big a place do you want?

For some years I found myself in the business of selling country-style land. The families who came looking were surprisingly similar; all much the same age, all with multiple children, all in a sufficiently comfortable income bracket so that the price of the site was not critical. All were refugees from suburbia. All were living on roughly a quarter of an acre.

In seeking more land to live on, these families of similar background were all facing the physical and mental leap from a suburban area into semi-rural. Each family explained this to me in much the same phrases.

To each family I put the same question. How big a place do you want? Some of the families asked for one acre. Some of them asked for one hundred.

In making their widely varied requests, all of the families used the same words, with only the numbers differing. For one thing, they all said they wanted to be—

Isolated. I believe this word means to stand detached from others of a like kind. You don't isolate yourself from trees and grass, just from other people. These families all liked other people, but they sought that magic distance from others which would enable them to be distinctively themselves.

There was talk a little while ago about wanting our houses to be distinctively our own. I have seen areaways fifteen feet wide that told a story of distinction. I have seen houses in the middle of a thousand acres that had no distinction.

My own emotional definition of isolation is that if every house is out of sight of every other house, and beyond the range of annoying sound, there's isolation enough. How much distance is required to achieve this goal depends on terrain. Most people do not define isolation with quite this stringency. In the architectural sense, if houses stand far enough apart so that they do not interfere with each other aesthetically, that could be isolation enough to achieve all the distinction you yourself will seek.

Going back to the phrases used by my land-hunting families, none of them wanted to be—

LONELY. I believe this word means not having others of like kind near. Now you can see my difficulty in advising these people. In all good faith they told me they wanted other people near, and not near. This is perfectly all right. We're all the same way. We have to put our own boundaries at some distance about us.

To help you determine your distance, let's make scale drawings:

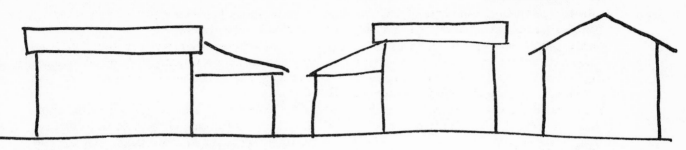

This feels crowded. Now take the same three houses and spread them out a little:

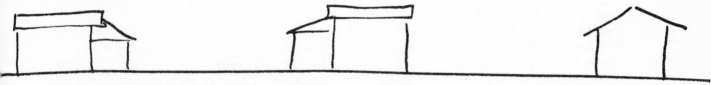

There is room in this sketch to build two more houses between the previous three. Would you like that or not? Now let's introduce a little hill and a couple of trees. I'm running out of acreage so there will be only two houses this time.

Do you want your neighbors across the hall, across the back fence, a stone's throw, within sound of a shout, dog bark, gun shot, or five minutes' drive away?

Before you answer, try the right-hand house in the previous sketch, by itself.

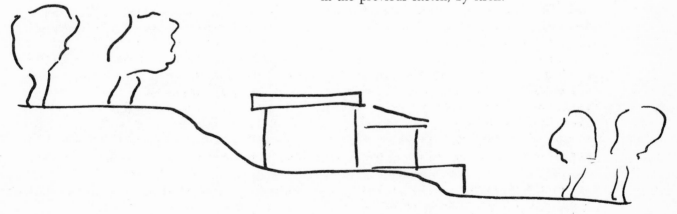

It's the same house, with the neighbors removed. Do you feel lonesome now?

My land-hunting friends all said they wanted to be—

SECURE. There are all kinds of security. In talking about house-siting I think it means free from fear or apprehension. You can argue yourself blue in the face, but if you remain apprehensive, that's it.

You can explain to yourself that an unlocked door is safer than a locked one. You can insist that a thief feels safer in a crowd, while an honest man is not afraid to walk by himself. You can tell yourself that the fire department will be here in three minutes.

You can believe all these things, and still be apprehensive. You can be even more apprehensive to see all those people crowded in close around. You have to explore your own mind to find that place between isolation and loneliness which will make you feel secure.

Here I am doing the best I can to describe a good house-site when, in fact, I can't even describe good weather. With one man wanting sunshine, another rain, and still another, snow; when one wants wind and the other wants calm; when some like it hot and some like it cold; how can I venture to help you find the place where you intend to spend the rest of your lives?

In terms of house planning, I can try. I didn't help you decide what hemisphere or country or state to live in. I did not help you decide what climate you prefer. I'm trying to stick to architecture while avoiding geography, politics, and psychiatry. It's a losing try. Since your house is an important part of yourself, these things will get into the act whether or no.

Starting with what state you will be in and what city, if any, you will be near, we have looked at the kinds of areas available; urban, suburban, semi-rural, rural, working rural, long gone, and double.

Pick your area, then we will get down to cases on what to look for. The discussion will involve real property, money, law, and emotion, in this order:

20.—The real estate
21.—The economic estate
22.—The political estate
23.—The personal estate
24.—Making it yours

20. The real estate

They call it "real" estate because that's what it is; the stuff you see and touch and walk on. Here are some things to seek in the physical reality of your proposed site.

SITE OPPORTUNITY. I said that WHERE is the most important single factor, apart from yourselves, in the success of your house. Of all the factors involved in choosing WHERE, site opportunity is the most important. It is also the hardest to define, because site opportunity will never be twice the same.

The site must have "something." Something to work on, to build around. Something to trigger your imagination, or if your own imagination is a slow starter, someone else's. The trigger something might be tree, grove, boulder, stream, hillside, rock wall, meadow, valley . . . anything, but "something."

The less obvious this something is, the less it will cost. Every man and his brother is out looking for the completed thing of beauty. You can save money by grasping the site opportunity that other folks have been too hurried or too unimaginative to see. If you do not happen to have an eye for seeing what can be made from what exists, take along a friend who has. Remember that the site opportunities which were easy to see have already been gobbled up by someone else.

Forgive me one personal instance of site opportunity. The last piece of real estate I bought was for one reason and one reason only—the presence of a small stream, and a constriction in the valley which begged to have a dam put across it. Being one who prefers his swimming water not over fifty feet away, the possibility of getting a big pond, cheap, was all I needed. We closed the deal in minutes. Aside from the site opportunity, which was obvious, and the name of the town we were in, I knew nothing about the property, which is a shameful violation of much of the advice from here on.

The moral of the story, perhaps, is that after the pond was there, people kept stopping by to tell me how they had thought of buying the place and creating that very body of water. I began making marks on the wall. This happened exactly fifty times.

Though not once did I say, "Why didn't you?", assorted reasons were offered. Too far from town (four minutes by car). Too brushy (the brush had hidden the pond site). Little traveled road (a state numbered route). No mail delivery (the mail route came our way two years later). No neighbors (you should have seen the crowd at our house last night). As the pond got prettier, the reasons dwindled away. With time most of the fifty people forgot that for a while they had hated us a little.

ORIENTATION. With site opportunity the most important item in the site selection book, I think orientation possibility is the next most important.

In Section 2 we discussed sun orientation; in Section 3, scenery orientation. There are other kinds of orientation—to storms and wind; to the road; to the placement of your driveway; to the sound of trucks grinding up that road; to the shimmer of moonlight on the pond—and these things don't always fit together.

The right place to locate your house with reference to the sun may not be the right place with reference to the scenery, or to the wind. None of these may be right with reference to the road. It is a rare site indeed which will be kind to you in all respects.

To pursue my own anecdote, I was happy to find a strikingly good site opportunity. I knew the place was oriented wrong. It lay like this:

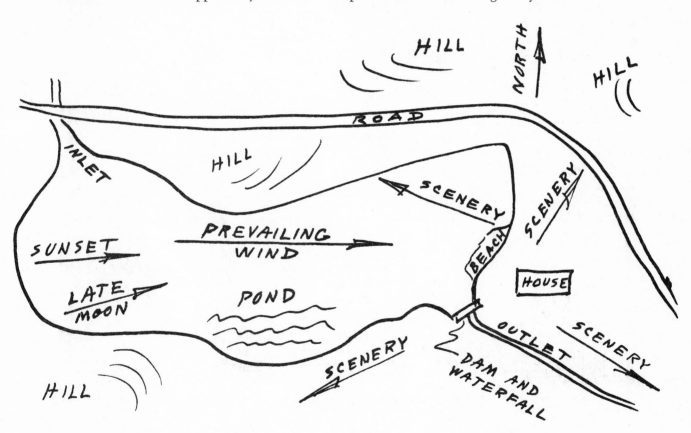

Scenery orientation is perfect. From the inside looking out, with scenery in all directions, you couldn't go wrong. Sun orientation is just fair. A big hill to the east delays the sunrise by twenty minutes. The sunsets are lovely, but only a late moon strikes the water.

The obvious flaw is in wind orientation. All winter long the prevailing west to northwest wind sweeps across the open pond area. The rest of the year, leaves, brush and natural trash in the pond all wind up on the beach. . . . Don't get me wrong. It's a beautiful place, at least according to the scores of painters and cameramen who have worked it over. I still say nature didn't fix it quite right.

In my dreams of perfect orientation, it would have been this way:

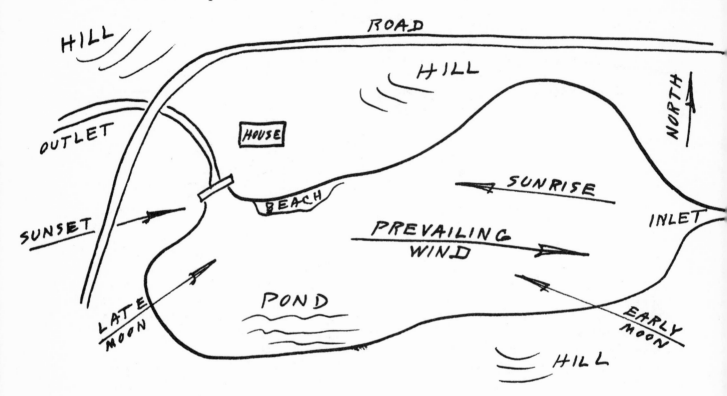

All I have done here is turn the pond and road upside down and backwards. The sun rises early. The wind keeps the beach clean. The sunset glows upon the waterfall, and the capricious. moon has lots of time to gleam across the water.

Notice, by the way, that the road orientation is good in either case, A house should be located on the inside of a curve, thus:

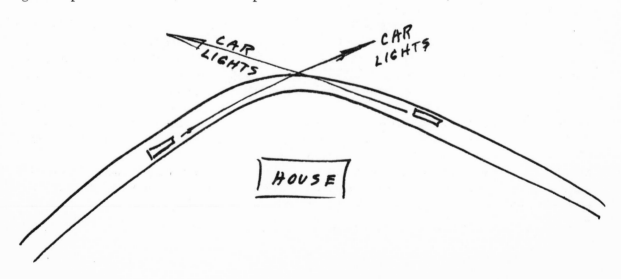

because a house on the outside of a curve is swept by car lights from both directions. It's a fine location for filling stations and hamburger stands, but not so good for living.

Speaking of road orientation, if the road going by us is a busy one, we hope that at least it will be fairly level. Look at this unfortunate fellow:

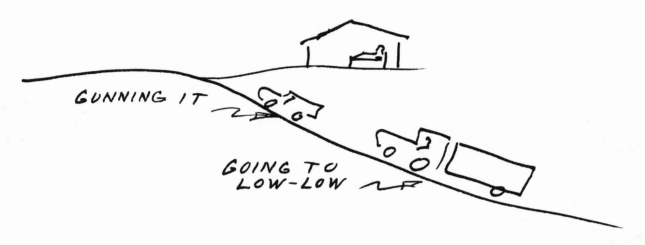

The hapless gentleman lying wide-awake in bed is listening to the rattle of crockery on his shelves.

Site orientation is a complex of many factors. There is orientation to sun, wind, road, scenery, moon, water, car lights, sewer lines, and the nearest telephone pole. Sites oriented perfectly to everything are rare or non-existent. I've never seen one. The gentleman lying awake in bed has made his compromise. Though the trucks wake him up, in all other respects his site may be perfect.

Carried to an extreme, one fault can be bad enough to make a site unusable, no matter how many virtues it has. A wooded, pleasant, well-located section that I know of, seemingly remote yet close to the city, was seized on eagerly by the builders of expensive houses. The area turned out to be in direct line with the only jet take-off runway at a military airport ten miles away. At ten miles out the jets were still at full throttle, not very far up.

In my own anecdote there weren't any trucks or jets, just the wind piling detritus on my beach. It was still a lot better than having no beach at all. Site opportunity is the most important consideration, then you choose the best orientation you can within that site.

PRIVACY. I discussed isolation a few pages back.

Isolation is an emotion. Privacy is a matter of sight lines. If people can't see you, you have privacy. As seen from the street, your front yard is public, your back yard is private. As seen from the neighbor's house next door, you have no privacy in either yard.

As said before, I like to achieve privacy by the simple device of having no other house in sight. Failing this, the architect seeks a distance great enough, or terrain hilly enough, or screening dense enough, so that the neighboring houses neither influence nor interfere with your own plans, either achitectural or personal. Only the site itself can tell you how far that distance is in feet.

My notion of a pleasant compromise between isolation, privacy, and loneliness is to have no one in sight, but to be aware through distant sound, a glimpsed roof, rising smoke, or just plain knowing, that neighbors are there. In this situation you can't hear the neighbors' radio going, but you can walk there to borrow a cup of sugar, and in disaster you could crawl there with a broken leg.

In any case, an increase in line of sight privacy saves money. It gives you architectural freedom to build as you please.

LAND AREA. Here is a house sitting exactly in the middle of an acre of land. Acres don't have to be square, but this one is.

I don't like square houses either, but this one is. It makes the arithmetic simpler. You will see that one square house, 37 feet on a side, sitting in the exact middle of one acre, which happens to be square, and thus about 207 feet on a side, is 85 feet away from the property line in all directions.

If I had two acres in a square, which would be

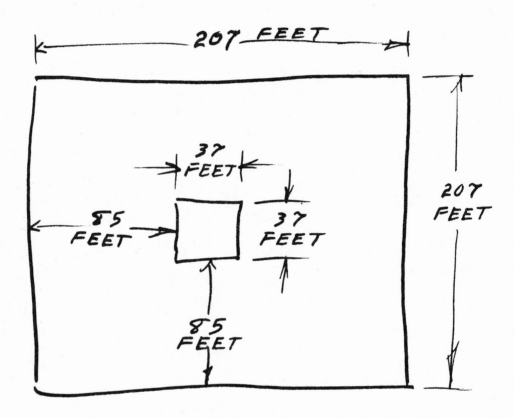

about 287 feet on a side, the distance from the same square house to the property line would have become 125 feet, or an increase of 40 feet.

In order to double my original 85 feet I would need a square 377 feet on a side, or a little under three and a half acres.

You will see that isolation is hard to come by through increase of land area alone. However, let's see about how big 377 feet square is, in terms of what might be put on it.

This is poor architecture and poor landscaping, but it gives you an idea of what three and a half acres will hold. An acre isn't nearly as big as it sounds. To crowd everything in, I had to dispense with the hills and the brooks. If you want to take long walks in your own woods, add upwards of ten acres to this sketch.

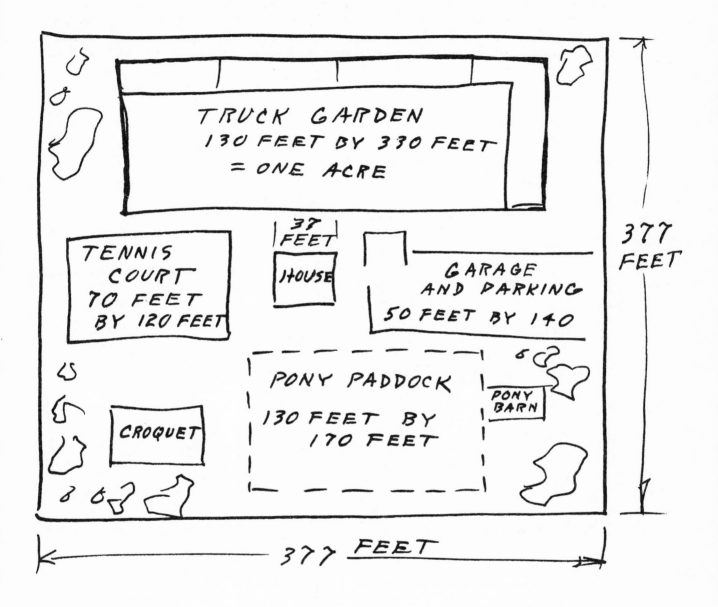

SCENERY, FAR AWAY. Early in the book I talked about designing your house to fit the scenery. At that time the scenery had not been selected, but I know without asking that you want a house with a view. Everyone says this. Before we take a hard look at some real estate, we need to find out what kind of a view you want. Views come in all sizes.

If you were raised with your only view the house across the street, you may now be thinking of view in terms of a hundred feet or so, but I doubt it. It is more likely that you dream of scenery in terms of vast distances, something that happens somewhere else. Something like this view of Bald Mountain—ten thousand feet high, seventy-five miles away, as seen on a clear day through the view window of hill-dwelling friends of mine.

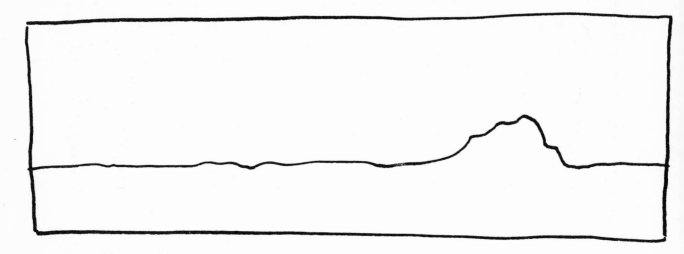

I prefer the view of Bald Mountain when it looks more like this:

with a bush four feet outside, a tree ten feet away, a hillside eighty feet on my left, trees marching down the valley, a church spire glimpsed in sunlight, beyond which I can sometimes see Old Baldy, many miles the other side of the river.

SCENERY, NEARBY. Near view, middle view, and far view combined are hard to beat, but if a choice has to be made, I think the near view is more important. Here is what I see from my office windows, looking south:

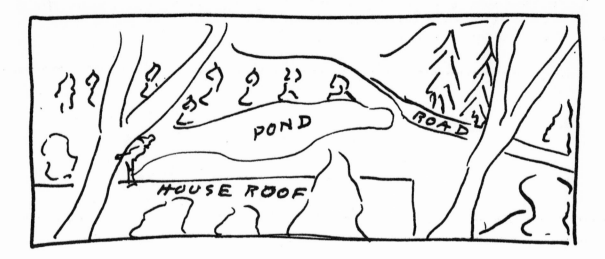

This view stops at the birch-covered hill across the pond, and the twin pines on the other side of the road. This year a pair of ravens sit briefly in the exact tops of those two pines. Robins graze below me, starlings fly by, and the downy woodpecker got himself into both pictures, because he has been hammering away all morning.

Near scenery is likely to be cheaper, easier to get to, more controllable, and somehow more satisfying, particularly if you own it. Incidentally, for scale purposes the area included in this last sketch amounts to about four acres.

SCENERY, WET. The desire to have some water to watch seems so nearly universal as to deserve a paragraph of its own. We arrange our scenery to include bodies of water all the way from a bird bath to the Pacific Ocean. Most site-hunters of my own experience have had as their first question, "Is there any water on the property?"

I have had to tell them that there is only so much natural water to go around, and most site-hunters are by now too late to get a piece of water at a reasonable price. Water is beautiful, enjoyable, inspiring, and lots of fun. It attracts people who fish for trout. They are welcome at my house. The people, I mean, as well as the trout. Water in any quantity also attracts people who own forty horsepower outboard motors. These are not quite so welcome.

It seems a shame that with ten thousand lakes in northern Minnesota, and more or less a million in Canada, we can't each of us have one little lake to call our own. Thirty years ago we could have done better, but as of now, the most satisfactory and probably cheapest way for most of us to arrive at wet scenery is to find a site where we can make some for ourselves.

In looking for a site, keep your eye out for a steady supply of ground water. The tip-off is a nasty swamp which has kept someone else from buying the property long ago. Running streams are prettier, but they are more expensive and they involve the legal rights of other people who live on the same stream. Swamps are loaded with water, which is the essential ingredient for making a pond.

I'd better stop here on the subject of making old swimming holes. How to make your pond is a big subject and probably belongs in another book.

Now that you are ready to start looking for real land to walk on, here is a summary of what, after having read this section, you just might be lucky enough to find—

A hillside, preferably facing south. A road, well but not heavily traveled, preferably to the west or north. A grove of trees, badly in need of thinning. A meadow, preferably covered with brush and briars. A swamp so dense it hides the brook running through it. A screen of hills or trees in the middle distance. All shrouded under an aspect of worthlessness which has kept anyone else from building a house on it long ago. I will later suggest that it should also be within three miles of the local fire station.

Good luck.

21. The economic estate

This section will continue with the topic of saving money. That is a poor way to put it. Naturally you can save money by remaining single, living in a furnished room, and warming beans in the can for your dinner. What I should say is that this section is about how to get the most for the money you do spend on your domestic estate.

DEVELOPMENT COST. I wound up the last section by recommending a brush-covered hillside, a briar patch, and a swamp.

Though this sounds like a madman's way to start saving money, take a closer look. The raw materials are all there for scenery, site, lawn, and swimming pool. The terrain is there, and the trees. There is probably plenty of loam, and with luck plenty of water. With a little more luck you may find your own sand, and driveway gravel, and rocks. You would be amazed how much rocks cost when you don't have any.

Of course I am describing a dream situation. The point is, the better your site, the more it can be left as you found it, bar a little slicking up here and there.

It costs something to move a truckload of dirt, but it costs more to heal the scars of moving it. A tree left where it is costs far less than the same tree either moved or removed. The briar patch, mowed for a year or two, may become a handsome meadow, but grass and loam, once skinned away, may cost you a dollar a square foot to replace.

On a really good site you can build your house and move in. There will be little or no scraping and cutting, ditching and piling, moving of hills and filling of hollows. There will be few of the raw piles of gravel that tell us someone has undertaken to rebuild nature in a big way. On a really good site, you can relax and let the earthmovers earn their living somewhere else.

After you have lived there for a while, mowed the briars and cut some brush and pruned some trees, you will have decided which projects are important to you and which aren't. You will wind up spending most of your site development money on something else.

Your new friends will not utter that awful sentence, "Gosh, looks like you folks have done a lot of work." Instead they will say, "Fine place. Weren't you lucky to have found it."

ROAD LOCATION. A road is a road, but whether the road is east, west, north or south, and up or down, can affect the whole design of your property, as well as the development cost.

I am assuming you will want your house to be gracefully far from the road. I can think of many reasons for wanting the house to be far (how far is far?) from the road, and no reasons, emotional or practical, for wanting to be close to it (how close is close?).

I am also assuming you will want your driveway to be as short as possible (and how short is short?). Depending on where you are, a good gravel driveway may or may not be expensive to build, but any driveway takes maintenance. Incidentally, the minimum proximity of your garage to the road may be fixed by local law.

You will have noticed that all through Chapter One I never made a sketch that didn't have the garage next to the road, the house away from it. To repeat, you want a short driveway and a remote house. Yet you unload your groceries in the garage, and you want a short, all-weather carrying route from there to the kitchen. At this point you have a problem which pulls two ways.

Throughout Chapter One, in most cases I have meant to sketch some kind of roofed passage so that garage and house are either corner to corner, or do not touch each other at all. In a situation where the best garage site and the best house site are some distance apart, we can stretch out our roofed passage. A little money spent here may save a lot elsewhere.

What constitutes a good garage site? This question can be answered rather precisely, not being subject to the emotion that goes into selection of a house site. You want the garage opening to face toward sun and away from prevailing wind. The driveway exit to the road should have an easy turn and good visibility in both directions.

Most important, the driveway should never pitch down from the road. Level is good enough. Up a slight grade is best. I think I would reject a house site if there were no way whatever to put the garage at least level with the road.

Why? In the first place, any road can become a gutter, and water runs downhill. Second, even if you never tried to buck out of a garage through snow, you certainly once in your lifetime had a car that wouldn't start. The ideal situation might look like this:

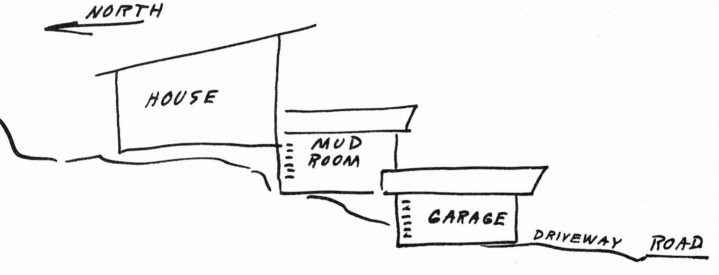

Ideal in all respects, that is, except the stairs to be climbed from garage to kitchen.

Granted that you have found the idealized site, complete with hill, and granted that the view from the top of the hill is better than from the bottom, I still suggest that a compromise site halfway up the hill is better for year-round living. On a gold-and-green day in May, length of driveway doesn't seem to matter. On a brown-and-white day in January, an extra ten feet can seem too much.

Roads bring other things besides automobiles. A reasonable proximity to the road saves money on your electric power connection, especially if you decide to have an underground cable. It saves money on your water, gas, and sewer connections, if you happen to prefer a site where they are available.

Proximity to the road is well loved by route delivery men, bearing milk, bread, fish, groceries, and special delivery letters. They may not come in at all if you are too hard to reach. Some proximity is also well-loved by your friends, who want to be able to find you.

Speaking of friends, don't forget they want a decent place to park, close to but not on the road. To belabor the ideal, we include a level area alongside our slightly rising driveway. But then I seem to want everything.

Summarizing this road business—up to a point, withdrawal from the road saves money, because it gives you more architectural and living freedom. Beyond that point it begins to increase the cost of services.

WATER. In this day and age the delivery of burning fuels can be had over much of the civilized globe. Even electric power, which seems to be almost everywhere, can be supplied by your own generator if you wish.

Water, as a commodity, deserves a very special place in our thinking. The problem of supplying it becomes more, not less serious, not only because our social habits have increased its use, but because every year there is less water to be had, and there are more of us to use it.

We want good water, clear, soft, pleasant-tasting, if we can get it, but good or not, we have to have the stuff. Loss of our water supply can be more serious than the loss of anything except the air we breathe. Water is cheap, if we have plenty; priceless, if we don't have any.

Urban and suburban dwellers, who are assured of a fairly reliable supply of inevitably bad-tasting water, may skip the next few paragraphs. Here we will discuss how the semi-rural and rural citizen finds his own water.

Dwellers in problem areas—where there is no water to be had except by irrigation, or by drilling a hole a thousand feet deep—may skip too. They have their own special worries.

What I will sketch are conditions which prevail where most of the earth's population lives. Here are some customary sources of domestic water:

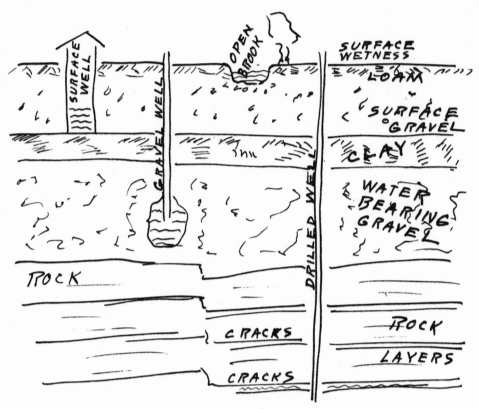

Under any point on the surface, all, some, or none of these water systems may be present. In pick-and-shovel days, those who couldn't get water from a running stream dug a hole in surface gravel. By digging far enough they generally could find some amount of water. Let's call this a surface well.

In regions once glaciated there is often a layer of clay under the surface gravel. Below that is found another gravel water system unrelated to the surface water. With power machinery a pipe can be forced into this water-bearing gravel. Then a heavy pump removes water and gravel until a cavity is developed. This procedure gives rise to the phrase "developed well," or "washed well," or simply "gravel well."

If water can be had from no other source, and you are desperate, a hole is drilled into solid rock. The rock has cracks in it, and sometimes water lies in the cracks. The driller keeps going until he cuts through a crack which holds enough water to suit you. This is called "rock well," "deep well," "drilled well," and if the water rises to the surface because of a higher source, "artesian well." I should warn you that this last phrase is often misapplied to an ordinary drilled well.

Our interest is money, not geology. Here is how the price per gallon of domestic water works out:

Gravel well: least expensive, largest supply, most reliable supply, inexpensive pumping equipment, best chance of soft water, best chance of pure water.

Surface well: could be more expensive if dug, fair supply but irregular in dry seasons, inexpensive pumping equipment, good chance of soft water, purity good to bad depending on environment, but requiring frequent test in a contaminated area.

Rock well: by far the most expensive, much smaller supply though fairly reliable, more expensive pumping equipment, water hard to the point where softening is desirable, purity doubtful.

A good well is a source of immense satisfaction. It does not necessarily save you money to be located on a city or town water service main. It may be more expensive, both in cost of site and meter charges.

If you are going to have your own water supply, you will be way ahead in economy and enjoyment if you choose a site which permits a gravel well. Many well drillers will encourage you to believe that a rock well is necessary. In some places it is the only possible source, but it always takes longer, costs more, and gives a less satisfactory result.

SEWAGE. The urbanite does not know how much of his rent dollar goes for sewage disposal. The city fathers build sewers and he pays taxes. The suburbanite has a sewerage assessment levied on his front footage. These are so-called open-end sewage systems, where the stuff is carried away, eventually to be disposed of with tax dollars.

The semi-rural and rural dweller has to plan his own closed-end sewage system, but winds up money ahead. Once his disposal system is properly installed, approved by the local board of health, and paid for, his maintenance should be low. I said "properly" installed. Once again the nature of the site can save or cost you money.

You will want a good place for your well, preferably close to the house, and a good place for the sewage system, also preferably close to the house. But the well and the sewage system want to be as far apart as possible.

Let's sketch the problem:

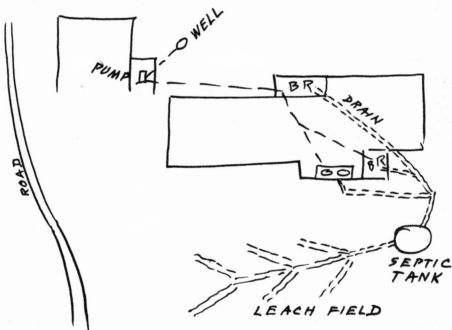

Safe, cheap leach fields are made of drain pipes laid in gravel. A clay field is not so good, because the leach areas must be larger for a given amount of water disposal. The building of a leach system involves a certain amount of tearing up the ground, which we argued against a little while ago.

We can now write idealized specifications for the site which will provide good sewage disposal for the least money. There will be a level piece of ground, preferably lower than the house site and away from the well site, underlaid with gravel a few feet deep. Digging up this area will, we hope, not hurt much of anything. Then, so that nothing is wasted, let this be the spot where you decide to put your garden.

It becomes a ritual to say—other solutions are possible, but the solution which enlists the co-operation of nature is cheaper than the one which does not.

LABOR. The farther we go into site selection, the more we seem to be talking about work. I'm not trying to sell you on the joys of labor. The building of a house is indeed a complicated procedure. It involves a lot of work, most of which will be done at your expense, but by someone else.

I think the cheapest way for you to get a house built is to hire an architect who knows you, and a boss carpenter who knows his business. Give them some sketches of what you want, then take a trip around the world. When you come back your house will be ready. You will have saved the cost of the trip by not being on hand to bother the help.

Failing this drastic procedure, the important thing to worry about is a good supply, nearby, of smart workingmen. Men who can drive wells and bury leach fields. Men who know how to lay footings without destroying the landscape, and who can remember where hammer marks will show and where they won't. Men who will handle pipes and wires and roof boards as if they intended to live there themselves.

It may suit your fancy to employ a general contractor. A good one—and that of course is the only kind you want—will in all cases save you trouble, and in some cases money as well. Do not ask the good contractor for a fixed price contract. He doesn't intend to lose money, and he will have to charge you extra for the risk. If the contractor is so bad you feel a fixed price is necessary, I would guess he isn't the right man for the job anyway.

Having selected the contractor, don't worry about whether or not he uses union-affiliated workmen. That's his business, and is decided mostly by where you are. Good workmen are where you find them. Some areas seem to be endowed with the spirit of good workmanship, of delivering an honest job for an honest dollar. Other areas do not. About the only way you can find out before the fact is to ask people who got there before you did.

A mountain of alleged humor has been written about dishonest contractors and lazy, incompetent workmen. I am a carpenter. I have worked with carpenters, masons, electricians, plumbers, landscapers, and earth-movers. It may or may not be of significance that the area was semi-rural. It seemed to me that the intelligence, skill, and desire to save money on the part of the workmen was usually greater than the good sense and understanding of the customers who were asking them to do the work.

Once again, the business of saving money on a house is largely up to you. Ask most any craftsman for the right thing and you'll get it.

FUTURES. Change occurs faster than you can foresee or remember. Two questions haunt you: will you like your house twenty years from now? Will you be able to sell it twenty years from now? My first inclination is to say that you can't tell, so why worry about it. It still isn't fair to say that the future is blank. The qualitative nature of change can be predicted with some accuracy.

Barring catastrophe, the area where you live will be more crowded twenty years from now than it is today. The real value of your property will have increased, and its stated money price will have increased even more. Being twenty years older, you yourselves will be more reluctant to move. The winters will be colder, the summers hotter, the hills will be steeper, and your shoestrings farther away.

If twenty years seems a long while, take a look at the immediate future of your site. Is the town growing too fast, growing slowly, or standing still? Is the school system keeping up with its job or falling behind? What kind of neighbors are being attracted to the area? What will likely be built across the road? On either side of you? Speaking of roads, will a super-highway come through to wreck the neighborhood, or will it pass just far enough away for convenience and not damage?

If you are near a city, remember that the suburban fringe moves implacably outward, a fact which is good or bad, according to your taste. Whether you like it or not, the lines which you drew on your map, back in Section 18, will have moved by next year.

Moving outward around every city there is always an irregular but well-defined belt where land and property values are at a premium. As of the moment this is the "right" place to be. Being the "right" place, it is also the expensive place. I suggest that you do your hunting on one side or the other of this belt. You will save money now, for sure, and perhaps make a little money later on.

22. The political estate

Once upon a time towns had precise boundaries. You knew when you were in town and when you left town. Jim James lived in the last house on James Street and beyond that there wasn't anything. You could guess the population of the town by counting the number of stores near the corner of Cross and Main.

You used to tell people what town you lived in. Now you tell them how far you are from what numbered highway. You drive along these limited access routes, vaguely glimpsing signs reading "Entering Roundapple Corners." Within these long and gas-embroidered boundaries you owe allegiance to nothing but the turnpike, the registrar of motor vehicles, and the patrolman in his unmarked car.

This kind of citizenship persists only until you get home, at which time you become once again citizens of a political unit stated in terms of nation, state, county, city, or town. Now do you like it at home or don't you?

Which town you live in is very important to you. They are most emphatically not all alike. Towns can be distinguished one from another in many different ways.

SIZE. The most readily discovered difference is population. How populous a political unit do you want to enter? To some people a community of ten thousand people is a metropolis; to others it is a crossroads hamlet. This is not debatable; you just feel that way.

The town I was raised in had one drugstore. The cities I have lived in had thousands of drugstores. The town I live in now has two. Here at least is competition. To my way of thinking a two-drugstore town is about the right size, but

you are welcome to your own opinion.

The character of people remains as diverse as usual, wherever you are. Most of us respond to a pleasant smile. You will have friends wherever you live, because you are that kind of folks. A community, however, takes on a character of its own, apart from the diverse character of its individual members. You, as members of the community, are affected by its character.

Size of community has an important bearing on the character which it develops. I don't know what size you will prefer, and will venture only to advise you that smallness does not necessarily mean inadequacy. I suggest you pick a size range which appeals to you, then consult any road map for population figures.

LAW. In some communities there seems to be nothing illegal except making a loud noise and driving over twenty-five miles an hour down the main street. A hundred yards away, but across a political boundary, no action seems permitted until you have held a public hearing and then invited the mayor to dinner.

We law-abiding people, who stop at stop signs and make the correct signal for a left turn, can be woefully surprised by some of the traps that local ordinances have set for us.

A man I know bought a farm. He built a barn and filled it with hay and horses. In the beautiful pasture he built a paddock, in which he intended to spend his spare time teaching his friends and his friends' friends to ride. The barn is empty now because there happened to be a law which said that plow horses are agricultural, and welcome in an area zoned for agriculture, but riding horses constituted a stable, which was not allowed.

Another man I know bought a remote hillside. He was a small-arms enthusiast and wanted a place to practice pistol shooting. He was a real nice fellow, therefore it was with regret that the police chief had to tell him the discharge of weapons was forbidden except for hunting game.

I know still another fellow, namely me, who pulled the legal blooper of all time. I had always wanted to live on an island. When a lovely little island, within swimming and shouting distance of good neighbors, came up for sale, I bought it. I spent some time wondering why that lovely island had remained vacant, and eventually found out. It seems the island was covered by a law forbidding a septic tank within a hundred feet of open water. The island was only a hundred and fifty feet wide.

Once you have been warned, avoiding these legal traps is not too difficult. Talk to the police chief or the town clerk or the mayor's secretary. Say, "I like the looks of your community. I'd like to spend my money here. I plan to build an aviary and raise Canadian geese." Your informant will take it from there.

TAXES. Most automobile-shoppers kick the tires and slam the doors, having fun but learning nothing. Most land-shoppers inquire about the tax rate, in itself a meaningless figure. Tax rate is nothing but a multiplier on assessment. Until your property has been assessed, you can only guess what your actual tax will be. Many assessments take area into consideration, in which case the neighbors, if any, can help you guess.

I can suggest a couple of ideas about local property taxes, though they may not apply in the town of your choice. Tax assessment provides an argument for building rather than buying. If you buy, the assessors usually accept the price you paid as the real value of the property, a figure likely to be higher than their appraisal would have been. If you build, the assessor usually gives you the benefit of any doubt in his mind.

In many towns, appraising for tax purposes is done by professionals according to their own formulae. These formulae are based on convention. The more conventional a house, the higher it will be taxed in comparison to what you and I might consider to be its real worth. Without exception, every building technique suggested in this book results in a relatively lower tax. There is nothing underhanded about this. After all, if in one way or another you spend only half as much money, you should be taxed no more than half as much. My own town's assessors, themselves experienced builders, arrived at an astonishingly accurate idea of how much I spent. I pay taxes accordingly. Fair enough.

I don't object to taxes if I think I'm getting my money's worth. The proper inquiry for you, the land shopper, to make concerns the services

received for your tax dollar, whatever that may be. The real shocker is to pay lots of tax dollars and get no decent services in return. Here again the neighbors are as good a source as any on what they get for their money.

SCHOOLS. The public school system in one way or another uses roughly half of everyone's local tax dollar, or about as much as all other community services put together. Far from being distressed about this, I think the community which spends even more on schools will benefit.

After sheer population, the local school system does most to establish the town's character. Let there be a good school system, and word gets around. The kind of people you would like to know will come there to live. The school tax may be higher and property may cost more. It doesn't scare them a bit. Property is worth more because the schools are good. They won't be caught settling in the next town. Someone whispered that the schools there are punk.

Maybe I will recall this later on as an argument in favor of building a house instead of buying. It costs no more to build in a good school town than in a bad one. Once the house is built, it takes on a plus value from good schools, a negative value otherwise.

The school superintendent ought to be the most important man in town. If he isn't, he should be replaced.

SERVICES. We will all put good fire and police departments in the relatively non-debatable category. If they're on the job, we're all glad of it. In a one- to four-drugstore town you might even become a volunteer fireman or an auxiliary policeman yourself. Running hose lines at three A.M., when it's twenty below zero, is good clean fun, after you get back home.

Insurance companies change their rates according to the distance from the nearest fire station. I think we should worry instead about predictable minutes and seconds required for fire truck arrival. At sixty miles an hour on a country road, the fire truck travels three miles in three minutes. At a clogged street average of ten miles an hour, the same truck travels one-half mile in the same time.

A policeman sleeps, from time to time, the

same as anyone else, but good police coverage does not require hundreds of policemen. It just takes two—one to be awake while the other sleeps. As a prospective citizen, you may be happier to know that a policeman is always available when you pick up the telephone.

Having given the nod to law, order, and a fast fire truck, I am less certain about the other services. Road maintenance, for instance. Maybe yes, maybe no. I get quite fond of those old familiar curves and bumps. They don't bother me a bit, and they are better than traffic cops for slowing down the plus-sixty boys. Highball semi-trailers, garbage and gravel locals, all are smart enough to pick the best roads. I'd just as soon live on a not-so-best road. My answer is to hope that the highway department keeps my road just nicely passable.

Snow clearance, though, is a different story. Tropical readers may skip this point. In snow country, the semi-rural areas win all the way. Six inches of snow in the city is a major disaster. A foot of snow in the country is a breeze. In the first place, we have ten times as many snow plows per ten thousand people. In the second place, we have one-tenth as many people getting in their way while the snow is falling. In the third and most important place, we have room to shove the stuff around. Business goes on as usual in the country, while the city folks are still wondering what hit them.

Besides educating our children, providing fire and police protection, and keeping the roads open, what else is a community supposed to do for us? On minor services, opinions differ. Some people want trash and garbage collection. Others are willing to haul their own to the town dump, preferring to have the money spent on a good library.

The town I live in keeps the grass mowed in the cemetery. It keeps the roadside trees trimmed and the roadside brush under control. We have sprays; one kind for elm disease, another for poison ivy, a third to kill some of the mosquitoes.

More important than the sprays, we have sanitary regulations, and a forest fire watch on top of the highest hill. We have visiting nurses, care for the old, a community playground, veterans' benefits, a Red Cross chapter, a Mental Health Association, five different brands of churches, and parades on Memorial Day and the Fourth of July.

There is a lot of humor in a community. Ask the neighbors. They groan at the business of it all, but love it. If they don't love it, I suggest you go live somewhere else. These matters will become of intense concern to you, once you buy a piece of property within a political unit.

NEIGHBORS. As house-owners, home-builders, taxpayers, fine people, and citizens of stature, you will become part of the political community we have been discussing. Whether the community is large, medium, or small, you will have neighbors.

You know me well enough by now to know I am not an advocate of conformity for conformity's sake. Neither have you caught me advocating non-conformity for non-conformity's sake. Whether the neighbors are fifty feet or five miles away, they are more good to you, and more fun for you, if you like them. I certainly can't write any rules for what it takes to like a neighbor.

Residential zoning is not based on snobbery. It is the only possible attempt to guide people of reasonably similar tastes, inclinations, and diligence into reasonable proximity with each other. The advocates of zoning don't put it this way. Using the dollar idiom they say that the purpose of zoning is to protect the value of your property. Using the same idiom, I will say that the purpose of zoning is to protect the value of my property to me.

The basic purpose of residential zoning is to help you find yourself, now and in the future, among people with whom you have at least one thing in common, an interest in your homes and your property.

Your house is probably the largest single investment you will ever make. You are going to build it well, and take good care of it. You hope that your present and future neighbors feel the same way. Well-written zoning laws, far from being discriminatory or intolerant, are an attempt—and they can be no more than an attempt—to steer the newcomer into neighborhoods which he will enjoy. Let us, say the zoning laws, locate where we can feel neighborly.

BUILDING CODES. On the heels of residential zoning almost invariably comes its less welcome little brother, the building code.

The basic purpose of a building code for single family residential areas is to prevent the erection of structures which give offense to the eye. This is a difficult proposition to write into law. Most residential building codes begin with such innocent injunctions as staying back seventy-five feet from the street, and using some kind of exterior covering other than tar paper, both aimed at avoidance of visual nuisance.

It is when building codes start trying to tell you how to build your house that they themselves become nuisances. Their intentions are excellent; sanitary safety, fire safety, structural safety, all aimed at keeping you from pinching the wrong penny, getting into trouble, and becoming a nuisance to the community. The trouble with these stipulations is, many of them don't work.

They don't work because it is almost as difficult to codify safety as it is to codify aesthetics. For example, if the sanitary rule specifies fifty feet between well and septic tank, and is measured in horizontal feet, what became of the vertical distance? How can you define water purification in terms of feet without specifying the type of leach? How can you know what is going on down there, anyway? The only possible way to be sure your citizens are drinking pure water is to specify that each well be tested twice a year. I have never yet read any such code.

Fire-safety codes don't agree with each other. Some mention fire-retarding walls but say nothing about the roof. Some specify that outside doors be of solid wood, but allow hollow core doors on the inside. If the fire code were seriously concerned with personal safety, it would prohibit sleeping upstairs.

Structural safety rules attempt to control the thickness of earth-retaining walls, without mention of reinforcing and without examining the horizontal load. They specify wall stud spacing without reference to the weight being held. They insist on fir but prohibit spruce, or vice versa.

To the lay observer, what proves his building code to be a well-intentioned nuisance is the fact that the house across the road, lying in a different political unit, was built to an entirely different code. Wall thickness, material, spacing, kind of wood, footing width, roof pitch, soil pipe size, shingle weight, all are incomprehensibly different. Why, asks the layman, isn't six inches at my house as good as six inches across the street?

To an engineer, a building code may be unworkable because of the absence of loading and stress specifications which have to be the basis of his design. A code which specifies thicknesses but not stresses, or pipe sizes but not rate of flow, can do nothing for the engineer except worsen the results of his efforts. To the engineer, an electrical code specifying wire size for amperage has been properly written, because it equates load with capacity. A boiler code relating pressure to steel wall thickness is doing the same thing. Both deal directly with stress.

Most building codes dealing with structures are written in language not applicable to up-to-date technology and structural engineering. Codes tend to describe building techniques which were obsolete fifty years ago.

Engineered architecture does not violate building codes; it lies outside them. For instance, if the code specifies a basement wall twelve inches thick, what is the inspector to say if he sees no basement at all? If there were a basement wall, would its thickness change if the structure resting upon it were one, two, or three stories in height? The code and the inspector are silent. If the code specifies sixteen-inch stud spacing, and your architect hasn't used any studs, what do you do now?

All right, what do you do now?

First, and easiest, avoid a building code area. Though most such codes start out trying to be helpful, once codified they wind up being punitive. Avoid them if you can. However, avoiding them becomes increasingly difficult.

Second, if the community of your tentative choice has a building code, read it, or ask your architect to read it. If its language is aimed at the creation of a beautiful town, stick around. If it contains a long list of building specifics, think seriously about looking elsewhere. Not merely because of the money involved, but because the code will sit there glowering over your shoulder while you design your house.

Third, if you are committed to a community

which has a severe building code, live with it. Don't fight 'em, join 'em. The more severe the code, the more lenient the inspector knows he has to be with variations. Your house is going to be loaded with variations, in fact it won't be anything else but.

You are going to be an asset to the community. You have money to spend and will be able to pay taxes. Your house as planned will beautify the town, not sully it. You will find that the building inspector is a fine source of information on soil conditions, seasonal ground water changes, prevailing winds, and local sources of good quality lumber. You will find the members of the building appeals board most sympathetic with your ambition to put up a fine, big, handsome house by construction methods of your own choosing.

Don't ever sneak into town and start digging without letting city hall know. City hall will throw the book at you. Smile at city hall, ask its approval, and you'll get it, with growing friendship and a lot of good advice thrown in.

So much for politics and law, if not order. Don't laugh. You might find yourself running for mayor some day.

23. The personal estate

A while back I spoke of the house as a visible expression of what we ourselves would like to be. Now that we are actually looking for WHERE to build, we wonder if the site might not help us do what we want to do.

The passionate gardener will be interested to know that one acre of land, covered with loam one foot deep, represents 1,600 cubic yards of loam. To keep the arithmetic simple, at a dollar a yard that's $1,600. If the stuff is there already, it may not add to the price of the acre. If it isn't there, and you want it, you will be out of pocket about $2,000 to correct nature's deficiency.

On the other hand, suppose your passion is not gardening, but dog breeding. You may not want a lot of dirty old loam, but instead a set of neat gravel-surfaced runs. Gravel keeps the feet trim and the toenails under control. If you have loam, and your gardener neighbor has gravel, you can do one of two things, trade houses or trade dirt.

If you came across an undistinguished piece of flatland which was nothing but an unusable stretch of gravel, and rocks, and a claybank, you might wind up with something like this:

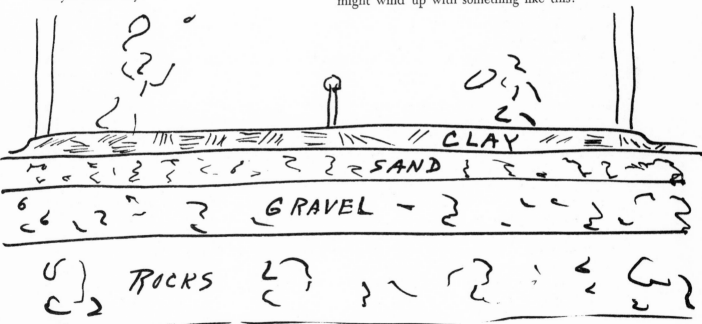

Don't look now, but it's a tennis court, splendidly surfaced and drained. And it cost you several thousand dollars less to build than it would have on top of your neighbor's fertile garden.

If horses are the thing with you, there should be a hilly exercise pasture, a level training paddock, some way out other than down a mile of pavement, and a nice place for the barn, preferably downwind.

If you are boat-hungry, why not look for a place on navigable water? Sure, lots of people move their boats back and forth to water and pay taxes a hundred miles away. But why? If boats are your life, live where the boats live.

I have heard that enthusiastic swimmers load themselves, four children, six bathing suits and a picnic lunch into the family car, then drive fifty miles to a swimming hole. This I can understand, but what stuns me is the thought of the fifty miles back.

If your hobby is playing the trombone, and the jam sessions get better right up to 2:00 A.M., you have an excellent reason for getting as much distance as possible between you and the nearest neighbor who is not stone deaf. Lacking distance, a heavy screen of evergreens is a good noise-killer.

If you are a home style astronomer, spending hours at your own telescope, you will prefer a relatively high elevation. Within that area, you will want a hill to shield you from the lights of the nearest city. Wait until night before you decide.

Some families, even though they realize that potatoes, milk, eggs and pork chops can be grown more cheaply by professionals than by amateurs, go for fun farming in a big way. They come up with a fine mixture of sweet corn, ducks, geese, tomatoes, goats, roses, fishworms, and a compost heap. This doesn't require as much space as you might think. Agrarian delights are available in semi-rural areas just fifty minutes from the office. It helps to have some fertile ground, some natural water, a pasture, and the willingness to build plenty of fence.

The most important thing of all in choosing your site is—what do you feel about it? The WHERE chapter by now has listed a staggering number of things to think about. Fear not. Not all of them apply specifically to you. It may be that just one thing you really like about a site will end your search.

24. Making it yours

In the dark all cats are grey. In the spring it is a rare bit of earth that isn't beautiful. In April the land-shopper is almost certain to say, "It's a lovely day, dear. Let's take a drive and look for a piece of land."

Don't. Please don't.

WHEN TO LOOK. "When" belongs in the next chapter, but in this case it bears heavily on "Where." Advance warning is in order.

In the spring the sap rises in trees, housekeepers, young lovers, gardeners, and home-hunters. Spring is the worst possible time of year to look for land, and the time when almost everyone does. The spring land-hunter will buy at the peak of the market, and generally a piece he doesn't really like at that, because he hasn't seen his new love with her make-up off. Beginning with a spring purchase, and in a hurry to get going, he will hire his architect, draw his plans, buy his materials, hire his labor, all at the peak of the market. Having suffered delays because everyone else is doing the same thing at the same time, he will move in at the peak of bad weather and wonder what happened to all his happy dreams.

The right time to look is late autumn, after the leaves have fallen, and into early winter. Not even then if the weather is sparkling and crisp. Always on days that are at least cloudy, and hopefully with the weather just about as bad as you can stand. Under these circumstances, a good piece of land will still look good; the poorer ones won't.

The seller or his agent will be so startled to see you out in bad weather, he'll try extra hard to find a place to suit you. He'll knock down the price too, because yours is the last money he expects to see until next spring.

Now you have all winter to draw your plans, line up the help, shop for, and order materials. Having gotten yourself at the top of everyone's do-it list, and with every carpenter for miles around running out of inside work to do, your dream-site will burst into activity at the first sign of workable weather. You'll be playing croquet on the lawn by the time the spring land-shopper has driven his first nail.

HOW LONG TO LOOK. Range far and wide, but do your hunting quickly. Compare one place with another while your impressions are fresh, and at the same time of year. If, on a cloudy day, with the leaves gone and the grass brown, you really like a piece of land, close the deal quickly. If it's good, and for sale, it won't be available next year, or if it is, I assure you the price will be higher.

By the way, do not land-look on Sunday afternoon, except in very bad weather. Wear hiking shoes and old clothes. If you aren't lucky enough to have an old car, borrow one. Bring your map, your checkbook, and leave the children at home.

WHERE TO LOOK. It is a fact that the more heavily traveled a road, the more expensive is the land next to it. To me this fact is incomprehensible. I think the land within sight and sound of a main road, let alone a superhighway, is blighted.

To my way of thinking the best buys lie on tributary roads, two- to five-minutes drive away, out of sight and sound yet easy to find and quick to reach. Preferably it will be a road that, although it has two ends, doesn't really go much of anywhere. The very presence of the main road, close by but not too close, tends to guarantee that still another main road will not logically be built through your living room.

This is a main road, where most people seem to want to be, where the choices are poor and the prices are high. You will ignore these signs.

When you have settled on a general area, you will hunt up a local real-estate agent, wave your hands in the air and tell him what you have in mind. If you honestly know what you want, and the agent is thoughtful, the chances are he will take you to the right place on the first try. Quite possibly the land you buy won't even have a "for sale" sign on it.

WHERE TO STOP LOOKING. I said earlier that the perfect site probably doesn't exist. Maybe it did a hundred years ago, or on some fresh new planet now. Try making a mental list, not only

of things you want but of things you are willing to do without. If you had your heart set on tall pines, but a good site offers you spreading copper beeches instead, give up and give in.

A couple I know—let's say a professional man and his dog-hobbyist wife—spent fifteen years hunting for the perfect site. Their original specifications, improbable at first, became impossible as the years went by. Their willingness to compromise increased, but not fast enough. They finally settled on an excellent site, built a beautiful house and are enjoying it tremendously. As of this writing, he is president of the Garden Club and she is secretary of the state obedience-training organization. Their home is farther from his work and much more expensive than it would have been fifteen years earlier. But what's money? The sad part is, they have had fifteen years less in which to enjoy it.

Personally, I am willing to compromise for less than perfection now, rather than hope for everything fifteen years from now. I just might not live that long.

PRICE. A site which permits and encourages a lot of house for a little money can be worth as much as the house itself. A site which requires expensive development and still gives nothing back is a liability, worth less than nothing.

At the end of Section 21 I spoke of the zone of inflated prices which creeps steadily outward around every city. By now you are aware of the distinction between real value and social pressure value. In the middle of the suburban fringe, land prices spiral upward. Everyone wants to live there. Naturally you will avoid this area entirely.

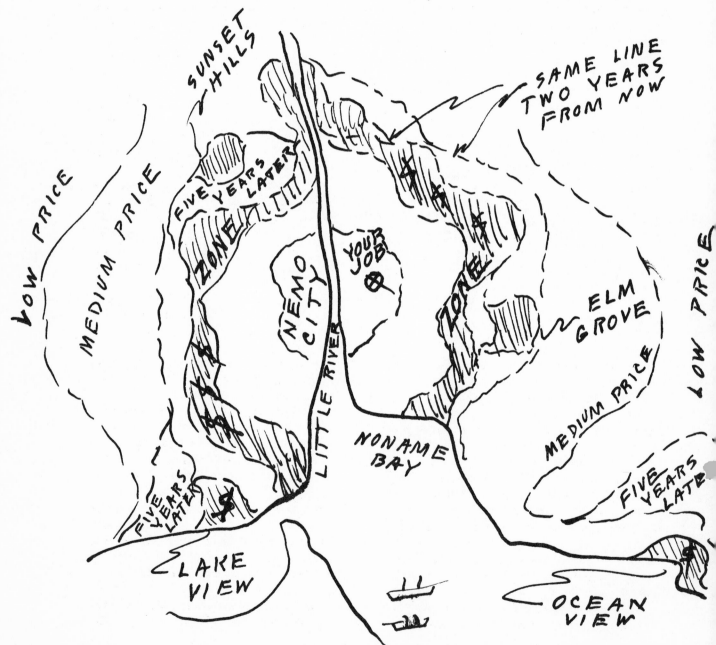

Here we are back at our old friend, Nemo City and environs. Today's "good," and therefore high-priced area has been shaded in the sketch. Tomorrow both inner and outer borders of that area will have moved out. It will sweep through the high-priced island of Elm Grove in a couple of years. Five years from now the beautiful golf course at Sunset Hills will be completely surrounded.

The trick is to leapfrog the dollar zone. It may take only a mile or two to leave the inflated prices behind. Once that is done, you can draw a deep breath and evaluate prospective sites on their merits, not on the length of the buyers' waiting line.

By merit I mean dollar merit, the site's ability to save you money on the total estate. On this basis the higher-priced site may, and in fact probably will, win.

I'll try to put some numbers on these generalizations. Economists suggest that the amount to spend on your entire domestic property—land, grounds, house, outbuildings, equipment and furniture—should be about four to five times your annual net income.

A very fine piece of land, representing few compromises on your part, requiring a minimum of development cost, and so delightful that it saves money on everything else, can easily be worth up to one-quarter of the total estate cost, or one year's income.

An acceptable piece of land, with charm but with flaws, with development expenses looming, might stop at one-eighth of the total, or half a year's income.

These figures will come as quite a shocker to the land bargain-hunters, who seem to be operating on the philosophy that if they save money on the site, they can spend more on the house. It doesn't work that way.

You surely appreciate the folly of spending—to name a figure—two hundred dollars for the foundation on which you intend to build your lives. You would not be foolish enough to skimp on land where you intend to spend, over the course of the years—and again to name a figure—from a hundred to two hundred times that much money.

The value of any piece of land depends first on how much money it can earn. An acre of corn land in Iowa is worth five hundred dollars if it can be made to earn fifty dollars a year. A square mile of corn land in Tanganyika might not be worth five dollars if there is no one to buy the corn.

Second is its value as a place to live. The price now depends entirely on how many other people want to live there too. This value is an imponderable, on which it is impossible to put any dollar figures. I have seen gorgeous residential sites for sale at twenty dollars an acre. I have seen land offered at five thousand dollars an acre that I couldn't in conscience recommend to a skunk.

Whatever you decide to do, please don't buy an obviously poor site at any price.

AREA. When you are ready to close the deal, get more land than you think you need, rather than less. Additional area, if made a part of the original transaction, will not represent a proportionate increase in cost.

Every transaction, large or small, carries its fixed overhead—selling cost, fees, time, title search, recording, as well as the plain nuisance value of doing anything except sleep. The seller knows this, and he should be willing to sell you twice as much land for much less than twice the money.

The seller also places a high value on road frontage; less on land away from the road. On the next page are some donkey figures which illustrate how land areas are priced.

My own formula for appraising residential land is something like this:

So much minimum charge for the first square foot, plus

So much per foot of road frontage, plus

So much per usable acre, plus

So much (less) per non-usable or screening acre, plus

An aesthetic extra for a strikingly good house site, minus

A development cost credit for obvious flaws, minus

A reduction for the trouble saved if the area is large, minus

An intangible reduction if the seller likes the buyer and thinks he will move in and build

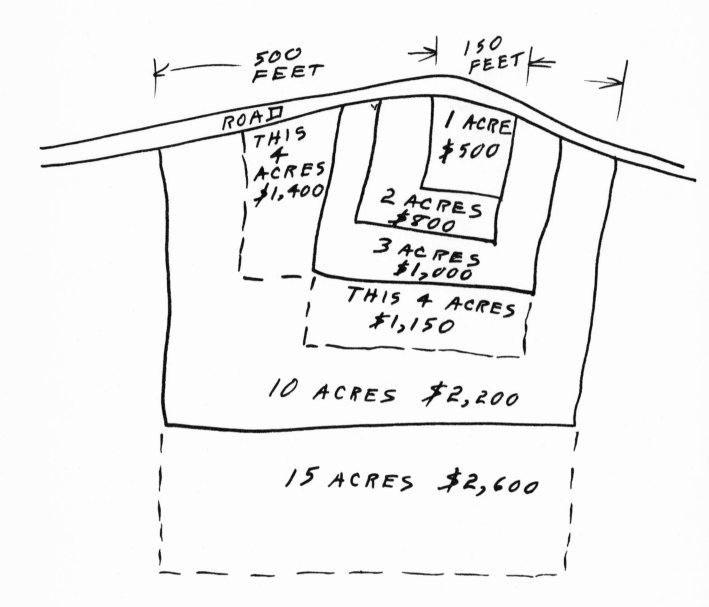

a nice place and pay taxes and behave himself and be a credit to the community.

Do without something else if you must, but buy more land rather than less. The better looking your house is, the more it will raise the value of the adjoining piece; the worse you will get stuck if you try to buy more acres after a while. Land prices in a good community never go anywhere but up, so scrape the bottom of the barrel and get more than enough while the getting is good.

CHAPTER THREE

When shall it be built?

25. When to pick the site

A few pages ago I got in ahead of schedule by talking about when to look for your site. I said that a late fall search permits planning in winter, building in spring, with time left for the children to get ready for school in their new town.

This is your best program if you are in a hurry. Most people, probably including you, are in a hurry once they decide to build a house.

It is not the best of all possible programs. Construction of your house immediately following purchase of the site may be necessary, but a slower schedule has its advantages.

Most people go about it this way. They dream about their house, look at magazines, clip out pictures, ask advice, doodle with floor plans, ask more advice, and save their money. When they can stand the dream no longer, they dash out to find a place to put it. The hammers are clattering before the ink on their deed is dry.

I say—to pick a number—that you should own your land, if possible, for at least two years before you start to build. There are many reasons.

AVAILABILITY. It's a pity we weren't all born a generation sooner. The planet is filling up. Every day there is less of it left for each of us. Good places to live within driving distance of Nemo City grow constantly harder to find.

We didn't ask to be born, and it isn't our fault we were born a little late, but it is our fault if we persist in the notion that there will be more and better places to live tomorrow. There won't. They get worse.

VALUE. As I said before, the value of a good piece of land, barring unusual circumstance, always goes up, never down. I said value, not price. In the constantly moving inflated price areas, which we already have agreed to avoid, anything can happen.

Since the value will go up, you can safely buy land and sit on it, while your plans, family, profession, prospects, and, of course, bank roll, mature. You don't have to wait to be sure. If the plans change, you can turn a nice profit and start over somewhere else.

Unfortunately, by next year you will be paying that same profit to someone else. A desirable site, even if it remains available, will cost you more next year than this.

INSTALLMENT BUYING. I keep bringing up the notion that it is easier, better, and cheaper to approach your total estate by easy stages, rather than trying to swallow it, washed down by a long-term mortgage, in one gulp. We have talked about installment building.

Lots of people forget that the price of the land is added to the price of the house, whether bought together or separately. Therefore getting the land bought and paid for is a form of installment buying. It eases the strain later on.

FAMILIARITY. It costs a lot less to go along with nature than it does to fight her. Yet to go along with nature we must get to know her, and she is as whimsical as a schoolgirl. She changes from week to week, season to season. Even the general pattern of a year does not repeat itself.

That patch of level ground which, seen in the fall, looks good for the garden, may turn into a swamp next spring. And where do the wildflowers grow? You might have been planning your driveway right through a priceless patch of wild orchids.

What trees come in leaf first? Which ones filter the light, and which give dense shade? What color are the lilacs, purple, white, or in between, and how soon are they gone? When do the grape leaves get big? Which of those old vines can be pruned and brought to bear? Are the birches white or gray? Will they show blight in a dry season?

What does a storm do when it comes from the west? Or from the east? Where does the snow melt first? Where does it leave an ice cover in the shade? Does that flowing spring dry up in the summer, and does that mudhole over there stay muddy all year round? Does the road gutter overflow in a heavy rain, and if so, where does the water go? If I dig a hole here, will I be digging in loam, gravel, sand, clay, water, or rocks?

You have bought your site, and you love it, but you don't really know it yet. I suggest that if your circumstances will permit a long courtship, a two-year get-acquainted time should provide most of the answers.

THE SUN. Much has been said in these pages about the importance of sun orientation. I have drawn sketches all over the place with arrows saying North, Sunrise, Sunset. More sketches have shown sun angle in summer, winter, morning, evening, ten o'clock and three.

I said that sun orientation is the most important single decision to be made, once you have settled in general where the house is going to be. This means both orientation as to time of day, which is described as an angle in the horizontal plane, and orientation as to day of the year, which is described as an angle in the vertical plane. Since the sun every day describes a different path across the sky, these angles change every day.

This is not all as terrifying as it may sound. You don't need a day-to-day set of angles. Close is close enough. You do need sets of angles taken, for a minimum, on or near June 21, September 21, December 21, and March 21. More is better. From these figures you can draw curves which will give you a close enough reading for any day and hour you care to name.

Let's suppose, however, that you, or your designer or architect, are trying to think about sun orientation on the strength of just one look at a proposed house site.

Not one person out of ten, whether he is selling land, buying it, or simply asking my advice on house-siting, has been able to tell me within thirty degrees one way or the other where south was. Three out of ten miss it by as much as ninety degrees, or one quarter of the compass. A few people have pointed straight west and sworn that was where the sun came up.

Given a map showing latitude and longitude, the time zones, and the services of a surveyor and mathematical astronomer, the sun angles for any given place can be figured out. This is a long and expensive task. The easiest way to get your sun angles is to take them yourself on the spot.

You can do it with two sticks, a tape measure, and a series of picnics at intervals over one year. During the first year after you buy your house site, here is what I want you to do. First, find south:

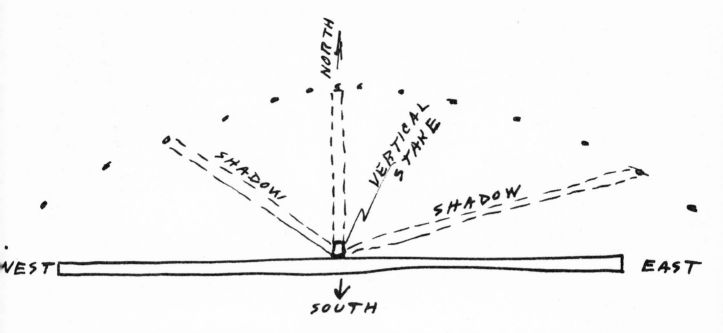

Drive a stake in the ground to some measured height. For convenience later, better make it forty-eight inches, if you are to build in feet and inches, or one meter, if you are to build in centimeters.

Every half hour or so through the day, and every fifteen minutes through the middle of the day, put a pebble or a twig at the end of your stake's shadow. The pebble which is closest to the stake is straight north. At least it's "sun north," which is all we care about now.

Next put a long, straight stick beside the vertical stake, straight down from its top and at right angles to the north-south line. This, of course, is pointing east and west, or anyhow close enough.

While all this has been going on, you will have kept a record of the time when each pebble was put down. Unless you are right in the middle of your time zone, the north-south line will not have occurred at twelve o'clock.

Measure the sun angles the way a carpenter does. You will be thinking like a carpenter when you use this information later. He measures, not the angle itself, but the distance out and over, or out and up. He can describe any line whatever in terms of all three; out, over, and up.

The "up" being fixed by the height of the stake

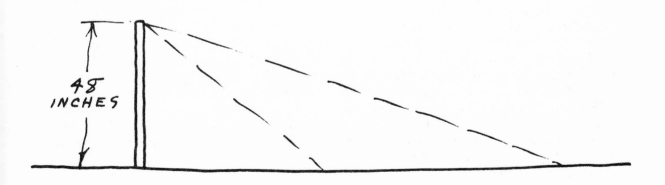

—you can forget about vertical measurements and use your tape only on the ground—

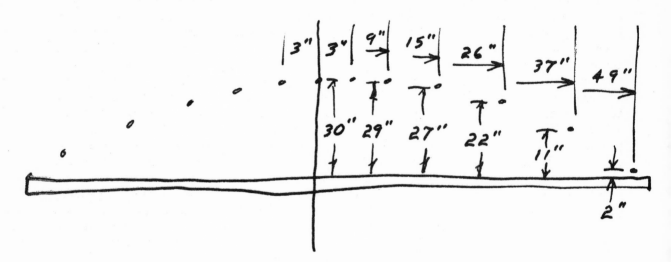

measuring east and west from the north-south line, and north from the east-west line.

At the end of the day, you need keep nothing but a piece of paper with this information:

	48-inch	Standard
June 21	vertical stake	time
7:30 A.M.	East 81″	North 3″
8:00	63″	19″
8:30	47″	32″
9:00	26″	37″
		and so on.

When you have done this once in a while through one year, the sun has been brought under control. To answer a question about last winter, drive your stake again, measure out and over. A stick from that point leaning across the top of the stake is aiming right at where the sun was.

It's a great argument stopper. Says Mike to Mary, "Look, hon, you can't put the sundeck there. It'll be in shadow until way after lunch."

"Why, Mike, you remember that picnic with the Jenkins' last August, well, we got here at nine. I remember that because I forgot the paprika, and right then the sun was just over a clump of birches. You can't have forgotten that because Dick Jenkins decided he didn't like the kind of beer you brought."

"You know Dick, hon. He was just kidding about the beer. Anyway, he was transferred in July, so it was June you're thinking about. Anyhow, I put the ice chest under the second oak tree, the little one, and it must have been still in the shade by lunch."

"Well, you know best, Mike, but just now it comes to me it wasn't the Jenkins' at all. . . ."

Do yourselves a favor, and lay hands on your house site as early as possible. Then spend your time keeping records on your own property, rather than clipping pictures of someone else's property out of the magazines. There's a lot of fun to be had, regrets to be avoided, and money to be saved.

26. When to buy

Don't go land-shopping on Sunday afternoon. That's when everyone else does. In some states it happens to be illegal, but the Sunday land-shopper doesn't get sent to jail; he just types himself in the eyes of the seller.

The seller assumes that you aren't serious. His lips are smiling, to be sure, but his mind is turned off, worn by the Sunday streams of station wagons, their occupants best-clothed, high-heeled, child-burdened, traffic-weary, who seem to be there only because they couldn't think of any other way to kill off the afternoon.

Reviewing in one paragraph the stern warning of Section 24: go land-shopping in bad weather, at a time of year when nothing looks good unless it is good, and at a time of day and week when you and the seller will have a chance to get acquainted. Buying land is not like buying a refrigerator. It's more like getting married.

Having done everything right, having gone land-shopping in your old clothes on a reasonably rainy Tuesday morning, and having traded your money for an excellent piece of empty real estate, you should then study your land for two years before you build.

Not the least important reason for your deliberate approach is that you will have given yourself time in which to buy a multitude of things. There are many big and little things to buy before your house is even started. More to be bought before your house is complete. For most of these things there is a right time and a wrong time to buy.

You know and everybody knows that the truism of buying is to buy out of season, or simply, when other people aren't. Everybody knows this. Very few do it. That's what makes the truism true.

Did I say I was smarter about it than anybody else? Oh no. I know perfectly well that one week before the grass starts to grow the lawn-mower repair man is sitting in his shop, twiddling his thumbs and quietly starving. But when do I take my lawn mower to be serviced? Ah hah! One week after the grass starts to grow, of course. By then the line of lawn mowers stretches around the block.

On some things I have managed to smarten up a little. After all these years I can at least remember that Saturday afternoon is a poor time to get my hair cut.

I can remember, when building a house, to buy my lumber at a time when the loggers and saw-millers and lumber yards are hungry. Next to labor, the total expense for lumber will be your largest single cost.

Plumbing and fixtures are a big item too. We wash a lot nowadays. Talk to your plumber and plumbing supply man when they aren't busy.

Make your selections, pay a deposit, settle on a far away delivery date. They'll love you.

Roofing is another thing you can buy off season. It's a big item, but easy to pick out, easy to store when delivered. The price of roofing rises steadily through the builders' year, then drops back in winter and starts over again. Maybe you'll get it through the hardware store, lumber yard, or supply house. Tell the man what you want as far in advance as possible, and let him do the shopping. Don't you do the shopping. Pick out a trusted supplier and stick with him for as many purchases as possible from one source. He'll break his neck to see you get treated right.

When doing the actual building, remember that fast construction is inherently cheaper than slow construction. Buying materials is just the opposite. The more time you can take to round up the stuff, the cheaper it should be.

I don't really expect you or me or anybody else to do it this way all the time. We are humans, which means that our wisdom and patience are less than infinite. These words are no more than a hopeful push in the right direction, and I wish I were smart enough to pay attention to them myself.

27. When to plan

You bought, or will buy, a site because you have certain things, vague or well-defined, in mind. Your general planning actually began before the purchase of the site. Your specific planning should not begin until after your real estate has become real. From there on, you plan all the time, with major plans coming first and lesser ones later.

I suggested a fairly long courtship with your site. A better analogy would be a long honeymoon. This is the most fruitful planning time, when mistakes can be corrected with a word or a pencil stroke. You need time to worry about where to put your perennial border so that you can see it from the kitchen sink. Time to decide how to get a plow into the garden and where it is going to turn around.

Planning time is a fun time. You may never enjoy the rest of the marriage quite so intensely as you did the honeymoon—I'm sorry, I mean the real house quite so intensely as the dream version. In dreams, neither the roof nor the faucets ever leak.

During the planning time, you work. "Work" is used here to mean play. You cut brush and trim the poplars. You get a forgotten apple tree back into blossom, and you sort which of those thorny things are briars to be cut and which wild roses to be pruned. The weed patch that used to be a plowed field is tilled, leveled, and seeded to clover. While you play, the major decisions, which at first seemed agonizing, turn out to be not so difficult after all.

The following un-Socratic dialogue may illustrate how the decisions come about.

Scene One: Mike, the assistant gardener, has just dug up a shovelful of loam and is standing there holding it.

"Where do you want this dirt?"

"Oh, any place."

"Where is any place?"

"Well, put it in the wheelbarrow."

"Where do I dump the wheelbarrow?"

"Over there."

"But hon, I'll just have to pick it up again and move it somewhere else."

"Let's use it to help plant the flowering crab-apple."

"What flowering crabwhattle?" Mike puts the shovel down.

"The one in the shrub order we gave the man last fall."

"Oh. Where's it going, hon?"

"Outside our bedroom window. I thought you'd like to look at it while you're taking your exercises."

"Say, I'm getting enough exercise now. Where was the bedroom the last time we looked?"

"Well, I thought you decided it ought to be close to the brook."

"Sure, hon, but the brook won't be worth a darn until it's dug out, and with the bedroom going that way instead of this way how can a back-hoe get at it?"

"Well Mike, if we decided . . ." Long pause while Mike puts the rest of the dirt in the wheelbarrow. "If we decided on the sedan instead of the convertible, would that be enough money to have the back-whatsit now, and then the dirt that comes out could go on the garden. Maybe?"

"It's a thought, hon. I'll ask him. Guess I'll dump the wheelbarrow over where you just said."

In this little story we are stumbling toward another axiom of house building: It is always cheaper to make major site changes before the house is built.

The extreme example of the failure to recognize this principle—and you'll laugh, but it happens often; people *do* build boats in basements and *do* saw off limbs behind them—is the case where the newly built house prevents doing the site work which had been planned. Something like this, for instance:

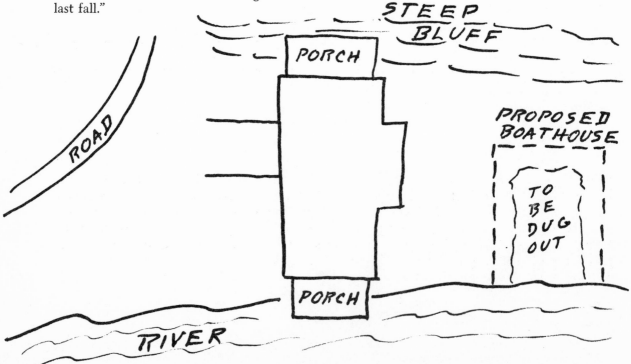

In this striking use of a beautiful setting, the owners made just one mistake. They built the house first. After that the boat bay had to be dug by hand, and every board, nail and sack of cement for the boathouse was carried through the living room and out the kitchen door.

This one is less extreme, but so frequent it hurts:

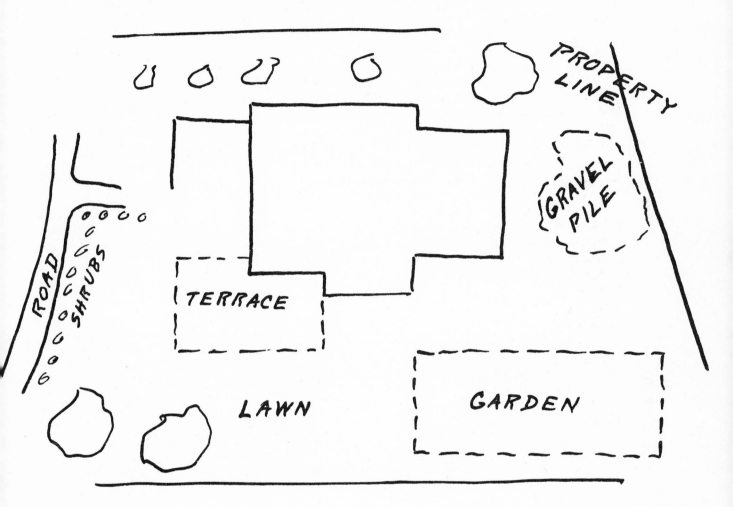

Let's say the gravel pile came from the basement excavation. Millions of people still dig basements, just to spite me. First they build the house, then, working in from the road, they polish up the lawn, the terrace, the garden. Two years later they want to get rid of the gravel pile, which by now is covered with briars and poison ivy. There are just four choices: one, make two thousand trips with a wheelbarrow; two, bring the trucks in and start over next year with lawn and garden; three, carry enough stones around by hand to make a rock garden; four, wait till it snows and sell the place.

Here's another. Tree surgeons make more money from this stunt than from their regular business:

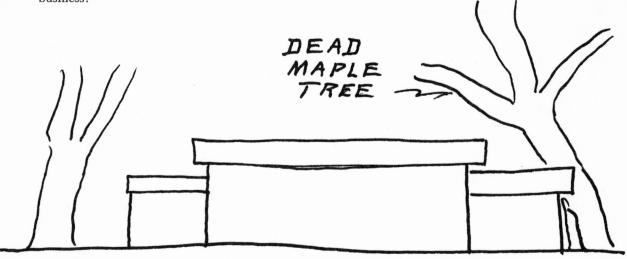

The dead tree could have been removed for nothing before the house was there. Left until later, the bill came to several hundred dollars. Ridiculous, you say, but other folks do it every time.

Anything whatever requiring the use of heavy equipment can be done cheaper if you do it first.

The next step is to get in your slow growth planting, those trees and shrubs with which you plan to correct nature's inevitable imperfections. Wait, wait, wait, I seem to be saying. But not with tree planting. In doing your long-range planting early you will be years ahead. You can build a house a lot faster than you can grow a tree.

Nine years ago I planted a larch. It was three feet tall. Seven years ago, when it was five feet tall, it turned out to be in the middle of the driveway. I moved it. With fine brainlessness, I transplanted it directly under where the power line had to come through two years later. Five years ago, at seven feet tall, it could still ride in the wheelbarrow, but just, and I moved it again. After two mistakes (mine, not the larch's) it is now in the right place, twenty-two feet tall, growing lustily, and not far from being the prettiest single tree on the place.

The moral, if any, is that if I had waited to be sure exactly where to put it, there wouldn't be any larch tree there at all.

I deny having drifted off the subject. We are talking about When. In summary, the recommended order of events is buy early, plan early, dig early, plant early, and build later.

28. When as it affects you

When in the years of your life should you embark on the building of a house?

The answer can be provided only by you. I can help you a little, but not much. I don't know how old you are, how many children you have, how much money you make now or how much you may be making ten years from now. I don't even know what country you live in. I do know that you are more courageous and able than most, otherwise you wouldn't be reading this book.

I can point to a few guideposts which may help you decide. The first guidepost says, *Get Going.* All other things being anything like equal, the sooner you start the better. There are many reasons. Here are a few:

The cost of desirable land goes up faster than the cost of living.

The selection of desirable land goes down at

an alarming rate. Most of the buyers I have talked to were anywhere from five to twenty years too late to get what they wanted. In consequence they had to take less, pay more, travel farther, or give up.

The cost of domestic construction also goes up faster than the cost of living. This is not an argument for buying rather than building. The price of any property, new or old, rises with the cost of new construction.

Paying rent does not accumulate any equity for you.

Your own muscle power can go nowhere but down as the years go by. Right now, whatever willingness you may have to heave, hammer, and dig is worth many dollars in the end result. You aren't getting any younger.

Here's the clincher: from your point of view the total effort required to build your estate must be divided by the number of years you have left to enjoy it. This simple calculation gives you your pleasure cost per year. One year of fun is worth any effort, if you think so, but more years are that much better.

The next guidepost seems to point the other way. It is labeled *Money*. The younger you are, the less time you have had to accumulate any. The older you get, the less time you have left to enjoy it.

We're all in the same box. Whether the calendar reads twenty or seventy, practically everybody has too little money and all of us have too little time. It is not the purpose of this book to tell you how to make money quickly. It might not be good for you, and I don't know how either, and if I did know the secret, I would keep it to myself.

My purpose is to help you make do with what time and money you have. I do not insist that you build a house at all. It may be the wrong time in your life. I do not suggest that you harness yourself to a housebuilding project, then spend the rest of your life doing nothing else and paying for nothing else, including interest charges spread over thirty years.

Back in Section 14 I suggested an extreme method of installment building, starting out with a house shell, one large room with bath, and going on from there. Some modification of this technique, depending on how hard up you are

and also how ready, willing and able you are, is one answer to the money dilemma.

Take what money you can reasonably spare and do what you can with it. Put the house dollar ahead of, let's say, the new car dollar or the fur coat dollar or even some of the dining out dollars. Then settle for something less than absolute completion and perfection on the day you move in.

If you will do these two things, my conviction is that the money problem can be licked, and you will have a decent place to live years sooner than you might think.

Lower on the Money guidepost is a sign which reads, "A dollar down and thirty years for the rest." This technique of acquiring a house doesn't seem like a bargain to me. Whether you pay rent or interest, neither contributes to your equity.

Still lower down, almost hidden in the grass, is a sign which reads, "Be sure of yourself." Money and interest charges can give you a hard time, but so can uncertainty. Better, perhaps, to rent a house or live in a trailer, if a major change looms in your life pattern.

Few young people go at one job and stick with it forever. It would pain me to think that you had closed the door on opportunity by tying yourself to a housebuilding project too soon. If, however, you are feeling strong and can see three or four years ahead, go to it. The experience will pay off, because just around the corner the next guidepost reads, in green letters—

"Build the first one."

Your first house will probably not be your last. Everyone starts out to build his dream house. It does not discredit dreams to admit that they are made of changeable stuff. Two tries is par for the course. Some folks build five or six houses and have more fun with each new dream as they learn from those gone before.

I think this is perhaps as good an argument as any for getting started early.

The last guidepost on When Street reads, "What about the children?" The right time is not, as is often said, "when the children are through school." By the time this comes to pass you've begun to slow down and the children have missed a lot of excitement.

If children thrived best in a stationary setting, the offspring of essentially migrant professions—teachers, preachers, army officers, and junior oil company executives—could hardly manage to survive.

I submit that children, as well as their parents, thrive on an occasional transplanting. They are hardy, adaptable, and interested. They will enjoy sharing the new house fun with you. They will enjoy a part in making their house grow up around them.

29. When to build

It was hard to deal with the personal question of When in your life to build. When in the year to build is easy. The carpenter knows exactly when. I am not talking about thousand-house builders, who work all year round. I am talking about one house. Yours.

Yours is the house that you want to build for the lowest cost possible; therefore keep the weather working for you rather than against you. It is expensive to move frozen earth, to pour concrete in below-freezing temperatures. Roofing doesn't lay well when it's cold, but has to be handled with extra care when it's hot. Rain is always a nuisance to builders, until the roof is up and they can work under it.

If you have more money than you need, you may declare that because the carpenter is being paid, he should work in any kind of weather. Certainly he will, but for an equivalent effort, the carpenter does more and better work when he is neither too hot nor too cold. Bad weather also means that the workmen need wind screens, sun screens, and special heating; that they have to spend expensive time covering materials, drying out wet lumber, or filling mudholes. These are costly diversions which do not contribute to the final product.

Here is the prescription for a day on which both carpenter and materials can give you most for your money. The weather will be fairly dry, mildly cloudy, with a light breeze, and the temperature between 55 and 65°.

The only thing that makes this prescription hard to follow is that everybody else is trying to build at the same time. The carpenter is working somewhere else.

On this ideal day, everyone wants him. Good-weather building seldom fits with the principle of off-peak buying. Where I live, for instance, late autumn is the ideal building time. Cool, dry, and pleasant but not too pleasant. In theory this time fits well with a program of getting the shell up and then working indoors through the winter.

In practice you never make it, because everyone else is trying to do the same thing. Carpenters, plumbers, electricians, masons, earth-movers, hardware stores, lumber yards, contractors—the whole force of labor and supply is dashing madly around saying yes to everybody and trying to keep everybody happy. Everyone wants to get finished up before the winter and no one quite does.

Obviously some compromise between good weather and good buying practice has to be found. In this compromise you can put human nature to work. Since no one ever gets things done as fast as he thinks he's going to, the time when he gets started to build is usually about two months behind the time he intended. There is a lag of two months between the best weather and the peak of building activity.

You will translate this phenomenon in terms of your own climate. In my part of the world, it takes us directly to early spring as the cheapest time to build. It's a little wet, to be sure, and a little chilly, but the leaves aren't out, the mosquitoes haven't arrived, the workmen are eager to get started, and the rest of the folks who intended to build in the spring aren't ready yet.

The happy compromise may be to plan for a start in the fall. Then with everything running four months late, it is suddenly early spring and away you go.

CHAPTER FOUR

How will it be built?

30. How to think

The subject of this book is how to get a good house for little money, but no pound of ink and paper can do more than suggest paths for your own thinking to follow.

Let's pretend that you are four years old, therefore not as yet possessed by a set of store-bought answers. At this age and in this frame of mind every one of your questions begins with "Why?" Why brings a "because" response. Somewhere between Why and Because you can learn How to build a house.

I believe this process is called thinking. Thinking is more readily observed when it is absent than when it is present. You can recall hundreds of examples of not-thinking, most of them committed by yourself, some by others. We are talking about houses, and when we talk about houses, not-thinking gets expensive.

Sticking to houses, let's take one sample of not-thinking. The following is not a made-up horror story; it is true. I watched these houses being built, a whole row of them. Once upon a time there was a beautiful, steep, grassy hill.

On the next page I have sketched what was done. The hill faces south, too. This is excellent siting, provided the house is planned to take advantage of the hill, not struggle against it. Provided at the very least that the builder spends ten minutes thinking before he begins to dig. Here he has taken a house intended for flat land and put it where it obviously does not belong. Whether we approve of the house itself is beside the point. The point is that not only has the builder wasted opportunity, he has also wasted money.

Think how much work went into carving up the hill before the basement forms could be set. Think how hard it was to get the concrete up there to build the earth-retaining walls, two-thirds of which had no earth to retain.

Think how every piece of material had to be manhandled up the hill. Think how precariously the bulldozer teetered as it shoved that fill against the basement wall, which, poor thing, couldn't become a proper basement until it had some dirt outside it. Think with sorrow of the front door, located inaccessibly on the road side, because that's where front doors are supposed to be.

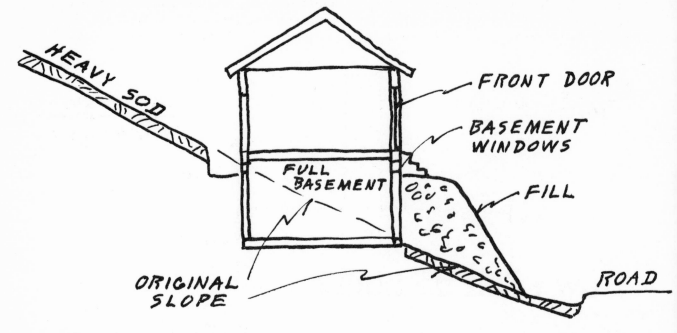

Think with regret that someone, having been told that front doors must face the road, failed to think about placing the entrance in the more readily accessible lower floor. Think with sorrow of the many windows which could have looked upon a beautiful view.

Think with anger that the laboriously placed fill, covering as it does the wall where the windows and doors should have been, now becomes an almost impossible maintenance problem. Think with nostalgia that the original heavy sod, which could have held a steep bank, is gone, lost in the digging.

Think to the future, when most of the fill will have washed down to be scraped off the road below, leaving the owner his choice of making an enormous rock garden, or remodeling the front of his house to a semblance of what it should have been in the first place.

If there is any humor in this situation, it is of the laugh-clown-laugh variety. The bitter humor stems from the attempt to force a given house plan, any plan, bad or good, upon an unsuitable site. In this particular case, the builder can not even say that he was following tradition. Ironically, there happen to be, right in the same neighborhood, some splendidly executed side-hill houses, built two hundred years ago.

Thinking is a subtle process, hard to teach, hard to learn. Not-thinking is easy. We are surrounded by things and influences that help us not-think. The best I can do here is to remind you of the more common causes of not-thinking. In housebuilding, the first of these deterrents to thought is—

TRADITION. To shelter himself for the night, a hunter builds his windbreak like this:

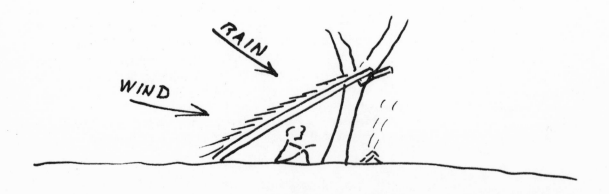

Thus in the New England colonies the early housebuilders were experienced in turning their roofs to the prevailing wind and rain. The Indians were threatening, with the settlers carrying an axe in one hand and a rifle in the other. The winters were cold. Many of the builders did this:

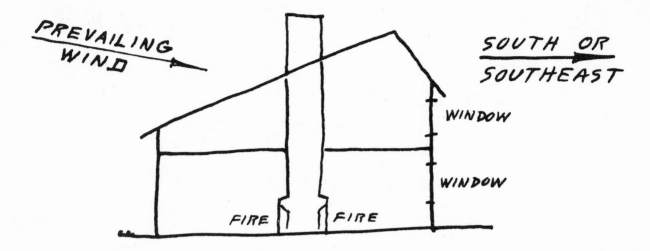

Here we have the hunter's shelter, raised off the ground to make a place for the children to sleep. The house was oriented to present as little of itself as possible on the windy side, as much as possible on the sunny side.

Someone thought the house looked like a saltbox, and an architectural style had been named. It became a tradition. As soon as this happened, people began building saltboxes all over the place, oriented east, west, and north, as well as southeast. The copying builders never asked themselves Why. The original builder, grinning and minding his own business, never troubled to explain to his neighbors that he had a good reason for placing the long slope of his roof to the northwest. The reason was forgotten. The shape had become a tradition.

Any architectural tradition can be traced by someone to its original reason, which was always good, or at least seemed good at the time. Subsequent copying of the tradition, in the absence of, or in the perversion of, the original reason, is likely to be unjustified.

I have not said that tradition is bad. If the tradition fits your problem it is probably better, safer, and cheaper to follow it than to spurn it. The danger of a tradition is that you will follow it without thinking, which means, without asking why.

CUSTOM. There are tremendous pressures upon you to do what your neighbor has done. For instance, the mortgage man at your bank will be much easier in his mind if your intention is to build a house exactly like the house next door, one which has already been bought and paid for. The mortgage man not-thinks that the second identical house will be worth the same amount.

Custom assails us from the outside. It gets written into law, into zoning rules, into building codes. It controls the not-thinking of government bureaus; it writes the rule books for financing agencies.

What is worse, it assails us from the inside. A lady said to me that she was "all through with this second floor nonsense. I'm too old to walk upstairs to make the beds." When I asked her why her house plans included a basement, she said, "Where else would I put the laundry? Every woman I know has her laundry in the basement."

The home craftsman put his first power saw in the basement because the basement was there, not fit for much of anything else. This is a temporary expedient. Custom then converts an expedient into habit, establishing the notion that you need a basement to make a place for your power tools.

The trouble with custom is that it makes you

pay for so many things you neither want nor need. Custom sows and mows front lawns that never get walked on, and front doors that never get opened. Custom creates fences that keep nothing in or out, and gardenless garden walks that lead to nowhere. Custom puts fireplaces in the homes of people who don't want fireplaces, then faces them with brick because everybody knows that fireplaces are made of brick. Custom puts non-structural plaster on the wall because everyone knows that a wall has to be plastered. With magnificent non-thinking, custom puts the washing machine in the basement, the bed upstairs, thus locating the clean sheets two stories away from where they are going to be used.

As with tradition, I do not say that custom itself is wrong. Custom misapplied is wrong. Custom misapplied is the most skillful pickpocket I ever met. To keep your pocket from being emptied, try asking yourself, "Do I want this because I really want it, or because it is customary?"

MAJORITY. Ten thousand people, all believing one thing, can be wrong, and one person who disagrees with them can be right. We all know this in our minds, though perhaps not in our hearts. We all can remember moments in history where one man was right and all the rest of the world was wrong. The standard treatment was to be burnt at the stake for being in disagreement with the misinformed majority.

Some parts of the world have given up burning at the stake, but most of us cling to the notion that "the majority is right."

Nobody that I know of ever meant to say that the majority is right. All we say is, in the science of government, "the majority shall govern." This is a political idea to which I subscribe. But when this political process is unconsciously carried over into either fact or beauty, I object.

Neither the reason for, nor the beauty of, a rainbow can be determined by majority vote. No one calls a meeting to determine the product of two times two, and how many petals you like to see on a rose is admittedly your own business. By the same token, I submit that although thirty families on your street have voted to have basement garages, it still doesn't have to be a good idea.

ADVICE. The advice-shopper is a lineal descendant of the man who believes in determination of fact by majority vote. The advice-shopper believes that if he can get enough people to give an opinion, he can add them all, divide by the number of advisers, and derive the right answer.

The real dyed-in-the-wool advice-asker never worries about whether the people he asks are qualified to advise on the subject. Since the advice-asker has no opinions of his own worth mentioning, he feels that a hundred opinions, stirred well, are somehow better than ten minutes of solid thought in his own behalf.

Ask a hundred people whether to paint your house blue or yellow. Statistically, you will wind up painting it green. My advice to the advice-asker is, ask one good architect, and leave your friends alone.

AESTHETICS VS. STYLE. I defend the right of any man to decide for himself what is beautiful, so long as he decides it for himself. When you are making up your mind what you consider beautiful, you are dealing with the philosophy of aesthetics. If you start peeking around to see what the neighbors are building, you are worrying about style.

You are entitled to change your mind about what you think is beautiful, but the chances are you will never change, or very slowly change, your approach to beauty. Style is a fickle thing; a monstrous mindless dragon in pursuit of the breeze-driven smoke from his own nostrils. We know for sure only three things about style: that it is never reasonable or thoughtful; that it is as quick as a kitten and ferocious as a tiger; and that it inevitably costs us money.

TECHNOLOGY. Domestic construction is the biggest single business in the world, and most of it runs about sixty years out of date. Tradition, custom, majority opinion, and friendly advice, used as substitutes for thinking, introduce this two-generation lag between what can be done and what is done. They are not reasonable guides toward getting a good house for little money.

Considering the technology they possessed, many of our forbears did a wonderful job of building. It is technology that has changed, not people. We've grown a few inches taller in the past six generations, because of vitamins and stuff, but we still eat, sleep, work, play, make love, and put on our pants one leg at a time. A well-designed, livable, thoughtfully sited house of two hundred years ago is well-sited, well-designed, and livable today.

Power machinery which provides heat, light, and water at the turn of a switch, gives us more opportunities than our ancestors had to achieve comfort and freedom of design. Power tools and factory-fabricated building materials give us the opportunity to build with more economy than our ancestors enjoyed. In both sentences I said "opportunity." The power machinery, tools, and power-created materials still won't do our thinking for us.

The trouble with technology is there's too much of it. Building was more laborious but simpler in the days when all we had was clay and rocks and trees and an axe and lots of elbow grease. If the builder made mistakes, at least they were his own. Nowadays, with the accent on buy, buy, buy whether you need it or not, a team of consulting engineers is needed to figure out whether any one manufactured product is what we want to use or is even fit to use.

Technology without judgment can go wrong as fast as it can go right. Technology can build a skyscraper two thousand feet high with less trouble than it takes to offer a valid reason for doing so.

Let us float back to earth for a more homely example. Technology is now able to improve the tenacity of the mortar which holds one brick to another. This development excited the science editor of a leading literary magazine. He explained that the new mortar now made possible a prefabricated brick wall. All you have to do is lay up the bricks in the conventional manner, encase the wall section in a steel frame, ship the massive result to a building site, call up a towering crane, and presto, you can have a brick wall sitting eight stories in the air.

The science editor missed two points. First, brick is and always has been a marginal building material whose only virtue is that it can be laid up quickly on the spot. A prefabricated brick wall makes about as much sense as prearranged dominoes.

Second, the strength/weight ratio of brick is exceeded by scores of other building materials, some new in technology and some old, so that the notion of hoisting a prefabricated brick wall eight stories up makes me wonder if the technologists have not lost sight of the all-important word, Why.

HOW TO READ ADVERTISING. When my father, a country newspaperman, ran advertising, it generally said, "John E. Smith Lumber Co. Sells Lumber," or "Gilchrist Has Groceries." These are transitive statements. As advertisements become more competitive, they tend to become increasingly intransitive.

When the sign reads "Meadowdale Farm, Corn, Beans, Tomatoes," it presents a statement of fact which allows me to buy corn if I want corn. If the sign says "better corn," or "larger corn," or "cheaper corn," my inclination is to drive on and look for a less intransitive advertiser. Some day the sign will read "low-calorie corn," and then I will drive by happily, having at last seen everything.

Yet there is much to be learned from the transitive residuum in advertising. We can't say that all advertising is vicious and must be ignored. Let's learn how to read the stuff.

Remember that the advertiser has one goal and one goal only: to persuade you to buy his product. This is a simple and completely obvious fact. Everybody knows it, and almost everybody forgets it. Successful advertisements are those which do the best job of making the reader forget the advertiser's self-interest.

When you set out to build a house, you are going to read a lot of advertising, buy a lot of things, spend a lot of money. You will be assailed by advertising that wants to sell you "style," except that it is always called "beauty." You will be told that technical things, machines and materials, are better because they are "new." You will sink in a quicksand of hung comparatives— larger, smaller, lighter, softer, cheaper, better, and more beautiful. You will learn to ask, "Larger, smaller, lighter, softer, cheaper, better and more beautiful—than *what?*" If you still haven't gone blind you will observe that most of these bought and paid for comparatives prove nothing except that they are in direct contradiction of each other.

This kind of verbiage you can discount easily. Much harder is to discover what isn't there at all. In the welter of claims and counterclaims between competing products, there is no money anywhere for advertising aimed at persuading you to buy nothing at all. For example, you never saw an advertisement telling you not to paint your house, and you never will. Nobody makes a nickel out of not-painting. Furthermore, if I wrote an article explaining why your house doesn't need paint, no magazine that carries paint advertising could possibly print it.

Here are a few tips on how to read advertising:

Most advertisers make their loudest claim about what is actually their product's weakest point. That is, if the product is too small, the advertising will call it "roomy," hoping you won't notice. If the product is really roomy, the fact is self-evident and need not be advertised.

In your reading, strike out all hung comparatives. Delete smoother, finer, safer, and easier. Read only the statements of purported fact which are left, if any, after these deletions.

Strike out such ersatz phrases as Autosyntronic and Magicentrometer used to describe new miracle methods of keeping the washing machine running.

Strike out all aesthetic judgments. "Beautiful" is an expression of the advertiser's hope, not necessarily your opinion.

If the advertiser asserts plainly that his product is good, useful, and expensive but worth the money—and it may well be—read to find out why, skipping most of the adjectives, and skipping assertions that the product is either "new" or "easy to use." If the product is really good—the wonderful thing is that so many of our products *are* good—a declarative statement of its merits should suffice, and no "free gift" should be required to persuade you to buy it.

THE MISNOMER. A lineal ancestor of the advertising man is the misnomer artist. To some degree we all possess the human penchant for calling things what they are not, for calling that thing dangling at our side a "limb" or "upper extremity," but never an "arm." The misnomer artist sees a piece of treeless flatland and automatically names it Willowdale Heights, thus escaping from reality in three directions.

The misnomer man decides that a rock well should be called "artesian," because few people can call him a liar and because the three easy syllables sit nicely on the tongue. He is the chap who decides that hens have quit laying small eggs, confining their efforts to super jumbo, jumbo, extra large, large, and medium. Women, he says, have quit wearing clothes, with garments being made now only for juniors and misses.

In the case of my favorite building material, wood, the misnomer artist has a field day. When we want to specify mahogany, we have to say "Honduras mahogany," because every other tropical hardwood gets called mahogany no matter what its name or attributes may be. "Maple," in the hands of the misnomer artist is neither maple nor maple colored nor solid anything, as opposed to "solid maple," which, although still neither maple nor maple colored, may with luck be partly solid, and still isn't "blond maple," which might be almost anything.

In fact, I can't think of a single named color bearing any resemblance to the natural color of the wood it is supposed to represent. Though a slow learner, I finally did figure out what "fruitwood" meant, only to be paralyzed by the appearance of the real baffler, "distressed fruitwood."

When it comes to architectural styles, the misnomer artist goes completely out of his mind. Or perhaps I should say, we are driven out of ours. For examples, see any page of real-estate advertising. Here, I'll mention one out of dozens. After years of watchful study, I learned that a ranch house had one floor and a colonial house had two. Now I'm back where I started because they've begun to advertise the "one-story colonial."

At the end of the How to Think section, I'm depressed. The roadblocks in the way of clear thinking about houses are awesome. There are tradition and custom to confuse us, the myth of majority opinion, too much advice and much too much mumbo-jumbo about style. There are machines that may or may not be worth the money, and advertising that must always be suspect because it originates in self-interest.

In a business as vast and complex as house-building, it is sad that there are many intelligent, sincere and honest people who are just plain misinformed.

Well, depressed or not, the rest of this section will be an old college try at how to understand, select, and build. Misinformed or not, if we keep asking why, we'll make out.

31. How to understand materials

Start to break a stick across your knee. Stop just after it pops and before you have pulled it apart. The broken ends will now look something like this:

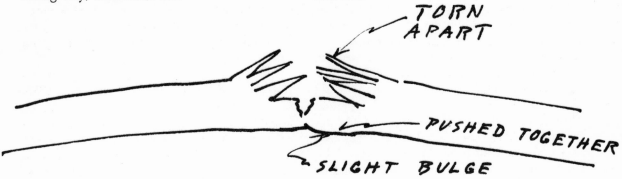

Back up and do it again, this time looking at the bent stick just before it breaks.

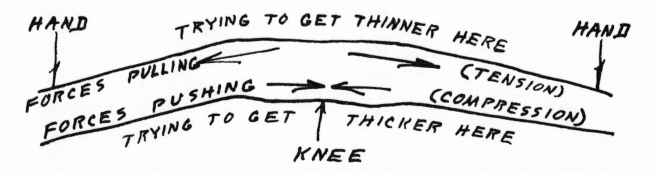

The forces pulling apart are called "tension." The forces pushing together are called "compression."

The stick which you broke is a "beam." It represents, among other things, the floor of a house. Turning the sketches upside down, the side on which the grand piano sits is·called the compression side, with the other side being the tension side.

You are now one-quarter of the way toward being a structural engineer.

To proceed with the next quarter, get, or imagine, three more sticks:

Take the little stick, a half inch thick by a foot long, and break it over your knee. That was easy. Now take the stick which is an inch thick and a foot long, and try to break it. Unless you are a professional strong man, you can't do it.

The difference between the two sticks is their "strength." You can take my word for it that, for the same material, the one-inch stick is exactly four times as strong as the half-inch stick. This holds true no matter what the two sticks are made of, whether it be pine, oak, aluminum, or steel. Strength depends on the square of the thickness.

Next, take the one-inch stick, four feet long, and break it over your knee. That also was easy. In fact, it took exactly the same pull to break the one-inch, four-foot stick as to break the half-inch, one-foot stick.

Since the stick ,represents the floor of your house, we are now talking about "span." We have learned that the one-inch stick is four times as strong as the half-inch stick, yet the effort required to break them is the same, because the one-inch stick is four times as long. Now we know that the ability to carry a load falls off in a straight line as the span increases, but comes up as the square of the thickness.

You are now one-half of the way toward being a structural engineer.

To go the third quarter of the way we need to do some measuring. (You can either do the measuring yourself, or take my word for the results.) It would be well to have a vise and a ruler, but once again we start out with the same three sticks. This time we will bend them, not break them.

Here is a rough picture of what we are up to:

Using the same push on the two short sticks, you will find that the half-inch stick bends (or "deflects") eight times as far as the one-inch stick. Yet we already know that the one-inch stick is only four times as strong.

Here we have observed the difference between "strength" and "stiffness." The one-inch stick is eight times as stiff, because stiffness depends, not on the square, but on the cube of the thickness.

Next, and this gets to be more and more fun, try the same load on the two one-inch sticks, one foot long and four feet long respectively. You won't even be able to measure the bend in the one-foot stick, but I can tell you that the bend in the long stick is a whopping sixty-four times as great.

The amount of bending depends on the cube of the length, and four times four times four is sixty-four.

Last, to check it all out, put the same load on the one-inch, four-foot stick and on the half-inch, one-foot stick. By now you know that the big stick, which is exactly as "strong" as the little stick, will bend eight times as far, and is thus only one-eighth as "stiff."

Applying all this to materials, we have learned from our three sticks that any given material, made twice as thick, will be equally strong over four times as much span, but will be equally stiff over only twice as much span.

Good carpenters know these things, at least in sense if not in numbers, because they have broken sticks and felt materials bend beneath them. A fair question now would be, why do we care?

We care, for one reason, because a floor needs not only to be strong enough to hold us up, but stiff enough to be free of annoying bounce. A roof, on the other hand, needs be strong enough to hold up itself and the snow, but no one cares whether it is stiff or not. In planning for a roof and for a floor, two different sets of criteria apply.

You, along with all good carpenters, are now three-quarters of a structural engineer, because you have at least a qualitative understanding of the difference between strength and stiffness. The last quarter includes information which might be called "characteristics of materials." Following are some of the more important words to think with.

ELASTICITY VS. BRITTLENESS. Elasticity means the ability of a material to bend or stretch, then return to its original shape. Every elastic material can be described in terms of the force required to bend it a certain amount, and every elastic material has a point beyond which it will no longer return to its original shape.

Squeeze a tin can a little bit and watch it go out of round, then return to where it was. Squeeze harder, and you will leave a dent. You went past the "elastic limit." Stiffness is not the opposite of elasticity, it is a measure of the force required.

In building, we like stiff materials, but all that means is we want the force required to bend the material to be high. Generally we want the elastic limit to be as high as possible, for beyond that point the material deforms permanently, and still farther beyond that, it breaks.

Much the opposite of an elastic material is a "brittle" material, which stubbornly refuses to change its shape, and then all of a sudden, under increased load or shock, comes apart.

This concept is important to us in the selection of building materials. For example, wood and steel have excellent elastic properties. Bows and springs are made of wood and steel, and will return to their original shape after bending thousands or millions of times. Plaster and cast iron are brittle materials. The first will break at a light tap, the second at a very heavy one. A brick or a stone will fall right in two, if you tap it at the right place. Let the foundations of our house shift but a little bit, and all plastered surfaces therein may crack, because plaster, though not strong, is stubbornly inelastic.

To erect a structure, we must use "structural" materials. The good ones possess both stiffness and elasticity. We then sometimes coat our structure with materials which have no stiffness at all. Roll roofing, for example, when warm, will assume the shape of anything it happens to be lying on. On a warm day, this is a non-elastic material. Unroll it, and there it stays. On a cold day, it is a brittle material. You can't unroll the stuff at all without cracking it.

CONDUCTIVITY. This characteristic, though not important to pure structure, does concern you in the choice of materials for your house. Materials with low conductivity help insulate the place. Here we run into an embarrassing difficulty. Most materials which make relatively good structure make relatively poor insulation.

Though some materials have lower conductivity than others of equal stiffness, the best and cheapest insulation of all is air, in tiny pockets or thin layers. The problem is to find or devise a material which embodies these air pockets without loss of stiffness. In a single, homogeneous material the problem can not be solved; it can only be compromised.

Advertising which says that a single material is good for both structure and insulation has to be re-read to say that it isn't too much good for either.

For building convenience, however, a product can be manufactured which we may describe as having a stiff surface on both sides, and a spongy interior. Remembering lesson one in our structural engineer's course, we see in this assembled material stiff skins on the tension side and the compression side, with the filling of the sandwich providing some insulation.

Having bowed toward the product designer, let's stick to fundamentals. At this stage of the game, let's keep on talking about stiff materials for structure, and special-purpose materials for insulation.

INSULATIVE MATERIALS. Another embarrassing difficulty presents itself, because conductivity is far from being the whole story.

Heat flows into your house, or out, in three ways. First, though least important, with the air entering and leaving the house. This is called convection. It is not a problem of faulty materials. If your house didn't leak air, you would have to make it leak on purpose, because you have to have a certain amount of air to stay alive.

The second and larger heat flow is by conduction. Warm air sits against the ceiling, and the snow on the roof melts. It melts quickly or slowly depending on the conductivity rate of the roof structure.

The third and greatest heat flow is by radiation, which is the way all the heat from the sun got here in the first place. On a cold night the process reverses itself and the whole house becomes a stove, warming up everything within line of sight.

Here is the difficulty. The materials which reduce conduction and the materials which reduce radiation are not the same. Radiation, the worst enemy, is defeated by shiny, light-colored materials which are both good at reflecting the heat back where it came from and poor at re-radiating it on the other side. Conduction is defeated by porous materials which trap air.

In the pure sense, anti-radiation and anti-conduction materials are totally unlike each other. Neither kind is generally acceptable for either the inside or the outside surfaces of your house. Therefore we have to enclose them between more serviceable materials.

As a possible solution, we can have another manufactured product which encloses a porous material between two shiny surfaces. This is almost a dead stop both to conduction and to radiation—but it creates other problems, as will be seen later. The best compromise or money-saving solution I can think of is to omit the porous material and simply trap air between two or three shiny surfaces. They make "thermos" bottles this way, and the same technique will also give you a very comfortable house.

FIRE-RESISTANT MATERIALS. Anyone who has tried to set fire to a pile of brush knows that his fire, to keep going, has to have three things: air, warmth, and fuel. To make the fire burn faster, you push it together; to put the fire out, you pull it apart. This amounts to adding or subtracting fuel, as well as controlling the amount of warmth versus ventilation.

You can put the fire out by pouring water on it, and thus cooling the fuel. You blow (add air) on the fire to get it going, but if you blow too hard too soon the fire goes out (it got too cool). Throw a wool blanket (or a foam blanket) over a fire and it goes out at once, having run out of air. Heavy, cool fuel added too quickly to a fire will put the whole thing out, because the temperature drops.

We were trying to burn the brush pile. By reversing the processes we can learn how to reduce the danger of house fires. The best way to keep a house from burning quickly is to make it long and low. A tall house burns as a torch burns, in its own draft; a low one behaves like a spread-out brush fire that keeps wanting to go out.

No material is "fireproof," provided the fire is hot enough. A masonry wall, itself fire-resistant, will help keep an outside fire from coming in, but it will heat up like an oven and increase the intensity of a fire burning on the inside. Masonry has a high rate of conductivity. The best materials for slowing down a fire are those which either reflect heat, keeping the rest of the structure behind them cool, or absorb heat slowly because their heat conductivity is low.

Insulation and fire resistance work together. Reflecting materials keep heat from getting into the supporting structure. You can check this for yourself with a piece of aluminum foil and two logs in the fireplace. Non-conducting materials take longer to reach the combustion point. It will probably surprise you to be told that post-and-beam structure, made of slow-conducting wood, will be standing long after a steel beam has reached its yield point and collapsed.

I have watched new/old buildings burn. The old part, built of heavy wood, remained standing; the new part, made of steel (even when encased in concrete) collapsed into a bonfire. The explanation is simple. The steel beam, which itself will not burn, loses its strength at around twelve hundred degrees Fahrenheit, or just a little more than the temperature of the match which lights your cigarette. It gets hot quickly, loses its strength, and dumps its load into the bonfire below. The wood beam begins to char on the outside at about the same temperature, but the inside remains cool for a considerable time.

We are plodding along toward the details of putting your house together. Characteristics of materials, weight, durability, cost, workability, appearance, fire resistance, cleanability, all have a direct bearing on how you will build your house.

In the next section we will look at the kinds of materials which are available.

32. How to select materials

We now share a vocabulary to use in discussing materials. We can communicate with each other on tension, compression, strength, stiffness, elasticity and brittleness, reflectivity and conductivity.

The next step is to make a rough grouping of the more conventional building materials:

Woody materials: softwood, hardwood, plywood, bonded chip, paper products.

Masonry: assembled masonry (brick, block, and stone); cast masonry (with and without reinforcing); and plaster.

Chemical products: glass and plastics (synthetics).

Metals: steel and aluminum, with other metals for specialized uses.

WOODY MATERIALS. If we were forced at this writing to discard all domestic building materials except one, we would keep wood. Given nothing but a pile of boards, there is very little that a good carpenter couldn't build if he had to. The tree-lover would say this is because nature, in designing a tree, achieved strength, permanence, and adaptability. The physical chemist might say that wood is workably soft yet flexible because it is made of long lignin fibre embedded in cellulose. The builder might say that wood is tenacious. It is easy to bend but hard to break. When a wooden building falls down, it falls down slowly.

Wood doesn't do any one thing quite as well or as cheaply as some other combination of materials which might be found, but it does many things well enough. It is the basic building material, as far as houses are concerned, to which we add a variety of other materials in order to take advantage of their special properties.

A sawed board, plank, or timber is reasonably strong for its weight. It must, however, be used with some intelligence, because its strength in tension appears only along, not across, the tree's growth rings. A board is easy to work, with inexpensive tools, and easy to fasten to another board. Its heat conductivity rate is low. It is elastic, a wooden structure being tolerant of natural assault, even the shifting of its own foundations. Wood has a pleasant texture, not bad acoustic properties, and to most eyes a pleasing appearance.

Wood supply is a tremendous industry. There are many varieties of trees, for which the claims, counterclaims, and misnomers are bewildering. In this confusion there is a common misapprehension. "Softwood" and "hardwood" are botanical terms, not physical descriptions.

Softwood is from evergreen trees. Some softwoods are very hard. Some hardwoods are relatively soft. There is a widespread though erroneous notion, based probably on the sound of the words, that for a wood to be hard is somehow better than for it to be soft. If anything, the reverse is true. It is the very fact of tractability combined with strength that commends wood to us as a building material.

Most woods used for structure are softwoods. Many, though not all, softwoods are easy to assemble, accept and hold nails well, and have some natural tolerance to weather. Insofar as wood is actually soft, it is light in weight and easy to work. Going back to our structural engineering vocabulary, it is less stiff per unit of thickness, but since stiffness increases with the cube of thickness, most softwoods figure out to be stiffer than hardwoods per pound of material.

Translating that into carpenter language, if you want a given stiffness, use softwood but use a bigger piece.

The wood from each kind of tree has characteristics of its own, some good, some not so good. To describe them is easily another book. I can't do it here. I will conclude with the general injunction to use nothing but softwoods for structure and for outdoors. You can use hardwoods, if you feel like it, inside the house.

Manufactured wood products take on even greater variety. Plywood, used in astronomical amounts, is three or more thin layers of wood glued together, with the grain lying alternately crosswise. This partially gets around the fact that raw wood is much stronger, in tension, along the grain than across it. It also partially gets around the fact that wood changes its across-the-grain dimension as the moisture content of the air changes.

The statement is often made that plywood is stronger than raw wood. This is not true. Plywood represents a compromise strength, nearly uniform in all directions, and can be used with less thoughtfulness on the part of the carpenter. It has less stiffness than raw wood per pound or per dollar, but properly used it saves on labor. It is less tolerant to weather and to mechanical damage.

Wood is also cut into chips, then bonded together in the shape of boards or sheet. The strength of this product now depends on the strength of the bonding agent. Both chipboard and plywood retain much of the essential character of wood, while lowering its quality of tensile strength along the grain.

Wood chip is made into paper products which are almost indispensable to the wall and roof skins of your house. Even when, a little later, we recommend aluminum foil, we will mean a thin layer of aluminum laid on a paper base. Be warned right here, however, that one paper product is not to be used—tar paper. Tar paper does everything wrong. It attracts heat when you don't want the heat, gets rid of it when you do. It feeds and spreads fire. It welcomes insects and retains water condensation. The direct replacement for tar paper, paper-backed aluminum foil, does everything right.

To conclude, it is very hard to build a house which meets all of your specifications, including charm and economy, without wood.

MASONRY. There are many kinds of masonry. The oldest existing works of man are fitted stone, laid without mortar. There is shaped stone, laid with mortar. There is fieldstone (unshaped), laid with mud or mortar.

A lot of building has been done with mud. There is dried mud, rammed mud, and baked mud. Bricks are baked clay mud, laid with mortar. With the invention of cement, which is ground and fired stone, came blocks, made of cement with various aggregates, put together in the same way.

I will call this whole group of materials the "assembled" masonries.

The monolithic, or cast, masonries are different. The invention of cement made it possible to cast structures more or less in one piece. This is called concrete, meaning a structure put together by the cohesion of separate particles. Assembled masonry uses large (brick-sized) particles. Concrete uses microscopic particles. I choose to list concrete as masonry, ignoring the size of the particle, because its strength depends on particle cohesion. Thus it belongs in the same family when virtues and faults are being considered.

The great difficulty with assembled masonry is its almost complete lack of tensile strength. It can stand lots of push, but almost no pull. With concrete this fault can to some extent be corrected by including steel reinforcing on the tension side. Concrete used in structures thus becomes a composite material, with one thing being used to correct the deficiencies of something else.

I also have to include plaster among the masonries. Plaster is masonry laid on with a trowel. My personal definition of plaster is "a disguise to cover deficiencies in earlier workmanship." Plaster, to me, is not a structural material at all. It has no tensile strength, little compressive strength, and no elasticity to speak of. In my opinion it is also heavy, dirty, troublesome and expensive.

In looking at the structural virtues of masonry in general, we soon see that they all have to be qualified. All masonry is heavy in terms of strength per unit weight. Most of it is expensive for what it accomplishes. Assembled masonry can be used only in compression, since it has no tensile strength. It has no elasticity and thus is not tolerant of shifting or shaking. Its heat conductivity is high, that is, for our purposes, poor, and masonries that are dark in color have, for all of our purposes except building fireplaces, undesirable radiation characteristics.

For a domestic structure, another big trouble

with masonry is that it is hydroscopic. It absorbs water. Any other building material used to complete your house has to be protected in some manner from exterior masonry, which is always wet. This can of course be done, but it is expensive and troublesome. If you don't do it, you'll be sorry.

I admit that masonry in its place is useful and charming. My house sits on concrete footings. The fireplaces are made of cinder block, though lined with steel and ceramics. We have a variety of earth-retaining walls, some of concrete block and some of fieldstone, and the garden wall, laid of irregular granite discards, is undeniably beautiful.

They say that masonry walls are fire resistant, pointing to the fact that part of the brick wall remains standing after the house burns down. A brick wall is fire resistant all right, but it makes a fine oven to hurry the burning of the roof, which usually burns first anyway. I think I'd rather put my money into a fire-resistant roof. Another thing they tell me is that masonry is permanent. It is, until something comes along to start it falling down, in which case it falls down in a hurry.

Reinforced concrete has many more virtues than assembled masonry, but it has two faults—limited elasticity and a propensity to absorb water. My conclusion is that we should use masonry where its special virtues commend it to us, and nowhere else.

GLASS AND PLASTICS. Chemical manufacture creates products which are essentially different in molecular form from the raw materials used. In this sense, these materials are "synthetic." The oldest of these is glass. In a structure the function of glass is to let us see our environment, yet not be a part of it. No other material does this anywhere near as well. It should be remembered that the purpose of glass is to see through, and keep the wind out. Beyond that, it has no structural virtues. The so-called glass brick violates every rule for a structural material: it has no reasonable purpose except that its texture can provide an occasional design accent.

If you want something that will let light in but still not be transparent, many plastic materials do the job better than glass. Already the versatility of this new range of synthetic materials has become apparent. They offer translucence or opacity, permanence, ease of shaping, light weight, built-in color, textural range, and low maintenance cost. Now that plastics are available in elastic rather than brittle materials, it is hard to see how they can fail to achieve wide use in walls, floors, and roofs of domestic structures.

The development and application of synthetic materials is, as of this writing, the fastest growing use of technology. The prime mover behind all this is the rapid depletion of natural materials. We are now wrapped, sealed, and to some extent tooled with synthetics. Soon we will be surrounded by them.

Already the vinyl family of synthetics has demonstrated that it can meet the conflicting requirements placed upon floor covering. Other synthetic formulations will be developed to satisfy requirements for walls and roofs. Machines will be designed to produce these materials at a price competitive with natural materials. The time may not be far off when natural materials, in diminishing supply, will become exotic. They will be used only for unique mechanical properties and aesthetic virtues.

METALS. Steel, contrary to popular belief, is inherently the most economical material of all. If you want the most building per dollar, and you are not too concerned about aesthetic considerations, the answer is to build with steel.

Steel is very strong, stiff, elastic, and—here comes a new word—isotropic. That means it has nearly the same strength and stiffness in all directions and thus can be used with less intelligence than a non-isotropic material. It can be manufactured in a vast variety of structural shapes, at little extra cost. These shapes are easy to put together. In theory, steel's major flaw is that it has to be protected from rust.

Although the all-steel factory has become almost an axiom, the all-steel house doesn't seem to catch on. It doesn't even catch on with me, and I know exactly why. Steel does not lend itself to my goal of revealed structure. In a bridge, yes, but not in my house, my personal haven.

For the steel house to become both actually and aesthetically warm, acoustically quiet, and in the domestic sense "pleasant," every bit of it has to be covered with something else. This involves "decoration," a costly process to which I object.

The next step, already being taken, is to combine steel with other materials in hybrid manufactured products which retain the virtues of steel (including, we hope, its economy), yet escape its excessive structural functionalism.

Aluminum is quite different. Light in weight, light in color, and rust-free, aluminum in some form or other has become an essential part of every house. By the pound, aluminum is expensive. Used in the right place, a few pounds go a long way. It reflects heat, stops air flow, controls condensation, discourages insects, and is fire resistant. It sheds no dust and it is easy to apply.

Aluminum is not an all-purpose material (for airplanes, yes, but not for houses), but the things it does well it does very well indeed. I buy aluminum foil by the dozen rolls, and use it everywhere. Whereas on many materials I have said, use with caution, aluminum foil is one of the "if in doubt, do" materials which can do no harm and may do a lot of good.

Having taken a fast look at the virtues of some basic materials, in the next chapters let's go to work on how to use what materials where.

33. How to build a footing

The ground beneath us is not necessarily stable. Its willingness to move around varies from point to point. Its ability to stay put depends on the load we put on it. The Washington Monument, they tell me, loads the ground beneath it at something around 18,000 pounds per square foot, and it is settling slowly, though uniformly. Pisa's leaning tower is an example of non-uniform settling. The ground under one side happened to be softer than under the other.

We have all seen sway-backed houses. Old houses, and some new ones too. The sway-back is usually caused by excessive ground loading. I worked on a house where the architect had specified an extremely massive chimney block at one end. Instead of leaving it hollow, as drawn, the builder chose to fill it with concrete. The ground loading in this case rose to about 10,000 pounds per square foot. The chimney block settled so fast, carrying the end of the house down with it, that the plaster cracked before it was dry.

With light ground loading, there should be no trouble. At a thousand pounds per square foot almost any ground, unless it's an outright swamp, will hold you up. In case this ground loading business bothers you, imagine a two-hundred-pound policeman, with flat feet and wearing number twelve shoes, walking softly across a patch of mud. His ground loading is not far from a thousand pounds per square foot. If he breaks into a run and begins to stamp his feet, the figure goes up to around three thousand.

The vertical footing, sitting on its narrow edge, creates excessive ground loading. Under multiple-story houses, loadings of five or six thousand pounds per square foot are common, or about twice as much as our policeman in a hurry. The fact that the vertical footing has been dug several feet into the ground serves only to increase the weight of the footing itself and thus makes the loading worse.

Six thousand pounds might be all right at one point, and not all right a few feet away. The easiest way to stay out of trouble is to keep all loadings low.

Here are profile views of various house footings. The first one, a full pad, has the lowest ground loading of all.

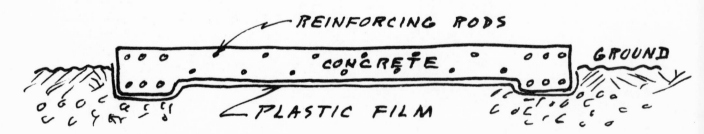

This footing floats the whole building on a concrete platter. In doubtful situations, perhaps involving deep loam or ground water close to the surface, the full pad is the best guarantee against irregular settling.

The full pad is also a bargain in that it provides a completed floor for shop and play areas, or for the whole house if you like it that way. My personal preference is to see the living area floor raised sixteen inches (two steps) above the pad. The resulting space can be used for pipes and wires, and if you choose as one big heating duct.

The first pad-builders buried all pipes and conduit in the concrete. I don't care for this technique. It violates flexibility, leaves nothing fixable or changeable. The early pad-builders made another mistake in omitting the plastic film moisture stop. This gave pads a bad name because they got wet and stayed wet. With the plastic film below, they still get wet from the air above, but not so badly.

In my opinion the full pad should be used only in cases where the ground loadability is doubtful. I don't think it is the best way to begin building most houses.

If you are sitting on good solid ground, there isn't much need for a continuous pad. Here is a view of a multiple pad footing.

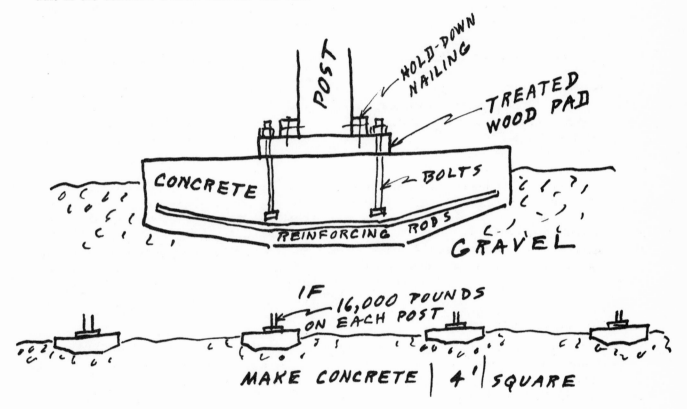

The lower small-scale view shows a pad for each post. First scrape away the loam and save it for your garden. Make each post-supporting pad big enough to keep the ground loading to a thousand pounds, then put some smaller pads in the middle of the house so the floor joists can be small. For level ground, it's hard to imagine a cheaper footing, or one which disturbs the terrain any less.

Pad footings, either continuous or multiple, are your best bet for use on newly placed fill. But don't build anything on recent fill if you can avoid it. Undisturbed ground is likely to stay put. Disturbed ground tends to shift around before it settles down.

The wall footing needs to be talked about only because so many millions of them get built.

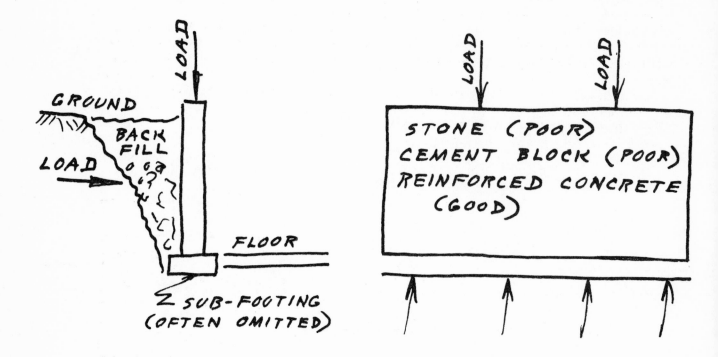

You will recognize this as one wall of the conventional basement. Let's take another look at history. The full basement, now an anachronism, used to be needed. Great-grandfather, having dug a hole in the ground, put a wall around it. He built his wall of rocks because that's all he had. With the wall sitting there, he used it as the footing for his house. Whether he knew it or not, he had done several things wrong, mainly because he had no choice.

First, because the masonry wall is heavy, and is vertical instead of horizontal, the ground loading is too high. Today, this can be corrected with a big sub-footing, but great-grandfather had no means of making one. Second, he had to build with assembled masonry, which has no tensile strength, therefore no power to resist local failure. His footing was liable to sag in spots. Third, he had to build an earth-retaining wall which was straight up and down, and thus was loaded from the outside only. A properly built earth-retaining wall should lean into its load. Fourth,

ground water was free to come in and turn his basement into a pond.

Having turned up my nose at the full basement wall-footing, I admit that the single earth-retaining wall, as sketched, can be a good architectural device if used properly. It lets you set a shop or garage into a hillside and perhaps cut down on driveway steepness, or on stair climbing. If, however, this wall is to be used as a footing for additional structure, please make it of reinforced concrete, not assembled masonry.

How many square feet of footing do you need? I have already suggested that you hold the line at 1,000 pounds per square foot. Now you may ask, how much does a house weigh? That's the same as asking me how long is a piece of string, but I will do my best to give an answer.

For a minimum weight of house, contents, and extras, use 100 pounds per square foot of floor and roof area. A two-story, 2,000-square-foot house with 3,000 square feet of roof would, by this formula, have two times two plus three, or

7,000 feet of horizontal areas, adding up to 700,000 pounds of possible ground loading.

Anything can happen in a house, however, and for a safer formula use 150 pounds for the floor areas, staying at 100 for the roof. This comes to two times two times 150, plus three times 100, which gives us 900,000 pounds, or roughly a million.

Now let's assume that 2,000-square-foot house is 70 feet long and 30 feet wide. Around the outside it measures 200 feet. Divide a million by 200. The result is 5,000 pounds to the running foot. Add a thousand pounds for the weight of the footing alone and the answer shows that the load is too great.

I do not criticize grandfather's vertical footings. I do criticize builders who have imitated him without asking why he did what he did. Even after the basement is dispensed with, the notion persists that a footing has to be a vertical wall. Here is an example:

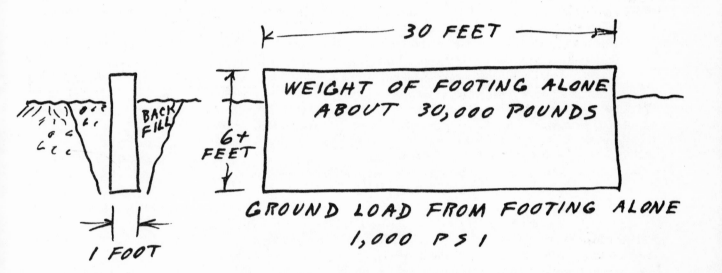

Imagine a house sitting on top and you can see how the ground loading has gone up. If you took the same piece of concrete and laid it out flat, you would have a far better footing.

Exactly at this point you may ask, "But what happened to the frost line?"

To answer your question, let's go back to grandfather. His house was heated only in the center, around the fireplace and the kitchen stove. A bucket of water close to an outside wall would freeze. Our houses now are vast though low-temperature ovens, even when we go south for a month and leave the thermostat at forty. Given a little insulation, such as a house sitting on it, the natural temperature of the ground below us is a uniform forty-five or better. The ground beneath and immediately around a heated house simply does not freeze.

The footing which I suggest for your dream house, is the one which in my experience has proved to be most reliable and least troublesome to build, a set of posts. Even while the cries of amazement and the screams or rage are rising, I continue to insist that this to me is the most versatile footing of all. It can be used almost anywhere. It probably goes far into pre-history as the foundation of the first recognizable man-made dwelling. Architects have rediscovered it time after time, and as of this writing, are discovering it all again.

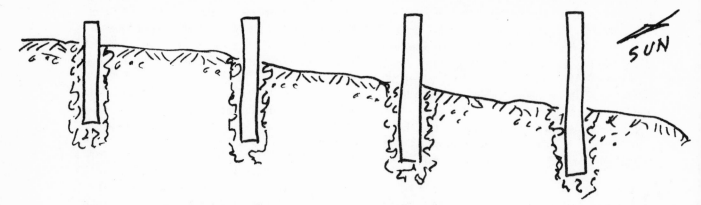

Here is a picture of the footing underneath the office where I sit at this moment. I dug some holes, throwing the top loam aside, and in the holes set heavy, chemically treated timbers. I filled the holes with clean gravel and tamped it down. No power machinery was required, just me and a shovel. Then I nailed the first set of floor beams right across the sides of the posts, and the building went up from there.

Having talked so much about ground loading, I should explain here that a post, called by the builders of docks and skyscrapers a "piling," picks up ground loading area from its sides as well as its foot. I'd rather not go into the reasons for this right now, but if you don't believe it, just try to pull a well-set post out of the ground.

Most builders will prefer cast-in-place concrete posts rather than wood timbers. If you do, don't forget to include steel reinforcing, plus bolts for holding down the floor timbers on which the house is built. Nevertheless, my sketch remains the same whether you use timbers or concrete.

The sketch shows the sun coming in on the long dimension of the building rather than crossways. The preferred location for a post-footed house is a south-facing hillside. On a winter day, the sun, coming in at a low angle, warms up the ground beneath. At night the ground tries to re-radiate heat in all directions, but finds little to cool toward except the house above it. Solar heat storage material, in this case the ground, has been provided for nothing.

Man's original intention in building himself a post-footed house may have been to keep away from prowling lions. Few of us are seriously troubled by lions today, but post footing does neatly help us to escape another natural enemy, ground water. Setting posts does not disturb the physical structure of the earth beneath. In most cases it requires no earth-moving machinery heavier than a shovel. It creates almost no disruption of environment. Nothing is moved which has to be taken away or put back. Best of all, there isn't any water in the basement.

In the scramble for living space, the post footing allows you to build your house wherever you like, at the lowest cost. It also gives you the greatest freedom to create a house which looks as if it belongs where it is. Of all possible footings, I like it best.

34. How to build a roof

In post-and-beam construction, as soon as the footing is in place, the roof goes up on its supporting posts. This is a very important advantage. Immediate shelter has been provided for both materials and workmen. Therefore the roof comes first, but we have not as yet designed it.

The first thing to decide about a roof is its slope, if any. Both the structure and the covering of the roof are determined in large part by its slope, or "pitch." This is spoken of as the number of inches of rise for each foot of horizontal travel. One inch of rise to the foot is "one pitch," six inches rise to the foot is six pitch. Naturally, twelve pitch is one foot to the foot, or forty-five degrees, while a flat roof is zero pitch.

The flat roof is wrong on all counts, the most important being that gravity doesn't help it shed water. The weather surface has to be much more carefully built to avoid leaks. It becomes at least twice as expensive per square foot as a sloping roof. Structurally, the flat roof is also more expensive. A sloping roof lends itself to the design of economical beams and trusses, such as you observed in the classic A-frame truss. A flat roof goes back to the uniform section beam of our somewhat more remote ancestors.

Roof pitch is an important dollar decision. There are three considerations to balance against each other: area; construction cost per unit of area; weather surface cost per unit of area.

As the pitch increases from zero, the area at first shows little increase. A one- or two-pitch roof is not noticeably larger than a flat roof, but it does allow water to run off. A twelve-pitch roof is almost one and a half times as big as a flat.

Construction cost goes down until about three pitch is reached, then begins to climb rapidly. This is based both on beam cost and on boarding area.

Weather surface cost comes out much the same. The steeper the pitch, the poorer the weather surface can be, because water runs off

easily. A low pitch weather surface is fairly expensive for materials, although less costly for labor. At anything above four pitch, the unit area material cost remains the same, labor cost goes up rapidly because the carpenter can no longer stand on the roof, and of course the area increases. Remember that roofs cost more to build then walls.

The silliest fad I have seen lately are these ultra-steep roofs which come all the way to the ground. If they were intended to rear above the snow on a picturesque mountain top, I might get the point, but I couldn't design a structure which would give you less interior space for your money.

In any well-built house, the roof is the most important and most expensive part. The square-foot cost of roof coverage is largely determined by its pitch. I have already admitted there are valid considerations leading toward raising or lowering the pitch. Someone has to flip a nickel and decide. I've decided. For what you know to be my favorite roof, a single plane lifted toward the south, I prefer one pitch.

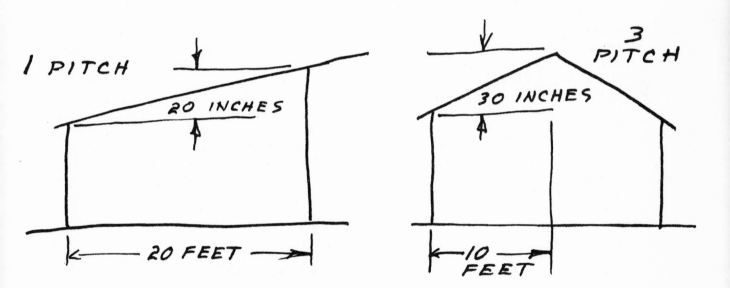

The first sketch shows one inch to the foot, on a single slope. The sketch at right shows a low-pitch version of the more conventional A-frame roof, to which you might be forced by location, building code, or just plain preference.

For the A-frame roof I prefer something around three pitch, as sketched. A relatively low pitch of this kind gives the effect and has all structural advantages of an A-frame, plus a pleasing interior, but doesn't waste much enclosed space.

Grandfather built his roofs like this:

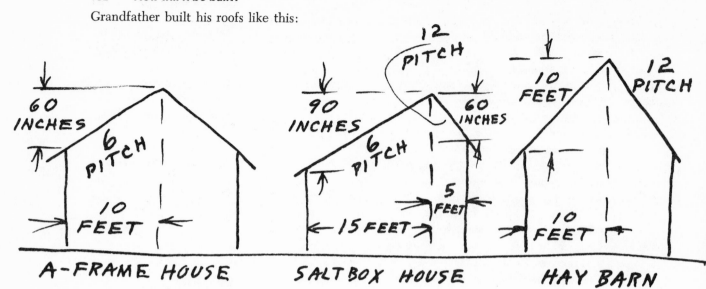

The feet and inches are there to indicate pitch, not the actual dimensions of houses and barns. Grandfather seldom built with less than a six pitch, and his roofs were often steeper. They had to be steep for they were put together with assembled materials; shingles, slate, tile, or thatch.

All assembled roofing materials depend entirely on gravity to shed water. Take shingles, for instance. Wood shingles will shed water at six pitch, but not much lower. Imitation shingles made of tar paper can be used, at your peril, down to four pitch.

The more broken up the roofing material the steeper the roof has to be. It was thatch for the poor and slate for the not-so-poor that gave rise to the extremely steep roof lines of ancient villages. We find them picturesque. The dwellers found them expensive.

By the way, great-grandfather usually put an even steeper roof on his barn than on his house. He needed room in the haymow. He kept his hay upstairs so he could fork it down to the cows in a hurry at feeding time.

The steeper the roof the more expensive it gets. There is more frame to build and more area to cover. Above four pitch the carpenter can no longer walk around comfortably as he works, but requires something extra to stand on. The scaffolding costs money and the carpenter works more slowly—thus adding to the cost in two ways at once.

Out of necessity, great-grandad started another architectural detail. His steep roof, which had to be steep to be waterproof with a shingle skin, created a big V-shaped space which he couldn't afford to heat. So he built a ceiling. Sometimes he put a floor in the Vee and the space above became an attic.

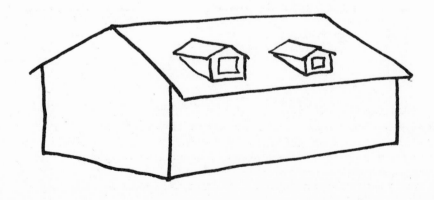

Being there, the attic became a useful shelter. In pursuit of gracious living therein, grandfather cut holes in the roof, covered them with little sub-roofs, and Aunt Mary and the extra children had a place to sleep from which they could see out. It was expensive, but necessary. The dor-

mer window had been invented.

Having been created out of necessity, steep roofs and dormers became a style, the right way to build a house.

Eventually this curious architectural form evolved.

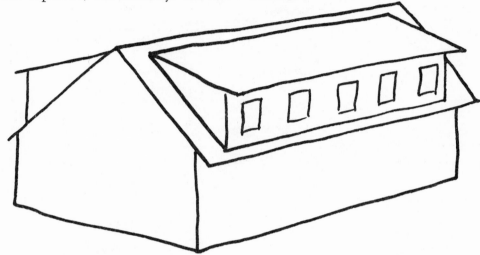

The dormer window has grown unti it almost, but not quite, engulfs the entire roof. The builder has gone to a low pitch on his dormer, to make more room inside, then has left a foot or so of token roof showing on each end, just to prove he knew what was "right" in the way of rooflines. You can see that having two roofs complicates the structure and costs a lot more money.

I drove down a street last night where these things stood row on row, all with full dormer roofs on both sides, all with a useless scratch of shingled roof on each side of the dormer, all with a token foot of roof above and below the dormer.

There were scores of them. Had each of the

owners contributed the two thousand dollars of wasted dormer money in his house, the people on that street could have endowed an orphanage.

The roof is the most distinguishing feature in a house. It is also the most expensive part—in first cost, in maintenance, and in heat loss. It behooves us to think carefully about how to get the most roof for your money.

Whether you are building a house, a factory, or an auditorium, you have a choice between a combination of structure and skin on the one hand, and the alternate combination of basic structure, sub-structure, and skin. Here is a picture of structure and skin:

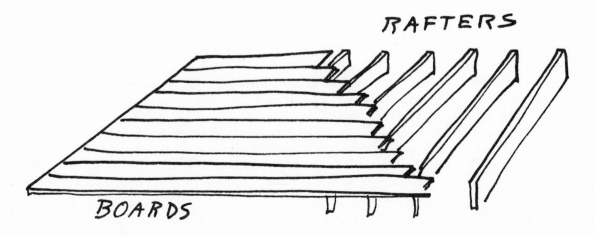

I have broken away the roof boards to show the conventional rafters underneath, and to illustrate how the rafter supports, the skin encloses.

Here is the alternative—basic structure, substructure and skin.

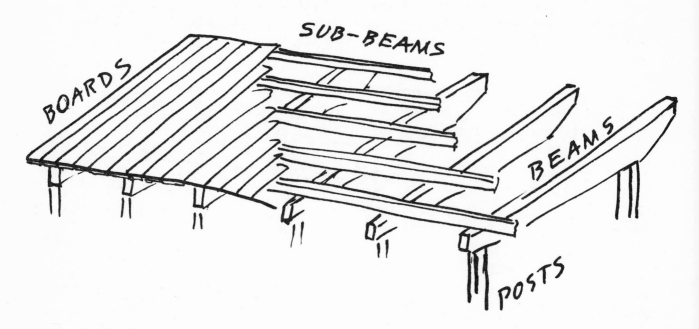

The posts and beams, spaced far apart, constitute the basic structure. Sub-beams running the long way of the roof, spread the load and support the skin.

This three-unit structure, or beam, sub-beam and skin, is a very old principle, and mathematically sound. What will surprise you is that it is actually cheaper than the two-unit, or rafter and skin arrangement, because it takes fewer pounds of material to support a given load over a given span.

Not only is it cheaper, but it makes a handsome structure, nice to look at just as it is. Now that we have decided to reveal structure and dispense with cosmetic decoration on the interior, this is an important point. I wouldn't care to look at rafters all day every day myself, but the pattern of beam and sub-beam looks good.

I also point out that the board or panels on this roof run in the correct direction, with the slope rather than across it. The stiffness of the boards thus is added across the greater span, and the board immediately above each beam becomes a part of that beam and increases its effective depth.

As for the material of which your structure is to be made, I say quickly that in your most-for-the-money house you will use wood. Per unit of strength, wood is more expensive than steel, but it can be exposed to the eye without apology and without covering.

What kind of wood depends on what you regard as attractive. Some kinds of wood are stronger, size for size, than others, but that tells you only what size timbers to use, and how many. I have never been able to understand why some building codes specify kinds of wood. The important thing in revealed structure is that you think the wood looks good and feels good. Some of the structural woods do not. For example, fir, a wood required in many building codes, and hemlock, equally stiff, are splintery and not of pleasant texture. I recommend instead almost any member of the spruce or pine families.

What you will be seeing of this structure are the posts, beams, cross-beams, and the bottom side of the first layer of skin, which will probably be either boards or plywood. You and your architect can have fun deciding what combinations of texture and color you prefer. Remember that if you accept what I have been saying about useless and expensive decoration, you are not going to paint or even stain your overhead structure. The colors will stay light and handsome if you leave the wood alone. With the money you don't spend on cosmetics for your house you can buy a second car or build a bigger dwelling.

The roof skin has to keep heat from moving either way, by conduction or by radiation, and it has to keep the rain out. This task is complicated and expensive. Some compromise between total success and economy has to be made. Here is an exploded view, in profile, of the best roof I know, all things considered.

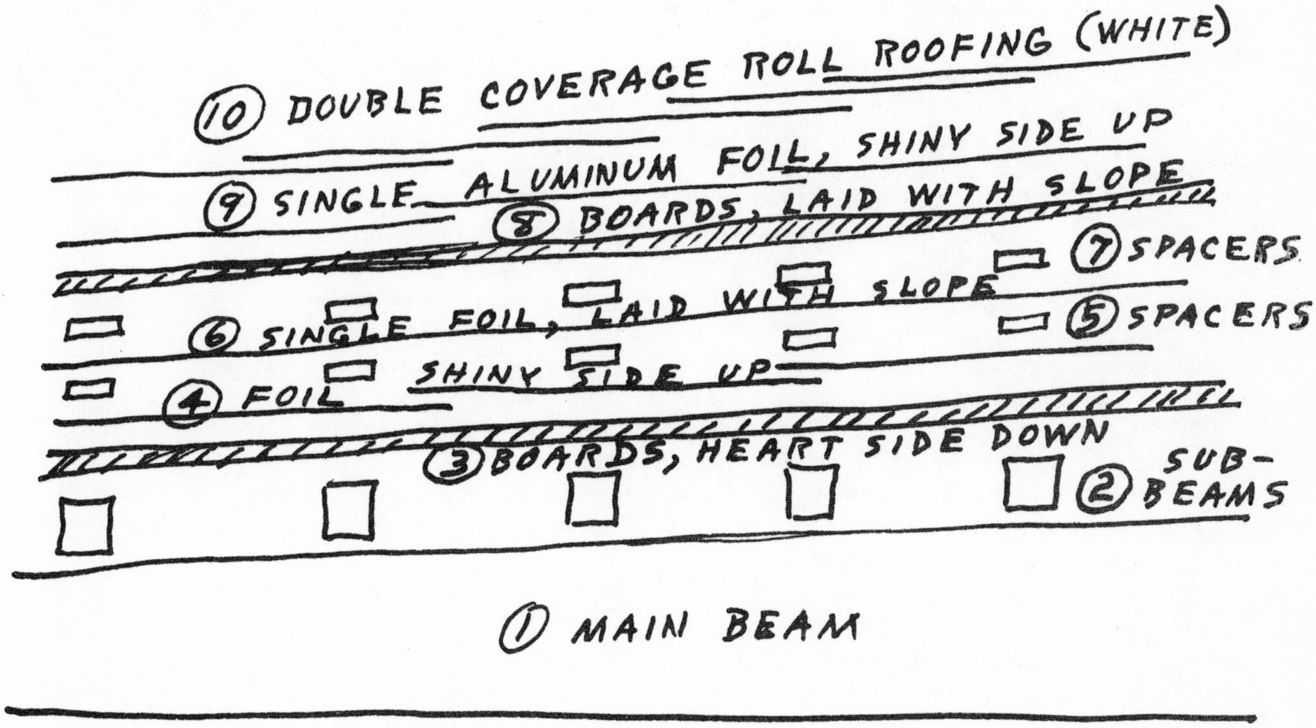

This may look complicated to you. It isn't. Let me explain how it works, and how easy it is to put together.

You know that it is much easier to work down than to work up. I mean gravity-down, not prestige-down. My wife rests the iron on top of the ironing board, not underneath. In my roof assembly the carpenter spends all of his time nailing down, not up.

It goes together like this:

1. is a main beam. Its shape and design will be determined by roof slope and span and are not shown here. The main beam sits on posts.
2. are sub-beams fastened to the top of the main beams.

3. are the visible boards, which you may call the ceiling if you wish. They are nailed to the sub-beams. They run with the slope of the roof, and add to the strength of the beams.
4. are strips of aluminum foil, laid shiny side up, shingle fashion, lengthwise of the roof.
5. are one-inch spacers, placed on top of each sub-beam, and nailed through the foil and ceiling boards into the sub-beams.
6. is another layer of aluminum foil, laid shiny side up, with the slope. One layer of foil is enough to keep outside heat out, but two or more layers are required to keep inside heat in. The layer of trapped air is a conductive insulation.

7. is another row of one-inch spacers, again set directly over the sub-beams. By adding to the effective depth of the sub-beams, they are adding substantially to their stiffness.

8. is the outer layer of roof boards. Since it is out of sight, the boards can be of lower grade than the ceiling.

9. is still another layer of aluminum foil, laid shiny side up, the long way of the roof.

10. is "double-coverage" roll roofing, laid as the name implies with a little more than half its width overlapping. Its surface color should be as light as possible. The kind I use is labeled "Snow White," which you can read to mean a fairly light gray.

I have found one variation on this scheme which doesn't greatly reduce its effectiveness and perhaps saves a little money. For layers 5 and 6 you can substitute a layer of the cheapest available insulating "board." I don't advise the substitution, but if you are pushing hard to save nickels, it will work.

I'd rather see you use the three layers of foil and get the benefit of the two layers of air. The second one reduces both conduction and radiation to as near zero as it's worth trying to get. The foil used here is not, of course, the kitchen variety. It is builders' foil, a sheet of aluminum on a backing of kraft paper. We use it shiny side up because we want drips and condensation to run off easily and cleanly.

At this point I have to answer a question from the floor. "What happened to the glass wool, rock wool, or mica flake that are often recommended as insulation?"

Answer: you may if you wish double the thickness of the spacers, remove the middle layer of foil, and fill the two-inch space with wool. You will get the same effect for about the same or a little more money.

I have three reasons for preferring multiple foil and air. The first concerns insects, who love to build their homes in the warmth and comfort of a wool batt, but are discouraged by the bleak horizons of aluminum. The second reason concerns fire resistance. If, by sad mischance, the lower layer of board burns away, the batt insulation will fall down of its own weight, exposing the upper layers to further damage. Foil will stay where it was put much longer.

To get at my third and most important reason we have to explore a whole new topic, dew.

Your weather forecaster talks about the "dew point." The ability of air to retain water vapor depends on its temperature. As air cools down, it reaches a temperature, depending on how much water vapor it had to begin with, where it has to get rid of some water. That is the dew point. Air, approaching its dew point temperature, then coming in contact with a cooler solid body, deposits its excess water thereon. This is dew, wetting not only your feet in the grass, but steel, wood, glass, masonry—in fact, everything at the critical temperature.

Dew doesn't "fall," it "forms." When dew is forming on the grass, it is also forming on the ignition system of your silent automobile. Worse, it is forming somewhere on or inside the walls and roof of your house.

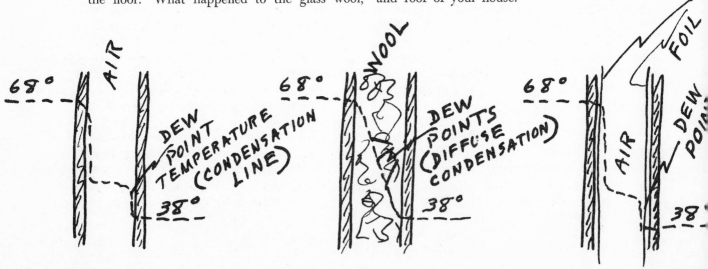

In these three sketches, the dotted lines represent a graph of temperature, same time, same place, same day, or rather, same evening, but three different houses.

The sketch at left shows in simplified fashion an "uninsulated" house, with an inner skin and an outer skin and some air in between. With the outer air cooling down, and heat flowing more or less freely from inside to outside, the condensation line almost always occurs on the inside of the outside. From there, in pre-insulation construction, the water runs down and soaks into the sill which eventually rots away, but at least the outer boarding stays dry and the paint stays on. All of us have seen extreme cases where the dew forms on the outside of the outside, where it does no harm at all, but only warns us that the house is losing heat at a great rate.

No one builds houses like this any more. There is always some pretense at insulation. When, a few decades ago, insulation became fashionable, there was a great wave of filling the air space with some kind of woolly or flakey material.

The middle sketch shows you what happens with this kind of insulation. The temperature at which dew forms is now almost certainly to be found somewhere in the middle of this semi-solid mass of insulative material. The dew is deposited there, and it stays there. The whole wall or roof gets wet and stays wet. A few weeks later the outside paint—this type of house is always, but always, painted—begins to peel off. In extreme cases, given a little more time, the inside plaster—this type of house is always, but always, plastered—begins to fall off too.

The third sketch, at right, shows you what happens when we go back to the original scheme but add two layers of foil. The condensation line will almost always be at the outer foil layer. Since water and aluminum are not even country cousins, the dew forms not so much as moisture but as actual droplets, which run down and away freely. If by chance you ignore my advice (many do), and paint the outside and plaster the inside of your house, both paint and plaster will stay dry.

But why, you ask, doesn't the water which runs down rot the sill? Answer: later you will discover that it runs out to the ground. In the first place, your ideal house doesn't have a sill. Second, if it did, the wall wouldn't be on it at all, but outside it.

Walls crept into the roof section because both suffer from this dew point business. I can now state my major structural (though not aesthetic) objection to the flat roof. There isn't any way for the dew to run out.

Go back, please, to my roof profile sketch. As we have said, each layer of foil is actually a skin of aluminum bonded to heavy paper. Each layer has its shiny side up. Though I can't predict which layer is going to be the dew point, I don't care, because each layer eventually drains to the back of the roof.

Another question that may arise concerns the double coverage roofing. This is shown on the assumption that our roof pitch will be somewhere between one and three, and there we are back to pitch again as the important factor in many decisions.

A flat roof requires the so-called built-up roofing, which is multiple layers of paper and tar, covered with gravel. With no assist from gravity to remove water, the job must be carefully done to be leak-proof.

From one up to three pitch, double coverage is required. This type of roofing can either be stuck on entirely with tar, or nailed first where the nails don't show. Unless something punches a hole in the roof, there is little chance of a leak.

From four pitch up you can use single coverage roll roofing. Single coverage roofing is laid on with only a narrow lap, and the nails show. This roof will keep you dry for a while, and it costs only half as much as double coverage, but the chances are that to keep the roof free of leaks another layer will be needed before too many years. Here, by the way, is a chance to do some installment building if you're short of cash. Single coverage now, with double coverage right over it when you can afford it.

For six pitch and up, aluminum sheet roofing has some impressive advantages. It is fire resistant, heat reflective either way, and permanent. Because of the difference in thermal expansion between solid metal and the wood underneath it, the aluminum sheet may loosen its fastenings and leak. Use it with caution except on utility buildings where an occasional leak won't do any harm. If and when someone invents a way to lay leakless aluminum, I will cancel this last statement and go for it as the finest of all weather surfaces.

You will recall that I shrugged off shingles as a hopeless and expensive anachronism. If by chance you don't believe me, or your heart tells you that it isn't a house if it doesn't have shingles on it, remember that four pitch is the absolute bottom limit. Below that, shingles leak.

After all this talk, the roof that I recommend is exactly the one shown in the sketch. That tells you about everything I know on the difficult and important subject of how to build a roof.

35. How to build a floor

Now that we have a roof over us we can work in any kind of weather. The next step is to build a floor. It makes a level place to walk around without stumbling.

Again we start with structure. Floors have to be stronger than roofs. Short of a snow depth running to very many feet, the heaviest load ever put on your roof structure is two carpenters walking around driving nails. Two feet of snow, with some rain thrown in, weighs less than fifteen pounds to the square foot. I use thirty pounds per square foot, plus the weight of the roof itself, in figuring required roof strength.

As for the floor, I can imagine a party going on with one person for every 10 square feet.

This averages the same fifteen pounds to the square foot. Now add a grand piano, play it, ask everybody to dance, and the figure goes up by somewhere between two and three. I use eighty pounds per square foot for figuring required floor strength.

However, and this is a big however, the determining factor in a house floor is not strength at all, but stiffness. We don't like the floor to dip and bounce beneath us. Stiffness, as you will recall from the second quarter of our structural engineer's course, falls off twice as fast as strength when span increases. To keep our floor structure light and therefore inexpensive, we want to support it at as many points as possible.

To illustrate: Let's say that a certain kind of four-by-eight timber is adequate for a sixteen-foot roof span. The same timber will prove barely adequate for an eight-foot floor span, the difference, very roughly, being at least two to one.

If the support is every four feet both ways, two-by-four timbers are good enough. The ultimate support being the ground, the decision as to the weight of our floor structure depends in every case on how far away the ground is and how often we want to reach down to it.

I'm almost afraid to mention rules of thumb, because every case can be different, but here goes. The hillside house, sitting on posts, is going to have a post every eight feet in both directions.

If the footing were instead a continuous pad on level ground, the shop and playrooms might use the slab itself as floor, with the rest of the house sitting on concrete blocks located every four feet. Like this:

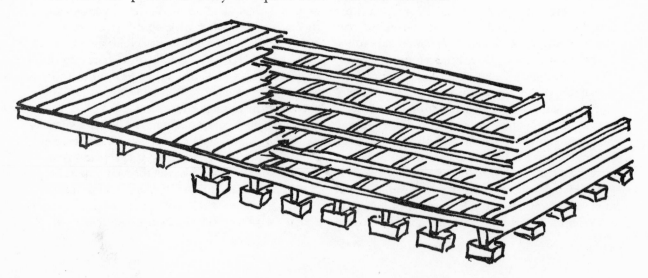

Note the similarity between the floor structure as sketched, and the recommended roof structure of the preceding chapter. The three-way system of beam, sub-beam and skin gives you more for your money, no matter what the load or the span, than a two-way system of beam (called rafter in a roof and joist in a floor) and skin.

The bottom of the timbers actually in contact with the concrete blocks is chemically treated, and no untreated wood is ever in contact with masonry.

If still more space is required for some reason, or if you want your floor to be a little farther off the ground, you can go up on another layer of concrete blocks, or on stubby posts. Always raise in even increments of eight inches, that being the step height which the human leg prefers.

The skin (some would call it the floor, as distinct from the floor structure) carries the final load. Assuming for the moment that you are concerned only with load and not with insulation, how thick shall the skin be? First you must decide whether the skin will be one layer or two. To arrive at a good decision we have to talk history some more.

The conventional floor is built up in two layers, a sub-floor and a finish floor. The first reason for beginning with a sub-floor, strangely, is plaster. The plasterers grind their dirt into the sub-floor, then the finish flooring, when laid, covers it up. Eliminate plaster, as I hope we have agreed to do, and one layer of floor skin, of the right thickness, is enough.

A second reason for the sub-floor comes from the lumber industry. The so-called "one-inch" board has shrunk through the decades until the present industry standard is $^{25}\!/_{32}$ inch. The same thing happened to the "two by four," which commercially is $1\frac{5}{8}$ by $3\frac{9}{16}$. The "inch" board today isn't even sawed an inch thick before planing.

Why is this important? Because, although the so-called "one-inch" board is about $\frac{3}{5}$ inch or a little more than half as strong as a true one-inch board, it is less than half as stiff. This means that two commercial "one-inch" boards, placed on top of each other and having a total thickness of roughly $1\frac{1}{2}$ inches, will bend more under your weight than a single board that is truly one inch thick.

I build my own floors with the lumber industry's next weight of board, called "five quarter," sawed to $1\frac{1}{4}$ inches thick. I have it planed to $1\frac{1}{8}$ inches. It costs 60 per cent as much as the two commercial "one inch" boards which it replaces, and is roughly half again as stiff. Also the single board won't squeak, the squeak being produced by the two boards rubbing together as they bend.

At this point the carpenters are walking on a floor made of $1\frac{1}{4}$-inch boards. The floor is stiff. Its durability cannot be improved by the addition of any other material. If you want to, you can run a floor sander over it and call it done. That is what I do. However, a bare wood floor will try your patience for several years while it converts dirt into patina. One coat of linseed oil right after the sanding will make localized dirt less obvious and speed up the patina process.

A floor does a lot of work. It is required to be soft to the foot, undentable by the tilted chair, quiet under the impact of high heels, impervious to cigarette ashes, stable under the hasty step, and easy to clean. A softwood floor achieves the best compromise between these conflicting requirements, but you may not want to look at bare boards. You may believe that with a covering, the floor will be nicer to the eye or smoother to the mop.

Whatever your choice may be, I suggested earlier that your floor should be lightly textured in smoothness, so as to be hard to slip on but easy to sweep, and heavily textured in appearance, so as not to show dirt.

Before covering your structural floor at all, remember that serviceable floor coverings are expensive. They will probably cost more per square foot than all the rest of your floor structure put together. My suggestion is that you use your wood surface for a while and see how you like it. You won't hurt it a bit. You can always add the covering later, provided the original walk-on floor was stiff. Here I rest my case for thick boards, and move on to the insulated floor.

Your idealized hillside house will have air,

not earth, beneath it. This will save a lot of money on site preparation and footings, but some of the profit must go back into a better floor.

Fortunately, the insulation requirements of a floor are not severe. Temperature differentials between house and ground are low, therefore heat flow by radiation is low. About all that is required is to keep the wind from blowing through. Here is a suggested floor structure, seen in profile:

NON-STRUCTURAL FINISH FLOOR, IF ANY

STRUCTURAL FLOOR

SUB-BEAMS

SPACERS, IF REQUIRED   SPACE FOR PIPES OR HEAT, IF REQUIRED

DOUBLE-SIDED ALUMINUM FOIL

INSULATION BOARD

BEAM

FOOTING POSTS

The floor structure is put together this way, always working from the bottom up. First the beams are fastened to the footing posts. Next a layer of insulation board, which has been made for low heat flow at the expense of strength. Here its only structural purpose is to hold up the aluminum foil. Next comes the foil layer, which this time, to simplify things, will be shiny on both sides. The insulation requirement is not severe. A single layer will suffice, and keep the wind out as well.

Above the foil layer, you have a choice. If you have not been able to achieve the central plumbing core which will be described later, there needs to be a space for pipes. In this case, raise the cross-beams on spacer blocks located above the main beam, and drive on.

From the cross-beams on up, our floor is exactly the same as before.

Here is one more reason for building the floor before the wall.

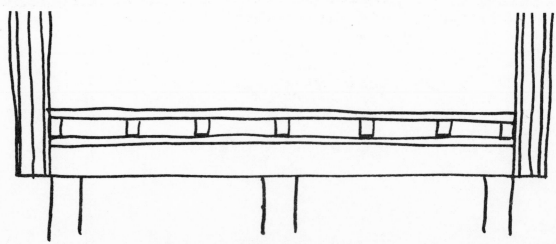

In the next section you will discover that your wall, instead of sitting on the floor, is going to come down past it. Conventional floors are finished last, and require fitting all around. Yours is built first, hangs over at the edges, and is squared off with a power saw. Then comes the wall, with no crack showing. And now you know why the dew water falls onto the ground.

All of which leads us to wall building.

36. How to build a wall

Architecturally speaking, walls receive a lot of attention, because they are at eye level, both from the inside looking out and the outside looking in. Structurally speaking, walls are the easiest and cheapest part of your house to build.

The architectural concern with walls—the pictures that have been drawn and the pages that have been written about them—is an aesthetic matter. What you do to dress up the inside and the outside is your business, but I suggest that for the time being you do nothing in the way of "decoration."

In a post-and-beam house, the walls are just hanging there, with their principal function being to keep the wind out. They are supposed to admit controlled quantities of air and light. Nobody walks or dances on them; no snow rests on them; water drains out of them easily. Being vertical, their major heat control requirement is radiation and not conduction. Their area is relatively small. As structure, they are required to hold up nothing except themselves and a few pictures.

Walls, I repeat, are the easiest part of the house to build. The carpenter doesn't even have to bend over. Among all the many ways to build a wall, here is the profile, looking down, of my favorite wall assembly:

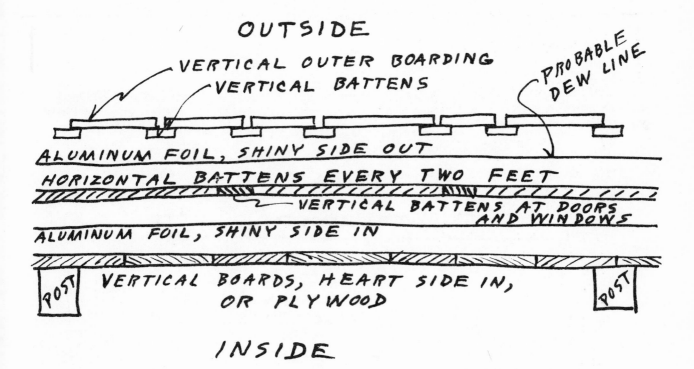

Having looked at the sketch, let's build it. This time we will work from the inside out, starting with the posts and working down past the floor, which, according to the preceding section has already been completed and squared off.

The first layer is what shows on the inside, at least until you get around to covering it up with whatever suits your fancy. My sketch shows it made of vertical boards or plywood. Holes are left for the doors and windows.

Since this first layer is nailed only top and bottom, into either the beam or the plate, it will seem perilously loose. At the opening for windows, where for the moment the boards are fastened at only one end, the wall will seem ready to collapse at the first puff of air. A nailing strip fastened at the bottom line of the windows may be helpful to the carpenter. It will serve more as reassurance than anything else, however, for it is not at all necessary to add stiffness to the wall—as you will see as the layers go on.

Next comes a layer of aluminum foil, shiny side in, running horizontally and overlapping from above like shingles. The wall at this point is practically waving in the breeze, just about stiff enough to stand up against the attack of the stapling gun that tacks on the foil.

Now we begin to stiffen it up with battens. A batten is a piece of almost-junk-wood, two or three inches wide and an inch (in quotes) thick. The battens are placed horizontally, two feet apart. Some carpenters use short nails to hold them on, as I do. Screws, though taking more time, hold better and in some designs are worth the extra trouble. The door and window openings are trimmed with battens all around. Our waving wall has suddenly become a lot stiffer.

Then comes another layer of foil, shiny side out, and an inch of dead air has been trapped.

The next layer is a row of vertical battens. The builder now has to get his head in the game, because the batten location depends on the width of the exterior board it is to support. The wall is now stiff enough and thick enough to nail to, and we hammer away merrily (using nails of the correct length), placing board on batten—leave a little space—place another batten and another board—figure how to break even at the window openings—another inch of air has been trapped—the condensation line is established at the outer foil with drops running harmlessly to the ground—and the wall, now four inches thick, is so stiff it rings under a hammer blow.

Building a layered wall is an easy but exciting experience. I get carried away every time. The materials are inexpensive; the completed product is structurally and thermally sound; the random width exterior boarding, in addition to being an excellent weather surface, has given us an aesthetic chance at variety of line and texture.

At this point you may say, I know all about board and batten. That's shack building. Here is what you mean:

OUTSIDE

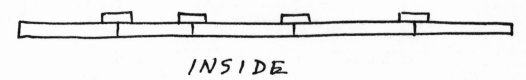

INSIDE

This is the board and batten you are thinking of, with the board put on first and the batten showing on the outside. It looks cheap, and is. All I do is turn the board and batten around:

OUTSIDE

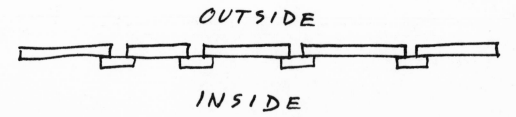

INSIDE

By doing that I add another inch to the effective stiffness of the wall, trap another inch of air, provide a free drainage channel for the dew. The whole thing remains cheap, but it looks expensive. If you don't believe it, come and look at my house.

The lower sketch, showing vertical, random-width boards spaced against battens, is in all respects the best exterior wall surface I can devise for a house. It drains well, both rain water and dew water. It ventilates itself. So far as the years of my own life have let me see, it will last forever. It is economical to build. It is so far out in front that I personally wouldn't think of building anything else. With all these advantages, it looks good too.

So far as weather is concerned, the house is now live-in-able as soon as it gets some doors and windows. The outside of the wall is complete for all time. The inside is completed or not, as you please. The wood inner skin retains the virtue of adaptability.

You can move in, live there in creature comfort, and retain your option on what you want to look at. If you want to decorate, the walls around you are ideal for trial and error experimentation. You can drive nails, hang pictures, display driftwood, or draw pictures in crayon, with no harm done. You can cover one wall with colored burlap, paint another wall white or decide on panoramic wallpaper, mix a little plaster or put up a little section of tile. You can decide that between two posts is a fine place to build a cupboard, or shelves for the display of Quimper pottery.

That good old wooden wall is an invitation to let yourself go. It didn't cost very much to begin with, and the chances are you can't do it any harm. If you want to—as I hope you will—you can just leave it alone.

37. How to build doors and windows

Here is the way the ordinary door is fitted:

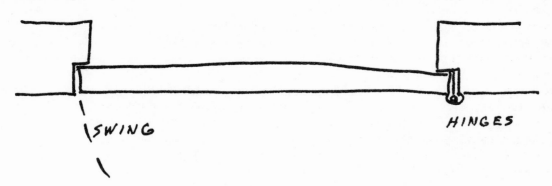

How well this door keeps the wind out depends on the accuracy with which it is fitted into a frame. In warm, wet weather, when there is no need for a tight fit, the door swells up and sticks. In cold weather everything shrinks and the door admits an invigorating breeze.

Refrigerator manufacturers are much smarter about doors. They build them this way:

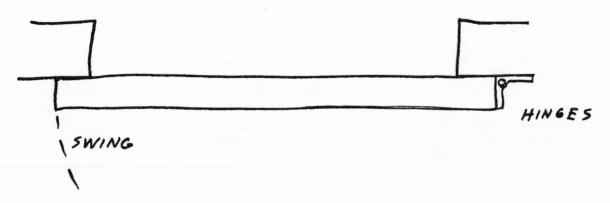

The moment you stop to consider it, I think you will agree this is the sensible way to build a door. It doesn't have to fit anything. It just closes, flat to flat, and there you are.

The domestic hardware people don't seem to have heard about the refrigerator-type door, so you will probably run into trouble getting hinges and latches that will work. When I can't find suitable hardware, I do this:

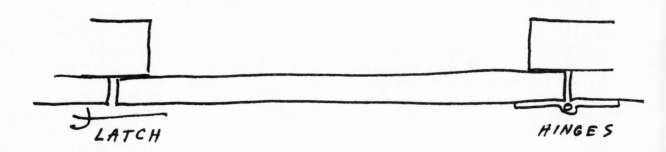

LATCH   HINGES

The next question is, which way should the door open, in or out? Well, one million out of one million house doors open in, and, flatly, every one of them is wrong. For once I find myself on the side of the building codes, which insist that doors, at least in public buildings, must open out.

The codes are based on one reason—rapid, unblocked escape from fire. There are many more reasons, all good, why doors should open out, and none that I can think of for their opening in. Here are some of the open-out reasons:

June bugs and mosquitoes collect on the door. Open the door out and they just sit there. Open it in, and happily in they come.

Comes the wind, pressing against the door. If the door opens in, it gets looser, maybe even blows open. If the door opens out, it gets tighter.

Comes the intruder, seeking admission against your wishes. The old "foot in the door" technique is useless when the door closes with the intruder's weight, not against it.

A door takes a lot of space, because there has to be an empty area somewhere into which the door can be swung open. If this space is inside, it costs you many dollars per square foot. If outside, it costs few if any dollars.

Without belaboring the dangers of fire, you will grant that getting into a house is never quite as urgent as getting out of it when things go wrong. Even something so minor as the cat being about to vomit.

If the weather door opens out, what becomes of the screen door? I have experimented with putting the screen door on the inside, opening in, but that doesn't work for the same reasons that the weather door doesn't work well that way.

The best of all solutions is the old-fashioned screened porch. If you don't like that name, we'll call it a "weather vestibule." It gets the arriving guest out of the rain, makes a place to put your overshoes and your umberlla, provides a chance to stamp the snow off your shoes or dry off the dog after a walk in the rain. It gives the mailman a safe spot to leave oversize packages, and it bewilders the mosquitoes who are trying to find a way in. There are a lot of comfort-inducing benefits in that list.

Assuming that we went a step farther and put the social-room door and the kitchen door in the same weather vestibule, the whole thing might look like this:

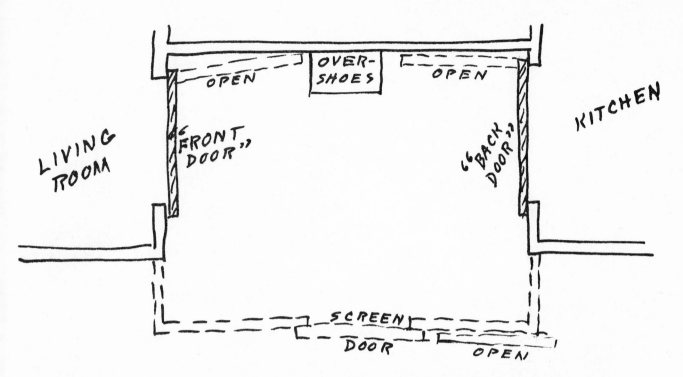

What happened to the good old "storm door?" You don't need any. The refrigerator-style door, with or without the weather vestibule, gives at least as much storm protection as two inset doors sitting back to back. I hope you have not forgotten to avoid putting any door where it faces into prevailing wind and snow.

I haven't said anything about how your door should look. Take your choice. They make all kinds. But I do want to utter a very loud cry about door widths.

A common standard width is thirty inches. Subtracting the stop strip, and assuming the usual situation where the door won't open all the way, you're lucky if you can clear twenty-seven inches. Yet many things are built to a standard width of thirty inches. A desk, for instance, is generally thirty inches wide and thirty inches high. You have a choice when the desk arrives; you can tear the wall down or send the desk back.

The refrigerator salesman asks, or should ask, about actual door clearance before he starts delivery. Appliances keep getting bigger. At least one door in the house should clear thirty-six inches. Not be thirty-six; clear it. This may re-quire a little shopping to find a store-bought door wide enough. For the rest of the doors, a minimum clearance of thirty-two inches will admit most furniture. This can be achieved with a thirty-six-inch door, which, happily, is a standard width.

Less happily, I report that although fire-resistant doors could be manufactured for about two dollars more than the cost of those usually available, they don't seem to have caught on. Up to now I've been fabricating my own. Short of that, the solid plywood door is a good bet, because it's massive. The so-called "hollow" door is a buck or two cheaper, and it's firebait. Nor does it close with that pleasant, convincing, "I'm at home now" thump.

WINDOWS. Some while back I defined a window as a piece of glass set in a wall for the purpose of admitting light and permitting you to see out, though not intended to be opened for the purpose of ventilation.

If you start with the wall structure described in the preceding section, here is the best way I know to get a lot of window for little money:

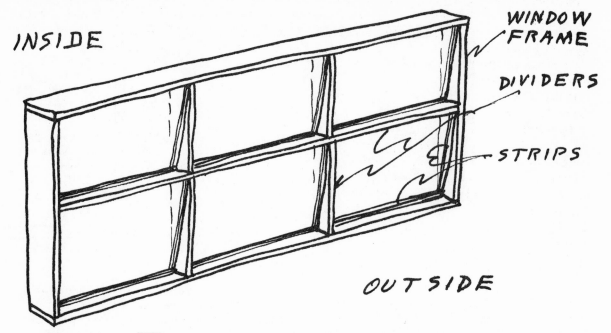

INSIDE

WINDOW FRAME

DIVIDERS

STRIPS

OUTSIDE

This is a carpenter's window, built right into the wall, using commercially available materials. It costs little if any more than a plain wall, without window.

First the carpenter builds a box, slanting the horizontal pieces a little downward so that whatever water collects on them will drain off. The box becomes part of the wall structure.

Next he cuts up or buys a lot of strips, about a half inch thick by five-eighths wide, and nails them in place so that the glass will have something to lean against. As we have learned earlier, the strips are to slant out at the top by about three degrees, or in carpenters' language about one inch in twenty.

Then the panes are set in and held in place by another set of strips nailed to hold the glass on the inside.

That's all there is to making windows. It seems almost too ridiculously simple to be any good. Perhaps because the window *is* simple (and we have come to believe that windows are complicated) many questions will be raised. Though it took only one minute to describe how to build a window, please bear with me during the many minutes that follow while I answer, not necessarily in the order of frequency or importance, some of these questions.

Question One: what happened to the putty? Didn't you know all glass is set in putty? Answer: yes, I knew it. When I began to build windows this way, I put glazing compound on both sides of the glass. That was quite a while ago. Then I got tired and put it on the outside only, and I asked every carpenter I knew if he knew what the putty was for. No answer. Getting even more tired, I quit using putty.

As far as wind coming through is concerned, I can't feel any difference. As far as protection from breakage is concerned, the only pane that has broken was the one smashed the time we got bombed by a partridge who was fleeing a hawk. (Picked up broken glass for a week.) I have concluded that putty got started in the days before power saws, when it was easier to stick the glass in place than to saw up another set of strips.

Question Two: why does the glass lean out at the top? Isn't that a lot of trouble? Answer: it is no trouble at all if the window is built in place. It avoids the use of rabbets, moldings, and close fits which make the conventional window expensive. Why is it tilted? Better vision, less glare, less dirt.

Question Three: how big are these panes, anyway? . . . Well, the smaller the pane the more material required to frame a given area. As a rule of thumb, it would seem that anything smaller than twenty by thirty inches is too small to fool around with.

At the large end, we have two things to think about: how large a piece of glass can one carpenter handle with comfort; and how big a piece can conveniently be replaced when it gets bombed by a partridge or little league home practice. My suggestion, not necessarily binding on larger and stronger carpenters, is something around thirty by forty-eight inches as a reasonable maximum.

Question Four: you say thirty by forty-eight. How come? Why not forty by forty, for instance. . . . The wider pane breaks easier and in most places doesn't look good. Remember that the window, being at eye level and extremely visible from inside and out, is a prominent part of your architectural detail, perhaps second only to the roof line in importance. The so-called "golden rectangle," that four-sided shape most restful to the human eye, is sixty-two somethings by thirty-eight somethings, or a little less than five-eighths as wide as it is long.

There is one little catch. Hang an exact square on the wall, and a hundred sets of eyes out of one hundred will declare it to be higher than it is wide. This is because the eye muscles make harder work of vertical movement than of horizontal. Therefore, if the long side of our rectangle sits horizontally, it can be fairly skinny, say, twenty-four by forty; but if it is installed vertically, we fatten it out to around twenty by thirty, and get the same effect. Graphic artists execute these proportions without necessarily knowing why. The rest of us can produce a better-looking result if we know the rules.

Question Five: how can I afford to buy all this plate glass? . . . Who said anything about plate? I use the so-called double strength, but otherwise ordinary window glass. It is rolled, not poured, and is very slightly wavy. Looking straight through, you can't see the waviness, but at an acute angle you can. Some people claim this bothers them. If they want to pay more for plate glass panes, my sketch doesn't change. All I say to them is why don't they rebel against the really acute distortions in the curved windshields of their automobiles?

Question Six: speaking of plate glass, what's wrong with these enormous single windows I see in all the magazines? . . . Nothing, except that I don't like them, and I don't think you will either after you've lived with them for a while. The caption beneath magazine pictures tells how nice it is to feel that you are living outdoors. This is obvious nonsense. Sometimes it's nice and sometimes it isn't. The first function of a house is to provide shelter from the outdoors, available at your will.

Let's look at my big window, as sketched, with six medium-sized panes instead of one great big one. The first contention of the big-window advocates is that the frames interfere with that old outdoorsy feeling.

Here is a sketch of anybody, male or female,

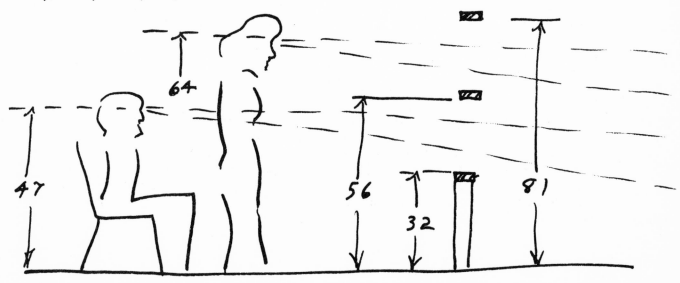

standing and sitting. Since all standard chairs are about the same height, 17 inches, and since people don't vary much from torso to torso, the eye height of almost anybody sitting down, is 47 inches, give or take a couple of inches. When people stand up, the difference increases, but the average eye height is about 64 inches, and 90 per cent of the world's people look out at a level not far from that.

The standard table height is 30 inches, rarely higher, sometimes an inch or two lower. Since we wish to preserve the option of putting a table against the window for flowers and stuff, to look good the window will begin at 32 inches above the floor.

Remember, please, that our field of vision is fairly flat, since we look sideways a lot easier than we look up and down. Also the normal field of vision, at rest, is inclined a little below horizontal, because we all carry our heads tipped a little bit forward. Starting at 32 inches, a 24-inch pane puts the divider at 56 inches. With your eye at or anywhere near 47 inches you can see out perfectly while sitting down.

Stand up, and unless you're very short, the divider still isn't in the way. At the other extreme, in order *not* to be able to see comfortably out of that upper pane, you would have to be at least seven feet four inches tall.

The vertical dividers are equally unnoticed, but for a different reason. When you look out, your eyes are focused on distance. Anything up close becomes a meaningless blur, and your eyes swing easily past the vertical dividers without even noticing them.

All I have argued so far is that the multiple-paned window is no worse than the single sheet of plate glass. Now I want to demonstrate why it is not only cheaper, but better.

Comes a bad day, or darkness, and that outdoorsy feeling is not for us. We turn our eyes away from an unbroken expanse of glass, hoping to avoid its coldness. Our eyes are no longer focused on distance, but on near things. We seek the feeling of enclosure, and our eyes rest gratefully on every physical thing that tells us the walls of our house are secure.

As a sub-question, you may point out that the magazines show lots of glass going clear to the floor, and isn't plate necessary in this case? To me, glass to the floor is inexcusable, except for the rare instance where the view lying far below our normal line of sight is too good to be missed. Even in this case, glass to the floor must be used with caution to avoid a feeling of insecurity.

Look here:

TO GLASS OR NOT TO GLASS?

This sketch explores the question of whether to start the glass at 4 inches up, or at my recommended 32 inches. You can see that the glass at the bottom does very little toward letting winter sun into the house. It's the glass at the top that counts in winter. In summer, glass to the floor requires more overhang to keep out the sun.

Glass to the floor does not trap more winter sun, but it does let more heat escape at night, radiation being proportional to area. It destroys wall space that otherwise could be used for tables, chairs, bookcases. Even if I live on the edge of a cliff and want to see the valley below, I'm willing to stand up to do so, preferring the feeling of fence between me and the sudden drop.

To summarize, I can't see how glass to the floor does any good. It may, instead, do considerable harm.

I'm trying to save you money, which is my apology for such a long answer to a simple question. To spend has become reasonable, accepted, compulsive. Not to spend seems to be the proposition which now requires the longer argument. Nevertheless, the way to save money in a house is to search out the things we have been told we need, but don't. If I have succeeded in convincing you that you neither need nor want enormous plate glass windows, I have saved you a good many hundreds of dollars right there. The answer to your next question may save you a lot more.

Question Seven: what about double glass for insulation? . . . Here we are really talking about money, and money which in some cases has been spent to do more harm than good. Once again we are discussing a widely advertised product that everyone tells us we can't live without.

My rejoinder is that I can live without a mortgage, so let's begin in the same old way to find out where we don't need double glass.

The obvious place where you neither need nor want double glass is on the south side, where at least half of your glass is going to be anyway. Probably not on the east side either, but that depends. If double glass keeps heat in at night, it keeps it out equally well in the daytime. In the course of a midwinter day and night you might break about even. In the meantime you have suffered, not only bankroll shrinkage, but a 20 per cent loss of vision, because every glass surface, inside or outside, knocks off about 10 per cent.

A better scheme for big windows on the south side involves use of curtains.

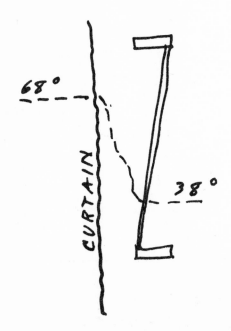

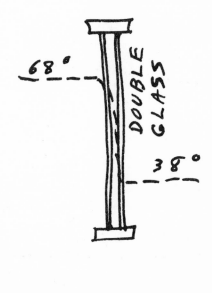

You intended to have curtains anyway. I ask that they become part of the insulative structure. The sun shines and the curtains are open, admitting heat. At night, you drop or pull them closed. Both the insulative and emotional requirements have been met. Not only have you won on heat, maintenance, and original cost, but you can go into the pipe and slippers routine without that black, blank wall of glass staring at you on a winter's night.

Double glass may be of benefit on a west or north wall, where we normally would not have many square feet of windows anyway. Even here it is questionable whether double glass will ever, in your lifetime, save enough heat to repay its original cost. Certainly it will not if you are willing to go to the trouble of pulling a curtain across it at night.

I can think of one situation where double glass is the right answer. Suppose that for good and sufficient reason you do indeed want to sit before a big northwest-facing window, gazing at the moonlight, without wearing a blanket. Here double glass wins.

Question Eight: what about condensation on the inside of a single pane window? . . . Those beautiful frost patterns you see on the inside of windows of a winter morning are a visual illustration of the condensation line, which I explained earlier. The same deposit of water has taken place inside your walls and roof, but you can't see it so you don't worry about it. That same frosty dew, when deposited on your windows, soon melts and runs down, changing from a thing of beauty into a puddle on the window sill.

The puddle is undesirable. As with all of our undesirables, the answer is to get rid of it or get it out of sight. There are at least two effective ways of dealing with window condensation.

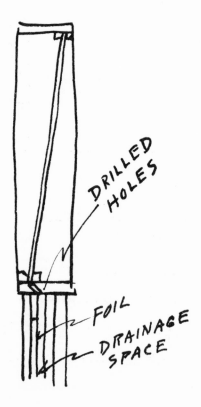

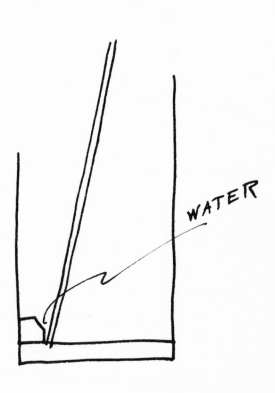

In the sketch at left, the strip of wood holding the inside bottom of the glass has been beveled to catch the water. Before putting that last piece in place, your carpenter drilled three or four tiny holes through the bottom board into the inside of the. wall, which was already loaded with condensation and has been built to drain. Exit the puddle.

In the sketch at right, the bottom piece of wood, beveled in the same way, retains the puddle but keeps it out of sight. Presently the water evaporates, and as it vanishes the puddle does its tiny bit to relieve the low humidity in the room.

VENTILATORS. You will remember that in the ideal situation, the ventilators are placed low down on the cool side; high up on the warm side. Since your carpenter is going to build the windows, he might as well build the ventilators too. Then, in that ideal situation, you might wind up with this:

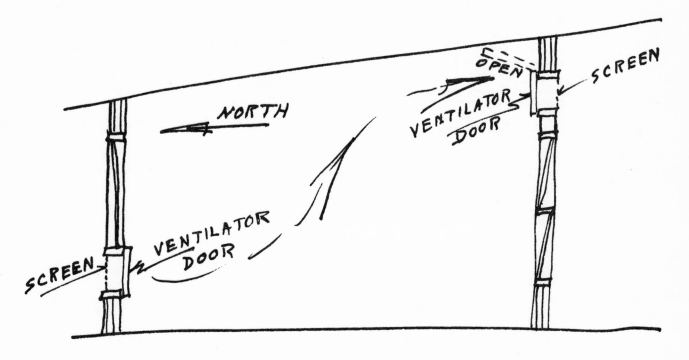

Here the carpenter has included the ventilator frame along with the window frame.

An alternate, space-saver arrangement for the north side looks like this:

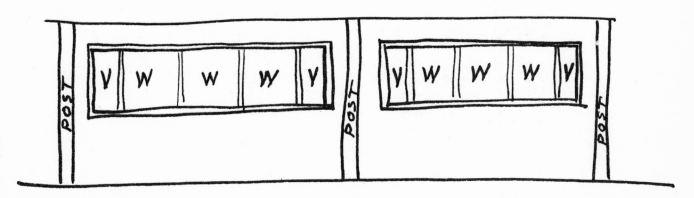

Here we have placed a ventilator at each end of the frame, with three panes of glass in the middle. This scheme, though departing from the ideal thermal arrangement, makes a lot of emotional sense. With the ventilators open in the summer, you do, as the magazines say, live outdoors. Close them, and your feeling of security at the line of sight has been increased.

Once we have decided that windows and ventilators are two different things, the location for ventilators, being independent of vision, is endless. We can place them where we like, hinge them in or out, up, down, or sideways. A ventilator, essentially, is a frame, a board, · two hinges, a latch, and a piece of screen. The screen stays there, with no nonsense about taking it down in the winter.

If the opening happens to be large in proportion to the rest of the wall, we will begin to worry about heat loss. I build my large ventilator doors like this:

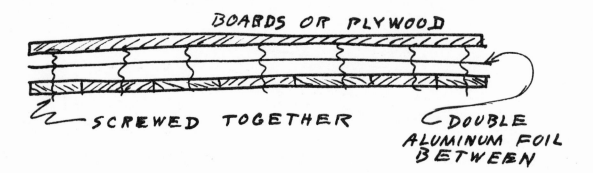

BOARDS OR PLYWOOD

SCREWED TOGETHER   DOUBLE ALUMINUM FOIL BETWEEN

Two layers of wood, screwed together crossways with foil between, are dimensionally stable, inexpensive, fairly non-conductive, and fire resistant. For very cold climates (or very cold-blooded people) use two doors, one on the inside of the wall, the other outside. Open the outside one in the spring, close it in the fall. You may call the outside one a "storm ventilator" if you like.

Ventilator areas can be surprisingly small provided they have been properly located with the inlets on the low, cool side and the outlets on the high, warm side. In building my own house I framed in three times as much ventilator area as has ever been used.

Specific figures at this range are always dangerous, but you need a rule of thumb with which to begin your own on-the-spot engineering. The outlet ventilator should be at least double the size of the inlet. Try making your inlet or cold side openings about one-twentieth the area of the wall they are in, your outlet or warm side openings about one-tenth the area of their wall.

You will find that the size of the openings required to circulate air will be about one-fifth the area of glass required to admit a satisfactory amount of light.

With the fixed window to see through and the ventilator to breathe through, you will have more light when you want it, more air when you want it, and better heat control than you would have with conventional windows. And for less money. The ball is now tossed to you, because you will have to do your own engineering to get light and air where you want them.

38. How to build partitions

Advice on partition-building divides itself neatly into three don'ts.

Don't build a partition as if it were an outside wall.

Don't use a partition to hold up the roof.

Don't build it at all if it really isn't needed.

IT ISN'T AN OUTSIDE WALL. The prime function of an outside wall is to protect the family from the world and the weather. The prime function of an inside partition is to protect the members of the family from each other.

To re-phrase, the outside wall must offer physical and thermal protection; the partition should offer visual and acoustic protection. The only time you need a partition is when you don't want to see somebody or hear somebody.

In spite of this perfectly obvious distinction between a wall and a partition, carpenters cling to their habit of building partitions as if they were outside walls. The convention is to use the same studding timbers and to complete the job with some sort of skin, plaster and decoration on both sides. This practice is used for partitions, clothes closets, linen closets and even the places where we hide brooms. Ironically, though partitions built this way are expensive, they aren't even good at their job.

To provide visual and acoustic protection, a partition should be a skin which is opaque to light, and a barrier which dissipates sound. Translated into structural terms, the partition ideally looks something like this:

Since the partition supports nothing, there is no need for strength. Stiffness is undesirable, because the stiffer a partition is the noisier it will be. Heat conductivity means very little, the worst situation we can imagine being a seventy degree living room on one side and a forty-five degree shop on the other. You will recall that heat flow goes by the square of the difference. In fact, if noise reduction is no object, there is no reason for the partition to be more than one opaque layer thick, just strong enough to hang pictures.

You realize that simply by being thick, a partition is robbing you of expensive interior space. The conventional partition chews up one square foot of space in just a little over two running feet of length. Therefore the single skin partition has much in its favor.

If, however, you object to the sound of trombone practice, squeaking bedsprings or the flush toilet, two skins are needed for a partition, if only to hide the acoustic insulation. To get the most sound absorption for the least money, the skins themselves will be soft-textured and not very stiff. The separators which hold the skins apart will be as light and infrequent as possible. The fluffy stuffing can be made of anything from rock wool batts to old egg boxes.

In choosing your materials, remember that a rigid structure is elastic, and thus transmits sound. The probably unacceptable goal would be two layers of burlap separated by cotton batting. A partition built that way won't transmit much of anything.

A closet full of clothes makes an acceptable approximation of these specifications. A bookshelf full of books does fairly well, and even a storage cupboard holding miscellany is not too bad. Therefore I suggest you put many of your partitions to work holding things. Closets are wonderful, provided they do not pretend to be outside walls and provided you can move them around.

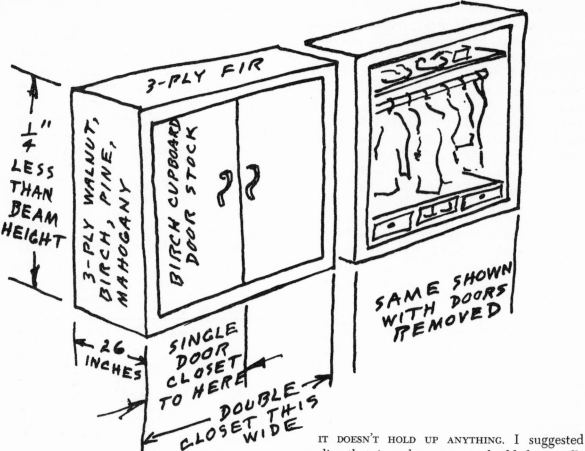

3-PLY FIR

1/4" LESS THAN BEAM HEIGHT

3-PLY WALNUT, BIRCH, PINE, MAHOGANY

BIRCH CUPBOARD DOOR STOCK

SAME SHOWN WITH DOORS REMOVED

26 INCHES

SINGLE DOOR CLOSET TO HERE

DOUBLE CLOSET THIS WIDE

SKELETON OF GAME CLOSET

IT DOESN'T HOLD UP ANYTHING. I suggested earlier that it makes sense to build four walls and a roof, move in, and find out by living there where the partitions should go. I think partitions should be made to justify themselves. They should by all means be easy to move, so that if a partition turns out to be in the wrong place, you can fix it.

In this section we started to build your house. We put the roof up first, before the floor or the walls were there, and of course before the partitions. We didn't build this way in order to avoid load-bearing partitions, we did it because it makes sense. Because it was done that way, however, you are left free to partition as you please from here on.

IF IN DOUBT, DON'T. My wife amuses her friends by telling them of the time when our flush toilet was surrounded by three doors propped together. Things are different now. The partition between bathroom and kitchen is all of five feet high, with cupboards on both sides, to boot, while early morning conversations proceed as smoothly as ever. We have thoughtfully provided a portable radio for the benefit of guests who remain acoustically conservative.

Naturally I don't insist that everyone adopt this relatively free-and-easy approach to partitioning. I do insist in all seriousness that partitions are not too good things to have if we can get along without them. Too many partitions promote darkness, bad acoustics, and inconvenience. It is much easier to add a needed partition than it is to take a superfluous one away.

So much for the don'ts. Now to the do's. Partitions are used to define rooms. The real-estate agent asks you how many rooms your house has, on the absurd assumption that an eight-room house is worth more than a six-room house. What you want is a house that you can describe to the real-estate agent as eight rooms, but to the tax assessor as six.

This we can do by using closets as partitions. The conventional closet is a full-partitioned, two-by-four studded, plastered inside and out room, too big for cats and too dark for chickens. Its walls are exactly as thick, stiff, and expensive as the outside walls of the house itself.

The movable closets on the opposite page can be used for clothes, or translated as you will into bookcase, kitchen cupboard, linen shelf or games storage. Built to beam height, it becomes a complete wall. It absorbs sound, stops vision, is easy to move around, can be modified at your convenience or thrown away if you don't want it any more.

Let's take the hardest problem of all, a square room, and see what we can do with it by moving partitions around.

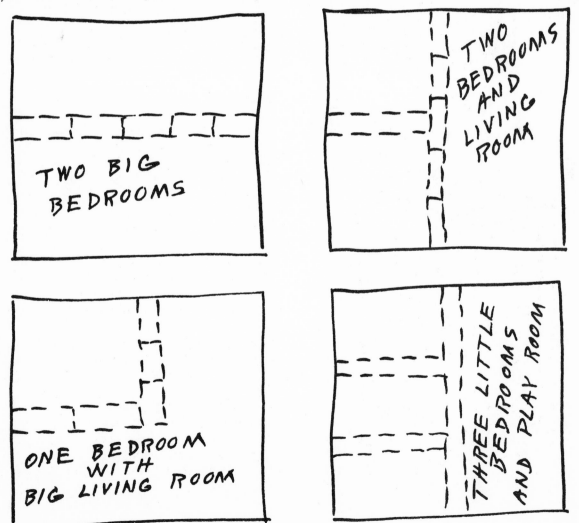

So we make a lot of movable closets and shove them around at our convenience. Where then is the feeling of permanence? With all these walls which are cheap and easy to move, do we not have an emotional need for a few things which stay put? The answer is to use masonry.

Most of the objections about outside masonry do not apply to its use inside. In an outside wall, it includes the condensation line, but it does not take on water when it is inside. It conducts heat, but inside who cares? Though it is heavy and expensive, when it is used inside a little will go a long way in charm, in texture contrast, and in the feeling of permanence.

Here is a partition made of two movable closets and a block of masonry.

Perhaps one doorway leads to the master bedroom, the other to a guest room. Turn one of the movable closets with its back to the wall, and you have a room for games, with storage cabinet. Take the closet away entirely, and you have an L-shaped living room. Turn the other closet with back to wall. You can have a reception, and still have room to hang up everyone's coat.

Somewhere a few things have to stay put. The fireplace is an obvious example. So are the bathroom and the kitchen sink with their associated plumbing. For islands of permanence, try sketching a few half-partitions of masonry. You may like them.

Inside doors are as different from outside doors as partitions are from walls. As with partitions, the need for a door should be demonstrated before it is actually put there. Most houses start out with far too many doors. You will see proof of that in the number of doors that later are taken off and made into picnic tables.

The function of an inside door is to be a visual and acoustic barrier, not to provide physical and thermal protection. This indicates that the inside door doesn't have to fit anything tightly. It should not be encased in the conventional door frame. It should clear the floor by half an inch to keep out of rug trouble. It doesn't even need a latch, if you don't think so. If it needs a lock, there may be something wrong with the family members' attitude toward each other.

Be that as it may, we do not have to consult a psychiatrist to arrive at the prime argument for a house with light, movable partitions and few doors. First reason is money. Move in as soon as the house will shelter you. You can spin your personal cocoons, if you still want them, after you get rich.

39. How to install machines

Your house has become very much a machine. Here are some of its mechanical chores:

To provide heat, at several different places and in varying amounts, with a minimum of effort on your part; also, in some cases, to take heat away.

To provide hot and cold running water, at several different places, for several different purposes, and to take same away when you're through with it.

To provide means for the storage of food, over short and long periods.

To provide means for the preparation of food —warming, frying, boiling, broiling or baking; and to do much of it automatically without the actual presence of the cook.

To remove and safely dispose of sewage, and in some cases garbage and trash.

To provide electric power at almost every conceivable location for a vast variety of purposes.

To accomplish these chores, the domestic machine must have a number of external connections:

A source of water.
A source of fuel. (Sometimes the same as the next one.)
A source of electric power.
A sewage disposal point.

From a tenth to a fifth of the cost of the finished dwelling normally goes into establishing these external connections. In other words, the first square foot of house costs at least a tenth as much as all the other square feet put together.

To convert these sources into services, your domestic machine requires a massive array of sub-machines: sinks, tanks, faucets, pumps, fans, valves, washers, dryers, burners, blowers, grinders, and traps.

I don't propose here to advise you on what sub-machines you can get along without, or which models to buy. My point is that these things all come to you in crates. Aided by a small army of plumbers, electricians, and appliance maintenance men, you install them and try to keep them running. If a sub-machine fails completely, you take it away and install another.

These sub-machines are all nourished by pipes and wires. If the sub-machines are the muscles of your domestic body, the pipes and wires are the nerves and the alimentary canal. The muscles can be taken out and sent back to the factory for repair, but the pipes and wires remain with your house and have to be fixed on the spot.

Therefore when I talk about how to install machines, I don't mean which ones to buy; I mean how and where to put in the pipes and wires.

We have three things to worry about: economy of installation, ease of maintenance, and flexibility.

From here on, your plans and sketches should include still another area, the machine room. If you plan carefully, you can put into this room everything around the house that groans, whirs or blows. You can also arrange the equipment so that most of the pipes and wires are exposed to your view and the hand of the mechanic.

Around this utility room will be grouped as many as possible of the sub-machines that use water. Wires are relatively cheap so we don't care much about where they are, but every extra foot of pipe is that much more money and trouble.

Finally, in principle, wherever possible pipes and wires will be left get-at-able, so that you can fix them or change them easily. As few as possible will be buried. All pipes and wires will be one size larger than required for your assumed needs, because those needs will always grow.

Economy of installation, our first goal, depends largely on arrangement.

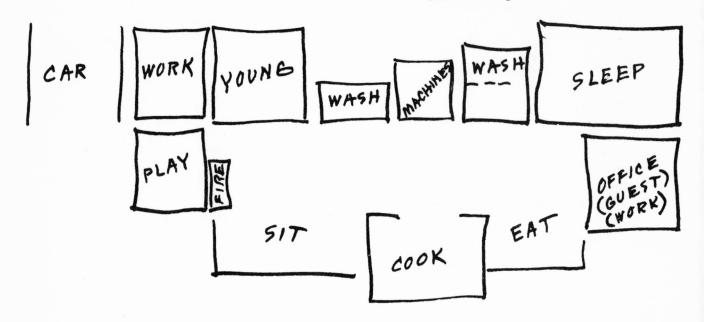

While talking about arrangement, I began a technique of sketching little squares to illustrate functions. In one sketch I began with the machine room smack in the middle. It didn't turn out too badly. With this area in the middle of the north side (our machines care little whether the sun shines or not) the head cook winds up in her customary position in the middle of the south side.

Your plumbing distances, assuming two bathrooms and a kitchen, can be shortened still more by doing this:

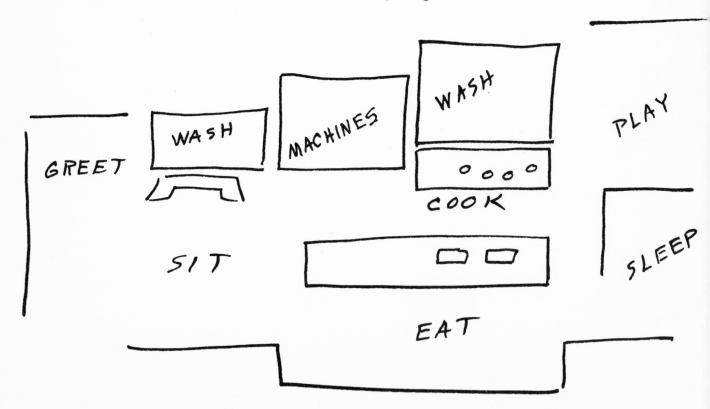

In this plan, piping approaches the irreducible minimum. The arrangement for living is also quite splendidly compact, if you want to live compactly. One thing is required—that the head cook enjoy scrambling eggs before an audience. I built one like this once, and the particular cook in question enjoyed it very much.

With the first objective, economy, defined as a matter of arrangement, the next two goals, maintenance and flexibility, are similar in that they both demand maximum accessibility. Here we run into the conventional habit of burying pipes and wires within walls, which makes them about as inaccessible as possible and requires expensive cutting and tearing whenever anything has to be changed.

The electrical suppliers have done a good job of making switches, panels, conduits and outlets accessible and at the same time not unattractive. Materials are available with which to cover the whole house with electric service, without hiding anything and without cutting holes in the wall. Naturally, the speculative housebuilder will be the last to use surface outlets and wiring, but these components are to be had by telling your electrical contractor that you want them. For once, an industry has provided a sensible service before its consumers demanded it.

The plumbing people have not done nearly as well. They cling to the notion that folks who use water don't want to see how it got there. It must be admitted their problem is more difficult. A wire is easier to package attractively than a pipe, but the need to keep plumbing exposed is greater. However bulky and inconvenient pipes are, they must be inside the house for two reasons: water freezes and pipes sometimes leak or clog and require maintenance.

The pipes go inside, but we try to hide them more or less artfully from view. The solution is simple for water-use areas which abut directly on the machine room. These areas always need cabinets, so we put the pipes in a false bottom, like this:

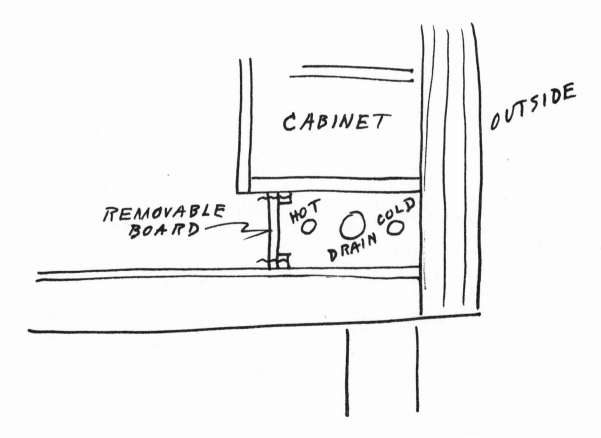

The plumbers will love you for simplifying their problems. Besides, this arrangement gives you an excuse to have plenty of cabinets.

Sometimes—for example, when pipes cross an area of open floor—you will have to forget the non-burying principle and fall back on the method sketched in Section 35. There the pipes run beneath the floor beams. They are still removable, but with more difficulty.

If your water is hard, make the buried pipe a size larger than it would otherwise need be. Keep joints and valves to a minimum. Speaking of valves, install the drain valve, which has to be at the low point in the system, in an accessible spot.

In locating sub-machines, especially those attached to plumbing, be sure to leave plenty of space around them. The maintenance man, whether he is a handy husband or a professional, must have room to swing his wrench. Your treasured appliances, wrapped in their baffling armor of enameled sheet metal, seem always to develop their major ailments at the back.

It does no good to say that, were the market not competitive, for 10 per cent more money a domestic machine could be made to run forever. First, the statement isn't strictly true. Second, the market *is* competitive and the consumers themselves are the ones who refuse to pay the extra 10 per cent.

The domestic machine does indeed wear out, stick, leak, freeze, wheeze, clog up and break down. You know the machine is going to need fixing. Therefore there's no sense pretending that it doesn't exist. Quit trying to get it out of sight and away from fixability.

The answer is a machine area with enough light and space for your present mechanical servants, plus a few more which someone will invent next year. Why not show the guest a machine room which in its way is just as handsome as your greenhouse, your swimming pool, your high fidelity living room, your pine-paneled playhouse, or even your kitchen stove with its little flashing lights.

The machine room with its steel and brass muscles chewed up about a third of your house-building money. You might as well be proud of it.

40. How to get it built

"Anything special is expensive." This statement will be quoted to you as an axiom by most members of the "building business," which includes craftsmen, contractors, financiers, real-estate agents, lenders, developers, appraisers, and pre-fabricators.

Happily, the statement will be denied by many skilled craftsmen, who are able to build, and would prefer to build something today that is different and better than what they built yesterday.

I have to accept the validity of the "anything special" statement as applied statistically to the whole building business. I deny that it must apply to any one particular individual or situation. My advice to you is to forget about it, because you are an individual, not a statistic.

Special construction influences building costs in more than one way. Here are three examples that indicate the range of effects.

SPECIAL CONSTRUCTION, low cost: Details are selected for inconspicuous economy. Low cost reflects low demand which, in turn, reflects the fact that few people know how to select wisely from what is available.

NON-SPECIAL CONSTRUCTION, medium cost: Details are chosen because it is assumed that they insure widest sales appeal. This is the area of peak demand because most people do believe that "anything special is expensive."

SPECIAL CONSTRUCTION, high cost: Details are selected for display and conspicuous economic waste, not for use. The demand is limited to those who can afford useless expenditure.

When the axiom equates special with expensive, it refers only to the area of conspicuous waste. In this area, the well-heeled buyer can put gold plate on his stone walls if he wants to, with no complaints from me. It's his money.

To those who quote and believe the axiom, the word special seems to mean something different for the sake of being different.

"Non-special" defines the customary, which is always the area of greatest demand. Commodities offered for sale are those which the seller believes most people think they want. Genuine bargains are never to be found in this area. There are reasons. First, bargains are not offered at times of or in areas of peak demand. Think about the day before and the day after Christmas and you will need no further examples. Second, mass production economies are often more than offset by advertising and distribution costs—which are an unfair charge upon the discriminating buyer—and by the addition of details which he doesn't want.

The addition of unwanted detail is especially significant in the non-special house, in which the builder has felt compelled to offer a little bit of everything, hence not much of anything. Special construction eliminates those features which to you are useless and expensive. You and I use the term "special" in the sense of the first definition above—something different and distinctive, but on the low cost side of the statistical average. To say it again, the whole point to this book is not what has to be added to make a good house, but what you can do without in order to afford more of what you really want.

Unfortunately, even doing without can sometimes be expensive. It depends on who does the work. If the craftsman, in departing from his habits, gets mixed up and spends most of the time scratching his head, you pay for every scratch. If, conversely, the craftsman is able to apply his well-learned skills toward the achievement of unique results, he will work faster as enthusiasm replaces boredom.

One hour of a carpenter's time is not a fixed commodity that results in a predictable economic benefit. A plumber friend of mine is a genius in the clutch. When my whole water system froze up solid, he came at once, hammered it back together out of old pipe fittings, and charged me ten dollars. If you try to engage his services for a routine job, he's available three months from next Tuesday.

A half mile to the west of my house lives a medical research man of considerable renown. This scholar can build anything. He asks me for advice, accepts a quick sketch, puts down his empty beer can, and departs. The next thing I see is the completed structure, put up exactly as I told him except better. His feeling for tools and materials, his intelligence and his muscular skill, relieved from prejudice by his total lack of formal building experience, produce an end result which is uniquely his own. Given the same problem, and building the answer to it with my own hands, I too would produce a unique result. It would be better than his, for me, and his is better for him.

The story of the medical man is not a plug for doing-everything-yourself. A mile and a half to the east of our place lives a financial type who doesn't know one muscle from another. All he does is line up a couple of friendly, well-adjusted carpenters and then go around saying put this here and put that there. He asks my advice but never takes it. The end product he achieves is not only beautiful but livable, and, to belabor the phrase, uniquely his own.

These two very different gentlemen have one thing in common. Both approach the construction of their domestic estates with this in mind; "What do I want?" Not, "What should I have?" The first man is able and willing to do his own work, the second man is able to persuade others to do it for him.

How does he do it? If you are an amateur plumber, you can talk about sweating pipe joints; if an amateur carpenter, at least you can hold the other end of a board. The second man owns no skill except to be a human being. The carpenters who convert his intentions into structure are human beings. They have skill to sell. He feels his way toward what he wants through his own creative process. He is willing to pay others to help him. It is an equal partnership. Being equal, the partnership operates quite efficiently.

How do you talk to a builder? That's easy. You remember that although the perfect builder does not exist, the perfect customer does not exist either. The most nearly perfect builder would be yourself, if you possessed the necessary skills. If you do not, the next best builder is the well-adjusted craftsman who interprets your dreams. In helping you with your dreams, he is content, because he is interpreting some of his own as well.

Since well-adjusted craftsmen are not always easy to come by, you may be inclined to engage the services of the friendly and businesslike builder, who at best is an artist attempting to meet a weekly payroll. He can produce, chargeable to you, carpenters and plumbers and masons and electricians at the snap of a well-worn finger. At this point, enter the architect.

Your well-adjusted architect is a bridge, an interpreter, and a catalyst. He is psychologist, structural engineer, business man, and client-quieter. He is, we hope, an artist as well, but artistry is only one part of the business of architecture.

Insofar as you are less than all-capable yourself, the architect becomes your brain and the builder becomes your back. The architect cannot write a specification which will govern every driven nail. The builder cannot decide the direction of every hammer blow. The house you will live in will be precisely the product of the craftsmen's hands.

Between the architect, your brain, and the craftsmen, your hands, stands the builder, your back. I suggest you choose him on the basis of sympathy and understanding. I do not suggest that you choose him on the basis of competitive bidding.

I can understand skyscrapers and tunnels and bridges being offered for competitive bids. I can but dimly understand the house you are to live in being so constructed. It seems to me that if the builder is not honest and able, you don't want him at any price. If the builder is human, as they all are, and has been compelled to offer a job-winning low bid in order to stay in business, you will have forced him to do less than his best in order to make a profit.

In not so charitable language, the less than honest builder, faced by a possible loss, can in the complicated business of building a house lick you in so many ways you'll never know what hit you.

This is the end of the How chapter. In terms of dollars, possibly the most important How of all is how to get it built. Not knowing where or who you are, I can offer suggestions in only the most general terms. In general, I think you will be better off if you employ an architect. In general, I think you will be better off if you do not ask your builder for a fixed price.

CHAPTER FIVE

Why will you build it?

41. Why own a house?

The title of this section must have limits put upon it. The whole book is a WHY book, even if you found it on the HOW shelves at your bookstore. Though *love* is the most important word in the language, *why* is in my opinion close behind. Of Mr. Kipling's six key questions, why is certainly the most important, because how provides the force, but why provides the reason, and reason is more important than force.

In our present context there is more money to be saved by asking why than by finding out how. The purpose of this section, then, will be confined to exploring the why of house ownership in the first place.

Question: Why own a house? Lots of people don't. Something around half of all the families are non-homeowners. Lots of people just plain don't want to own a house. Many others who do own houses aren't happy about it. Ignoring for the moment the emotional, geographical, and professional factors, let us examine house owning on a straight dollar basis. Here is a suggested tally sheet, which you can re-write to fit your own conditions:

WHAT IT COSTS TO RENT A HOUSE in terms of a family desiring a domestic facility, apartment or house, whose usefulness I will call One Eff:

Rent, at $150 per month	$1,800
Decoration and revisions not chargeable to the landlord	200
Metered services: gas, light telephone	300
Leisure-time expenses (renters dine out, play out more than owners)	600
Annual Total	$2,900

Insofar as you don't agree with my estimate of leisure-time expenses, you will have to play fair by increasing the quality of your living quarters, thus increasing the desirability of staying home. Strike out my last figure of $600, raise the monthly rental to $200, and you will find you break even at $2,900. Bear that figure in mind while we go on to examine:

WHAT IT COSTS TO BUILD A SIMILAR HOUSE in terms of a family desiring an equal domestic

163

facility, still called One Eff, but willing to buy it or build it, and assuming it will cost $15,000, with $5,000 cash down and the rest at 5 per cent interest:

Interest paid, $10,000 at 5 per cent, averaged over ten years, less income tax deduction—	$ 200
Interest charged to self, 3 per cent on an amount beginning at $5,000 and growing to $15,000 in ten years; no income tax deduction—	300
Taxes—	200
Fuel—	200
Maintenance—	200
Metered services—	300
Annual total	$1,400

Many people don't worry about the "interest charged to self" figure, but to play fair with yourself, you should. This is the income you would have had from your money if you hadn't spent it on the house. I use 3 per cent arbitrarily as being a compromise between the low yield of, say, a life insurance policy and the high yield of a common stock.

All the figures are arbitrary. I use them knowing that arguments will ensue. You will say, my taxes are more (less) than that, and so on. Please; the figures are intended as a numbers game to give us something to talk about.

From the numbers game totals so far, we find that owning seems to have shown a fifteen hundred dollar annual profit over renting. No charge is made against the homeowner for his capital investment, because he still has it. On an investment of fifteen thousand, a fifteen hundred profit represents a neat 10 per cent, to which we return the 3 per cent we already charged ourselves, making 13 per cent in all. Where can you do better than that?

But you say, "That's cheating, because we had something in mind a good deal better than a fifteen thousand dollar house." True enough. Remember that our numbers game so far has dealt with an equal domestic facility, labeled in each case One Eff.

Your dream house wouldn't be a dream if it weren't a lot more comfortable than what you have been renting. Now, how far up the owning scale can you go without losing money? You want something better, but how much better?

Let's try another set of donkey figures, this time shooting for a domestic facility labeled Three Eff, or three times as useful as the one above.

Interest paid, $30,000 at 5 per cent, averaged over ten years, less income tax deduction—	$ 600
Interest charged to self, 3 per cent, on an amount beginning at $15,000 and growing to $45,000 in ten years, no income tax deduction—	900
Taxes—	500
Fuel—	300
Maintenance—	300
Metered services—	300
Annual total	$2,900

The numbers game now shows that the break-even point in actual out-of-pocket dollars lies somewhere around Three Eff. In other words, the owner, for the same number of dollars per year, can enjoy a house three times as fancy as the one his neighbor rents.

Let's try it still another way. If you are now paying a hundred and fifty a month rent for a One Eff apartment, the chances are your spending patterns are geared to this figure. Call it a One Emm amount, and One Eff equates with One Emm. How many times One Emm can you afford to lay out over the years as the total cost of your dream house?

The answer looks easy. If a forty-five thousand dollar place is the break-even point when compared with a One Emm (monthly money) of a hundred and fifty, the maximum cost of your dream house can be Three Hundred Emm.

Three hundred times your present monthly rental, says the numbers game, looks like the most you can reasonably bite off as the price of home, fireside, and the hot and cold running water.

It would be nice if it were less. Three hundred, I said, is the most, the maximum. Let me quickly, though again arbitrarily, revise the figure downward to Two Hundred Emm, and stay out of trouble. There are two fallacies in the above argument that I want to expose before someone else does.

The first fallacy comes from the fact that you are still members of the human race. When you move from a One Eff to a Three Eff establishment, you will feel richer, which is one of the reasons why you wanted to move in the first place. Feeling richer, you will find it easy to spend more money. This throws my whole equation out of whack. I know, because I am, if anything, humaner than you are. If by chance you are one of those rare birds who can move to a Three Eff home without contracting a case of looser lucre, strike out fallacy number one.

The second and more serious fallacy may also be struck out if you had the good sense to select well-heeled parents or a rich Aunt Eliza who died young. The rest of us have to worry about where to get up the capital. Our numbers game could not, according to the rules, include capital as an expense. It isn't, yet we have to find some somewhere or keep on renting.

Most of us find it in the salt mines. We dig it out hour by hour along with the daily bread. At the end of a day's labor, it is hard to recall how many hours went toward the bread, which we ate, and how many toward capital, which we've still got.

Not knowing where you are or what salt mine you happen to favor, all I can suggest is that the capital may have to be budgeted as an expense, whether it is nor not. Let's take it easy and aim at a Two Eff, Two Hundred Emm place, or, in terms of the numbers game, a thirty thousand dollar house.

Having shed a tear for Three Eff, you're still way ahead. Your own house is twice as good as the one you were renting last year.

It would seem that the landlord has been getting rich at your expense, but that is another fallacy. He may be losing money too. For one thing, he can't build an apartment or a house exactly to suit you and only you. He has to keep renting it year after year to all sorts of people. Second, he fears that your behavior as a tenant will not be the same as your behavior as an owner. In most cases he is right.

The landlord's fears have shown you a solid dollar reason for owning your own house. You take care of it. You improve it. Whether the improvements are store-bought, or made by your own hands at the expense of Saturday golf, they remain yours, and your equity goes up.

Though ownership comes out ahead in the numbers game, the answer to why own a house still hasn't necessarily been given. I said before that lots of people own houses who shouldn't. Here is another checklist to work on in terms of who and where you are:

CONVENIENCE: are the ready-made limitations of an apartment worth more to you than the privacy of your own back yard?

MOBILITY: some people who move every three years make money by buying a house and then selling it every three years later. Do you want to go to this trouble?

INVESTMENT: house money, as we have seen, can earn 10 per cent or better, but it's frozen capital, subject to delay and dismay if you have to convert quickly. Maybe you would prefer to keep all your capital liquid, even though it earns less.

DOMESTICITY: maybe you just plain don't like to stay home. There isn't much point to building a Three Eff or even a One Eff house if you genuinely prefer huddling in a corner booth at Joe's Bar and Grill.

SPACE: is the extra space of a house and grounds worth anything to you? What are you willing to do without to get it? If nothing, forget the whole proposition.

PRIDE: can you put a dollar figure on the pride of ownership? What is it worth to you to feel like a king in your own castle? Once again, if nothing, forget it. You're better off without.

The checklist shows that owning a house has its perils as well as its profits. The reasons for owning a house at all have to be peculiarly your own. If you have good reasons, the chances are you will get a good house.

Please don't build a house just because everyone else does, or because it's stylish right now.

You might wind up living in one of these things that can only be described as a chunk of horizontal slum. Ask yourself what your house is supposed to do for you. You'll get a better house if you know why you want it.

42. Why build a house?

Now that those who aren't firmly convinced of the merits of house-owning have become spectators, we can discuss whether to buy or build. For a while we will keep clear of aesthetics and keep right on talking money.

There is a fairly general though quite erroneous conviction that only the well-to-do build new houses for themselves, and that they then hand them down some years later to a lower income bracket.

This error is helped along by the many products with a wide cost spread between "new" and "second-hand." Houses aren't like that. Most new houses, unlike new automobiles, will, if well-planned and well-built, increase in value during their first years of life, then level off for a considerable period, beginning to decline only if and when they are seriously obsoleted by technical advances.

I know people of energy and imagination who make practically a second living by building houses for themselves, well-planned houses on good sites. They live in each for a couple of years or so, getting the grounds planted and settled-looking, shaking the inevitable bugs out of the arrangement, getting the fireplace nicely blackened up, and then sell out at a good profit. It's a little rough on the wife, but if there's a streak of gypsy in her, she has a lot of both real and vicarious fun.

The point is, if you know what you are doing and if you behave yourself, it can be much cheaper to build a house than to buy one.

This should and does hold true for all price brackets except the very cheap, mass-produced jobs, and, at the other end, the needlessly and capriciously expensive. People in all income groups build and buy houses. A bargain is a bargain no matter where the decimal point falls. Granted equal skill, functional design will save the rich man as big a share of his money as the poor man. The poor man, however, working under a rigid dollar ceiling, may try harder and thus come up with a sounder design and a better bargain. That is, if he is poor because of youth or occupational choice and not because of reduced Why-power.

I didn't say that it would inevitably cost less to build than to buy. I said it *could* cost less. There are terrifying anecdotes of the dollar damage done to people who set out to build their own. I say it was their own fault, every time. They planned poorly, or not enough. They shopped for the cheapest builder and the cheapest suppliers. They thought architects dreamy, frivolous, and expensive. After construction began, they insisted on changes and changes of changes, without regard for the ease or difficulty of the work involved.

They had to have "the best of everything," with best always defined as most expensive. They looked at too many pictures in too many advertisements. They believed everything they read in the advertisements and in articles written in obvious support of those advertisements. They asked for and took advice from everyone except their own architect and builder who were trying to do a good job for them at a reasonable price.

They kept adding things, usually too late, then blamed everyone but themselves when the price went up. They eliminated nothing. Building your own house can cost more than buying one if you make it so. Nevertheless, in spite of all the perils, you have an opportunity to make it cost much less.

"New building costs more than buying." This hoary statement is still current—and it is still a fallacy. It contains its own disproof. Let's say you go out and buy a house. Somebody built it. You don't for one moment think the seller lost money when he sold it to you. All you have done is pay for his mistakes without the privilege of making your own.

Here sits a house already built. It is for sale, and its suits you; well, almost. You like the site, the neighborhood, the builder's reputation, and the plan of the house itself; well, almost. There is nothing distressed about the situation. You can be sure the seller has no intention of losing money. Why should he? He expects, and is entitled to, a profit. If you don't pay his price, someone else will. You know perfectly well you are paying the seller his profit because he has relieved you of the work and bother of building the house in the first place. All fair enough if this is what you want.

What worries me is that your opportunity to select what you want in a house has been confined to one choice. There sits the house; the money has all been spent, it's all done. Take it or leave it.

Several thousands of the already spent dollars have paid for things the original builder wanted but you don't. Yet you must buy the whole package if you want it at all. Some of the unwanteds will sit there, doing no harm; others will have to be torn out and changed. In the latter case you will have paid for them twice, once to buy and once to remove.

For example, the previous owner built a wall between kitchen and dining room, with handy pass-through and sliding door. You regard this as a holdover from the hired cook era. Out comes the door and wall, for which you have now paid double, and in goes the open bar which is what you would have built had you been doing it in the first place.

For example, the builder thought that most potential buyers would regard the house as unfinished without an asphalt driveway. You happen to abhor asphalt driveways, believing that crushed stone is more elegant. For some years you dream of the day when you will feel rich enough to have the asphalt torn out.

Or perhaps the original owner, seeking an honest profit but wanting to make the place look finished as soon as possible, went ahead with his foundation plantings. Being small, the shrubs and trees had to be put too close to the house in order to look good. This first year the effect is fine. In four years the plants will be so big they'll have to be moved.

Much of your purchase money will already have been spent at the behest of the real-estate agent, who has told the previous owner that he cannot sell an unfinished house. The frantic activity which immediately precedes your arrival will have been done at your expense, but much of it not to your liking. As a minimum requirement, the agent will have insisted that the house be freshly painted. One of the first things that you, as the new owner, will do is to have it repainted a different color.

"Building costs more than buying." Do everything you can to encourage people you don't like to believe that. The more people who accept it as fact, the greater will be the spread between new building costs and resale value, in case you ever want to sell. The more people who believe it, the greater will be your opportunity to build exactly what you want.

In new building, the key word is opportunity. You may not save money, but you will have the opportunity to do so. Certainly you will have the chance to make decisions, not only at the take it or leave it level, but at all levels. You will decide where the house sits. Which trees remain. Whether to tile the bathrooms. Where to put the sun deck. Whether to use area heating or central heating. Gas-fired hot water or electricity. And what to eliminate in order to increase the size of the master bedroom.

These decisions all concern how to spend money, and for what. In building your own house the most valuable opportunity of all is the privilege of deciding when and where not to spend it.

Both in spending and not-spending, you have the opportunity of behaving with above average skill, imagination, discretion, and self-knowledge at all levels.

If you do not have imagination, if you do not know what you want until you see it done, if you do not have the ability to reach decisions and then either stick with them or change them for good reason and with economical speed—if you don't possess these skills, please don't build your own house. Buy one that strikes your fancy, and pay the seller his profit.

43. Why not remodel?

Discussion of remodeling must run either to a few hundred words and stop there, or go on to several million. There is no sensible place to stop in between.

Our few hundred words here will be devoted to stating the general case against remodeling.

If you, for excellent reasons of your own, decide to ignore this generalization and plunge ahead with a remodeling job, the number of problem variations multiplied by the number of possible solutions becomes astronomical. In remodeling, sight-unseen advice is worthless. A million words wouldn't even get us well started.

By remodeling I do not mean normal maintenance or even normal updating to keep a house from becoming obsolete. I refer to major structural changes and major technical additions which are needed to make a building too good for chickens.

There is a persistent dream. It runs something like this. Beyond a grove of massive oaks sits a fine, sturdy and distinguished edifice. It needs a little paint, to be sure, but beneath the peeling paint one can discern, can't one, the mark of quality construction. They don't build them that way any more. The far corner may be drooping as you say, but that's why it's still on the market, and anyway we know that Bill Carruthers, when we catch him sober will be able to jack it up again for a song.

The dream continues after we go inside. These small rooms are really home-like, and of course can be enlarged by knocking out a few partitions here and there. We are not troubled with the location of the kitchen, because those stone tubs don't work and wouldn't do anyhow, and the kitchen is going to be two bathrooms as soon as the basement has been extended under this part of the house so the plumbing can be put in and the basement has to be a little deepened anyway to take a new furnace as soon as the basement wall has a hole knocked in it to bring in the furnace.

Well, naturally the plaster is all off because the roof leaked but of course the roof all has to be done over anyway but what can you expect with those awful old people not knowing what the place is worth and absolutely letting it go for nothing well really almost next to nothing.

If you think the above is an overly facetious report on what goes through the mind of a remodeling enthusiast, you haven't had to stand still and hear this sort of thing roll on, hour after hour. Here is the bargain hunter at work, trying to convince himself that he has found a bargain. "Next to nothing" is the habit-forming stimulant that makes bargain buying almost as incurable as the addiction to dice, horses, heroin or alcohol.

Even among the less addicted, the notion that major remodeling, though troublesome, saves money, is one of the most persistent fallacies of them all.

I grant there have been special times and places where houses of excellent basic structure were purchasable for less than their real value. There can be such special cases even now, and no one would be happier than myself to find one. I still grieve for some millionaire-built barns, retired by estate caprice from cow-housing, which were snapped up by someone else before I even heard they were for sale.

These are special cases. Once the seller puts his property in the hands of an agent, the chances are about sixty-nine to one that the bargain element has been removed.

I grant you that the very difficulties of remodeling can stimulate the imagination, sometimes producing an end result of great charm. If your imagination is like that, remaining silent in the empty outdoors but triggered by an assembly of roughly rectangular walls and roofs, a tumble-down barn is what you need, cheap. If these are your symptoms, my suggestion is that you buy the barn, stare at it for a while, draw your plans, then tear the barn down and start fresh somewhere else. I have already admitted that great charm can result from a major remodeling. Unfortunately, charm created in this manner is in most cases an expensive luxury.

The licking you take in remodeling is a stealthy one. It sneaks up on you. Thousands of dollars creep away in clearing the debris, in making room to work, in removing something you don't want before you can start to put back something you do want. The carpenter is cutting, trying, fitting, removing, replacing, and of course all the while expensively scratching his head. I never yet heard of a remodeling job that cost less than had been expected. It always costs more. Therefore, in general, give me an uncluttered field to start with every time.

We know, however, that all generalizations are false, including this one. Under what circumstances might it be emotionally if not financially sound to undertake a remodeling?

In the preservation, of course, of a minor historical monument. The house becomes a dinner-table conversation piece which can repay all the effort you put into it.

In using a site which is eminently satisfactory except for the presence of a building, yet you can't bring yourself to tear the old place down and start over.

In the use of enclosed space, the shell of which is in good repair. I'm a sucker for this one myself, because it keeps the carpenters in out of the rain.

In adding to an existing structure which is fine in its way, but much too small. You can build a new house for half the family and connect the two halves by a breezeway, leaving the old one more or less untouched. Strictly speaking, this is addition, not alteration. If you don't have to back up and start over, all is well.

Even beyond these exceptions, however, the idea persists that remodeling saves money. Because it does persist, the price of old structures available for remodeling remains higher than it should be.

Usually the seller of an old place knows more about what it is worth than the buyer does. Before undertaking a major remodeling, tread softly, look carefully, and shift your why-asker into high gear.

CHAPTER SIX

Who are you?

44. Who wants this house?

Though all men may have been created equal, they surely haven't stayed that way. Architecturally speaking, if all men were exactly equal they would live in identical houses, and wouldn't that be dreadful.

Whether you like it or not, your house is the visible, physical, static expression of you who live in it. At worst, your slips are showing. At best, the house is the considered, idealized picture of yourself that you would like the world to see and to think of as you, a tangible expression that still leaves you free to shrug off this idealized picture as the mood compels.

Come to think of it, a house is not quite static either. It gets up in the morning and goes to bed at night. It prepares for departures. It tells that the car wouldn't start. It says that the folks are home at last. Its complexion worsens with illness in the family. It warns that the occupants have had a hard night and are sleeping late. Without meaning to do so, I read my neighbors' moods with a passing glance. The signs have been posted.

When you begin to build your house, the signs for a while are in large print. Section 44, entitled who wants this house, becomes Chapter One of Volume Two, a description of yourself, written and paid for by you and your wife. You are Chapter One because you are the guy who has to get up the money.

You are the top banana. You are the meeter and the greeter and the mortgage deadline beater. You are the one who draws a deep breath and says it's mine and that's the way it's gonna be. Then you wonder how you ever got up the nerve.

You got it because you felt secure in yourself, or in your job, or both. Either one will do, but if your employment is essentially transient, you will need more nerve, or more self-security, than if you know where you are going to be working five years from now.

As a housebuilder, whether transient or not, don't sell yourself short. I assume you are a man of imagination and derring-do with one hand on your checkbook and the other on the escape hatch. If not, let me point out that many men who are short on derring-do still build houses.

Even if you do not believe the world is your oyster, you can figure out what to do if someone hands you an oyster to be opened.

If you are married, and statistically you probably are, I will assume that you are in love with your wife, a proposition on which no statistics can be gathered. To avoid saying "your wife" over and over, I will call this non-statistical female Mary.

Mary's happiness is one, though not the only one, of your goals. You realize that the house you are about to build will be Mary's house, that she will do most of the work and thus be entitled to make most of the decisions therein, while you will do most of the work but make fewer of the decisions thereout. All of this is all right with you.

You can hammer a nail if you have to. The greater your skill in this and related departments, the greater will be your satisfaction in surrounding yourself with the works of your own hands. Mary will like that, but even if your hands have ten thumbs, if you have domestic imagination, Mary will like that even better.

You, the alleged homeowner, will sometimes wonder where you are going to hang your hat, if you wear a hat. You may wonder sometimes why you drive an extra half hour to get to the place where you don't know where to hang your hat if you had one. The place belongs to Mary, but at least you know where to put your shoes.

All the while you keep a wary eye on Mary's indecisions, which you now know are biologically built-in. Where does she want to live? Does she know? If and when she knows, how much is it going to cost? Does she know that you want something out of this too? What you want, she ought to know, is something better than what the others boys have.

You, the perpetual interloper, will never occupy your own house in quite the same way that Mary occupies it. Call it cave, nest, dive, rooftree, castle, or pad, you will depart therefrom grasping your club (spade, axe, plow, or fountain pen) to challenge tigers, dig for worms, level the forest, till the soil, or get signatures on the dotted line. You are not unhappy about this and would not have it otherwise.

Your right to come home nights has been established by your combination of intelligence and imagination, energy and skill. Once home, if you can allow yourself to be proud of anything, you know that you can decently afford to be proud of your castle.

45. Who runs this house?

If your husband, who for convenience I will call Mike, is the one who spins the crank, you are the hub around which the wheel turns.

You are the queen bee, the executive director, the boss bird of the nest, the chief watch officer in all weathers. If you like your nest, all goes well; if you don't like it, ill befalls. My house, says Mike, is yours.

I am not concerned here with the color of your hair, your shoe size, or your taste in either evening gowns or nightgowns. I am concerned with your taste in houses, because it's your house we are talking about.

What you want is not always easy to determine. Your very womanliness, of which you are proud, includes a certain amount of indirection. Possessed of a number of wants, you will sometimes begin with the least important and work back from there toward the beginning. If some word discourages you along the way, you may never get back to mentioning the thing you wanted most of all.

I think you will agree with my proposition that your house should be the visible expression of what you want yourself to be. In common with almost everyone else, you don't always know what you want yourself to be. When you do know, you find it difficult to express the wish in terms of boards, beams, and plumbing, yet the whole thing is being built for you.

You, lady, are the key figure in this whole business of building a lot of house for little money. Without your help, the project fails. Here are some things which you can do to help the cause along.

You are essentially conservative, but you must be willing to take a chance once in a while.

You are conformist by nature, but on occasion you must allow yourself to be tempted by the green grass on the other side of the fence.

You are primarily interested in the comfort

and welfare of your family, but you may have to let them rough it for a while in the interest of greater comfort later on.

You will be happier with unfinished or imperfect things than with no things at all. You know that the completely finished and perfect thing has become unusable, while the things you use every day are not perfect and never can be.

You realize that your happiness is one, but only one, of your non-statistical husband's goals. His happiness is not your only goal either. This fact will help you to be uncompetitive with a concern which may, for the moment, override his undoubted love.

You will not demand perfection as proof of that love. You will not look at the pictures in the magazines and then say if I can't have one of those you don't love me any more. You know there is just about so much of Mike to go around, and therefore asking for marble under your feet may keep beaver off your back.

Above all, you will understand that the functions of your house are these: a place for your family to meet, work, play, wash, dress, eat, be comforted by each other, express love, and sleep. With these functions as your goal, you will be more pleased by the approval of your family than by the approval of your acquaintances. You will regard housekeeping as a necessary but minor aspect of homekeeping.

In designing a house which will help you carry out these functions, there is much to be hammered down about nails, varnish, floor lamps, laundry chutes, door knockers, faucets, panoramic wallpaper, thermostats, back fences, linen closets, old glass and new glass, trim, patina, foot scrapers, a mail box with your name on it, and the grapes growing purple in the kiss of the autumn sun.

While the hammering goes on, you can save or spend a great deal of money. Your decisions on what not to buy are the greatest factor in building your own nest at a bargain price. In not-buying, you will have your troubles. For example, being able to see the timbers that hold your house together may bother you at first, not because you see anything aesthetically wrong but because it's different. In a little while you'll be proud of the difference. You will exhibit pridefully your double oven, your soap storage cup-

board under the sink, your ballroom-size living room, your out-size mantlepiece and your built-in ironing board, all paid for by the wall-to-wall carpeting you decided you could get along without.

I want to tell another story. This one is about a woman who was wrestling with the question of where she wanted to live. It goes like this:

I'm standing in the woods, talking to a handsome lady who insists that she has always wanted to live in the country. She tells me, and her husband nods agreement, that the fresh air would be good for the chldren and she has been trying to get him to move to the outdoors for a long while now even though it would mean being that much farther from the office.

"I myself," she said, "have always enjoyed being in the country. Now how far did you say it was to the nearest drugstore?"

"Just three miles," I whispered. And that was the last I ever heard of that.

My own wife, Caroline, has a sense of proportion, a sense of what is important and what isn't. I'm spoiled. She is aware of what goes on. She is keenly responsive to people who don't have sense enough to come in out of the rain, but she herself knows when it is raining, and finds her own womanly ways to keep dry.

She even manages to be grateful when the roof doesn't leak. She has taught me that it is better to have a leaky roof than no roof at all, but then trying to describe my Caroline is harder than fixing the roof in the first place. Trying to describe a good woman is like describing the color and dimensions of the cloud the rain came from.

Two people in love can build a house. Two people are much more than twice as good as one.

46. Who builds this house?

When it comes to building a house, two people are more than twice as good as one, provided the two are in equilibrium. The funny thing about equilibrium is you never notice it. A teeter-totter going up and down all day long is assumed to be in good working order, but let it get lopsided and it calls attention to itself. Equal weight is needed on each end of the board.

Mr. Paragon might manage to be intelligent, aware, imaginative, compliant, energetic, persevering, skillful and versatile. If he could achieve all these virtues, he wouldn't have to get married at all. He could live alone. Indeed, he'd have to live alone since no one could possibly be good enough to live with him, and his superb genes would not contribute to the preservation of the species.

Cut the list of virtues down the middle and suddenly millions of couples can meet the specifications. Here is the list in diagram form:

Intelligence	plus	Awareness
Imagination	plus	Compliance
Energy	plus	Perseverance
Skill	plus	Versatility

Divide these columns between you as you will. Our society assumes that man is at the left, woman at the right. This may be biologically as well as socially correct, but you can swap the words around between you. If most of these skills are present in one or the other, you have an excellent building team.

It's like trying to move a great big rock. One guy heaves on a crowbar. The other guy pushes the rock sideways. Guy one has used energy, the other guy has persevered.

When the rock didn't move, the intelligent guy says that he should have been heaving on the light end rather than the heavy end, and the aware guy says that in either case the crowbar was slipping in the mud.

The rock moves a little, but not much, and the skillful guy says all right, he'll cut the thing up into little pieces. While he attempts to do so, the versatile guy finds his gloves, sharpens his chisel, and brings him a cup of coffee.

Several chunks having been removed from the rock, the imaginative guy detects a resemblance to Benjamin Franklin, and the compliant guy says yes, I see him too, and he's handsome, but I'll like rocky Benjamin better with some petunias planted around his base.

If between the two of you, you possess any four of these eight virtues, you're in good shape to start building a house. You may pick up the rest of them as you go along. Any more than four to start with is money in the bank.

If the word compliance appears in both virtue columns, you are indeed fortunate. I believe that in planning a house, compliance is the most important of all virtues. Compliance with a stubborn rock, with nature, with the weather, with your site, with your income. Most important of all, compliance with each other.

Compliance does not mean conformity, it means the rare ability to yield when the yielding is good. You can win an argument from a wise man. You can't win one from a fool. The fool is dead certain he is right; the wise man is not so sure.

In designing and building your house, I hope you will let yourselves lose an argument now and then. Lose an occasional argument to the architect and to the builder. Not all the time, just when they happen to be right. If you are wrong, on the evidence, say so quickly. This is the approved technique for coming out on top in the end.

Having practiced the technique for a while, try losing arguments to each other. This saves a lot of money, yet arrives at a house where all domestic functions are nicely in balance. Your workshop and kitchen, your office and sewing room, are equally well lit, ventilated, and equipped.

By the judicious loss of an argument here and there, you will arrive at a house which tells your story as you want it told, which looks the way you would like to look, a place which is better than what the other boys and girls have. The place will look as if you both lived there, and were pretty happy about it too.

CHAPTER SEVEN

Notebook

47. Notes on heat

Heat is always on the move. We find it convenient to say that the ways in which it gets around are by conduction, by convection, and by radiation. The greatest of these is radiation.

In one way or another, heat always flows from the warm thing to the cold thing. If you pour hot tea and cold beer into the same glass, the tea gets colder and the beer gets warmer. It never works the other way.

Heat is always trying to average out. If you sit on a hot rock, the rock gets colder and you get warmer. If you sit beside a warm rock, the same thing happens only it takes longer. If you sit on a cold rock, you will get cold in places, but after a while you yourself, being a producer of heat, will begin to warm up the rock.

Conduction: Touch a hot skillet and you get burnt. Conduction occurs when two things, solid, liquid, or gas, are in contact with each other and one is warmer. Rate of conduction is a matter of how fast the warm thing is willing to let go of its heat, and how fast the cold thing is willing to accept it.

If the handle of the hot skillet is made of iron, it will feel hot. If it is made of wood, it won't burn you. Though the two handles are the same temperature, the wood is less willing to let go of its heat, that is, it has a lower rate of conduction.

For housebuilding purposes, conduction is not very important. We spend most of our time either in air or on mattresses, both of which have a low conduction rate.

Convection: This word describes what happens when a fluid thing, liquid or gas, touches a warm thing, gets warm, goes somewhere else, touches a colder thing, and warms it. Convection is not really so much a different kind of heat flow as it is a method of transferring heat over a distance. It involves multiple conduction to and from a moving vehicle, the same as loading and unloading rocks.

If you admit cold air into a warm furnace, and then let the warmed air flow into your living room, you will be warmed at first purely by convection. After a while, when the walls have had a chance to warm up, they will begin radiating.

Radiation: This type of heat flow is quite different from conduction, or its big brother, con-

174

vection. Radiation is the flow of heat from one thing to another, over any distance, with nothing in between.

Most heat transfer over a distance is accomplished by radiation. It's going on all the time, all around us, in all directions. Radiation is how all the heat from the sun gets here in the first place.

The sun, sitting ninety-three million airless miles away, and a producer of heat even as you and I are, is able to warm a rock faster than we can. If, as many people do, you find the idea of radiation difficult to understand, just ask yourself why it is warmer in the sun than in the shade.

Better still, find a hot stove and hold the palm of your hand toward it, say, ten feet away. Instantly your hand feels warmth. Turn your hand around and let the back get warm too. This is radiation, pure and simple.

Now play this game with yourself. You are in a lonely cabin, on a winter's night. There is a ruddy stove at one end of the cabin and a window at the other. There is, though I don't know where it came from, a piano stool halfway be-

tween the stove and the window.

Sit on the piano stool, please, close your eyes, and spin around. Stop spinning anywhere you like, and now, with your eyes still closed, you can point directly at the stove and directly at the window.

That you can find the stove will not surprise you as much as that you can find the window. You will say that you can feel cold coming from that direction. What is actually going on is that the stove, a warm body, is radiating toward you, while you, a somewhat less warm body, are radiating toward the window.

If you want to play the game some more, have an assistant walk between you and the stove, carrying a big piece of aluminum foil. The foil came from the same place as the piano stool, but a white sheet will work almost as well. In either case, the stove will vanish.

Have your second assistant repeat this procedure between you and the window, and it disappears too. You're lost.

If, being lost, you would like at least to be warm, try this one:

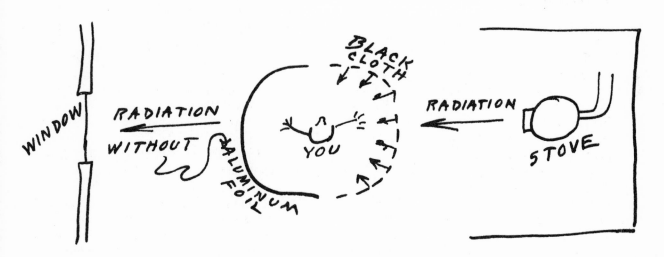

You won't be able to sit there very long, so I'll explain what's happening. The stove radiates heat to the black cloth, which accepts it quickly. The cloth re-radiates its heat on the other side toward you. The heat of your own body is radiating toward the foil, as is the heat from the

black cloth which went on by. The foil is a poor accepter of heat, but an excellent reflector. Almost all of this heat comes back.

We have built a heat trap with you in the middle. Get out quickly before you cook.

Having conducted this experiment, you now know more about heat flow than nine-tenths of the furnace salesmen who will call on you. Radiation works both ways, to and from, with rate of radiation being the same either way. Before you sign a contract for your heating system, ask the salesman to explain this to you.

The tenth salesman will really know his stuff, and we had better get ready for him too. Simply, though not quite correctly, the rate of radiation is determined by color, with black accepting and re-radiating heat quickly; white slowly.

Re-radiation and reflection are not the same thing at all. If a thing is poor at radiating, in or out, it is probably a good reflector. It won't absorb the heat; the heat has to go somewhere; it goes back.

Take that half circle of aluminum foil at your left, for instance. With its light color and shiny surface, the foil won't accept heat. Almost all of the heat coming from your body is turned back, with nothing being re-radiated to the cold window. Though aluminum is an excellent conductor of heat, in this case it hasn't any heat to conduct, because it didn't accept any in the first place.

The half circle of black cloth at your right is accepting the stove's heat greedily. It is an excellent radiator, both coming in and going out. Though it is not a good conductor (you can pick up cloth almost ready to burn without getting burnt), it is thin, and both sides become equally warm. Now some of the heat is being re-radiated away from you; most of it toward you.

Not only has the experiment indicated how to heat a house; it has even suggested what clothes to wear. If you want to be warm on a cold but sunny day, you will wear a coat which is black on the right side and white on the left side, and always keep your right side toward the sun. Since this idea isn't very practical, the compromise rules are these:

If you are galloping like Arabs across the desert, wear loose white robes, as they do, to keep cool. The sun is hotter than you are; the white robe keeps the heat out.

When hunting seals with your Eskimo friends, also wear white. Up there the sun isn't hot enough to make any difference, so the balance is again in favor of white clothing, which is slow to radiate your own body's heat.

While sunbathing on your front porch, if you're too warm, wrap up in a white bathrobe; if you're too cold, wear a black one.

Comes twilight, and you're still sitting there. Now, if you're too warm, use the black bathrobe. It will get rid of your own heat faster. If, as is more likely, you're chilly, put on the white bathrobe.

Heat gets me into no end of discussions. Though heat follows its own rules precisely, its behavior seems (but only seems) to be full of contradictions, such as that black and white bathrobe business.

We spend a mountain of money for heat: a towering amount for the installation, and over the years another towering amount for fuel. Naturally all this money to be spent brings in the advertisers and the salesmen, few of whom understand the principles behind what they are selling, and none of whom is moved by any interest other than to peddle his own product.

The "misnomer," which I discussed earlier, runs rampant in the heat business. A "radiator," that chambered hunk of iron sitting against the wall, is in very small part a radiator. It's designed mostly as a convector. The more modern "convector," a piece of pipe with fins on it, is closer to the truth in that it is mostly a convector, though something of a radiator as well.

The prolonged arguments about the difference between a "hot air system" and a "hot water system" are meaningless. Both refer simply to the means of conveying a warmed fluid (either liquid or gas) from furnace to destination. Both wind up warming a convector and in that way surrounding you with warmed air.

In order to be an effective radiator, a small surface has to be very hot, while a larger surface can be cooler. Carried to the ultimate perfection, radiant heating would warm floor, walls, and ceiling to exactly the temperature you yourself want to be. In this situation, you would care nothing about the temperature of the air.

The first reason we don't all build houses in this perfect way is because the installation cost for heating walls and so on is a lot more than the installation cost for heating air. Unhappily, in this case maximum comfort also represents maximum expense.

There is a second reason which I hate to mention, but in honesty I must. A lot of folks don't know when they're warm. The laws of heat flow are immutable, and our bodies are all constructed along much the same lines, but if you don't think you're warm, you're not. Many people of my acquaintance are conditioned to believe that they are not warm unless they feel a blast of warm air blowing in their faces.

Having equipped ourselves with the necessary theory, we are in good shape to arrive at specific decisions. I find that more people trot around asking advice about heating systems than any other feature of a house. This conveys the impression that heating equipment is controversial.

It isn't, except in terms of who you are and where you are. Right answers can emerge from an analysis of any given situation.

First, do you want central heating or don't you? To answer, we have to look at fuel supply. Of the four principal fuels available, coal, oil, gas, and electricity, the first two are suitable to central heating only; the last two are better suited to area heating.

Central heating came along when people wanted to reduce the nuisance of fire building by having one big fire and then conveying the heat there from all over the house. Conveying heat is troublesome and expensive, but for a hundred years the equipment for building many little fires, safely, was not available.

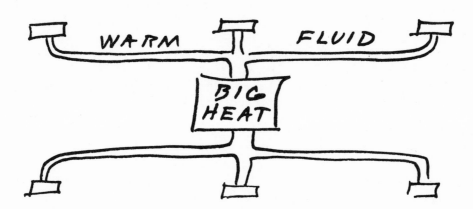

In central heating sketch, we have built one big fire and then pumped warm fluid through pipes or ducts. In area heating sketch, we have piped or wired fuel to the points where heat is

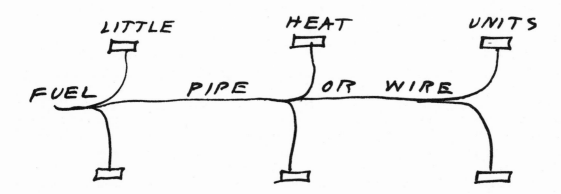

required, then built little fires. In the latter case, the fuel will probably be more expensive for each energy unit, but your increased ability to control heat use will result in a lower annual fuel cost. Certainly the installation will be much cheaper.

I am inclined to consider first cost as more important than fuel cost. Fuel cost is an installment payment, with no interest charge. First cost carries interest charges as long as you live.

I rate area heating as an improvement in all respects over central heating. Over a year and over a lifetime, fuel cost will be somewhat less, installation cost much less. Maintenance is easier, the heating system is much more adaptable to change, space requirements are lower, the whole structure of your house becomes less costly. This judgment assumes, of course, the availability in your area of some kind of gas, whether manufactured, natural, or refined, or of electricity priced at no more than two cents a kilowatt.

Area heating is not to be confused with what the newspapers insist on calling "space heaters." The so-called space heater is a portable kerosene stove, without controls, carburetor, or safety shut-off, which burns too fast or gets kicked over, sets fire to the shack and kills six children.

As of this writing the best all-around heating device I know of is a refined-gas burner built into the outside wall of the area to be heated. The vent being outdoors, it requires no chimney. It is cleaner than anything except electricity. Its installation cost per room is about a fifth that of central heating. Its heat can be turned on or off exactly as you need heat in that room. There is no lag time. It has to have a blower, which is noisy if you think so. Most people either don't notice it, or console themselves with the thought that the air being blown their way is nice and fresh.

The other important decision is whether to begin with radiant or convected heat. The gas burner spoken of is entirely a convector. Radiation is without question more comfortable than convection, but also without question more expensive to install. Electricity is best suited to radiant heat, that is, to the building of large, slightly warmed solid bodies around us. Gas works best warming air. We need to examine the cost of available fuels before making a final decision.

As of this writing, in most areas electricity will be more expensive than gas. It is also more convenient, more flexible, more pleasant to live with. Given more time for equipment development and lowered distribution cost, electricity may very well knock out every other means of heating a house. It's coming, but slowly.

For now, and for most of us, I will have to recommend gas-fired, convected, area heating. It isn't the best and it isn't the worst, but it may be the happiest four-way compromise between installation economy, operating economy, flexibility, and comfort.

48. Notes on light

In Section 2 I said that orientation to the sun is the most important of all decisions to be made in building your house. Nothing has come up since to change my mind.

In Section 9 I talked about arranging a house for maximum sun use. I'll stand pat on that one too.

In Section 47 I discussed heat. I had to admit that the subject is complicated, because in the case of heat several different things are going on at the same time. You can't conduct a sensible conversation about heat without knowing a little something of what you're talking about.

Light is simpler. Light, though itself heat, is easier for you and me to understand because it is visible heat. We can see it. We can make funny shadows with it. We can turn it on and off quickly. Therefore I don't need to discuss the technology of light.

Furthermore, I will not discuss light as an instrument either of mood or of decoration. Candles on the dining table may not let us see whether we're eating steak or cake, but with everyone looking so beautiful in the darkness, who cares? Similarly, if you want to buy two big lamp bases, set them on end tables, then cover the lamps with shades so dense no light can get out, this may be your idea of decoration but not my idea of illumination.

I will discuss light only as a thing to see by. Therefore, we will talk about the human eye, an instrument of enormous range. It can accept and use great brilliance, yet can receive limited information in the next thing to total darkness. Its cone of sharp vision is narrow, but it has almost a complete hemisphere of awareness vision.

Within this great range, both of brilliance and of area, the eye dislikes sudden changes. It hates to be moved quickly from light to dark, and hates even more to be moved from dark to light. Though a flat field of constant illumination would defeat the human eye entirely, excessive contrast within the hemisphere of awareness is also undesirable.

The eye sees best and with the least fatigue under conditions of moderate though adequate brilliance, and with illumination sufficiently general and diffuse to produce adequate but moderate contrast.

The eye does not enjoy looking directly at the source of light, or even close to it, if the light is strong enough to be usable at all. For seeing things, a light source directly ahead is the worst, directly behind next awful, and directly overhead only slightly less bad. The eye prefers two sources, both a little above eye level, one fairly bright and the other less so, one coming in from the right and the other from the left. Under these circumstances the shape of things can best be seen.

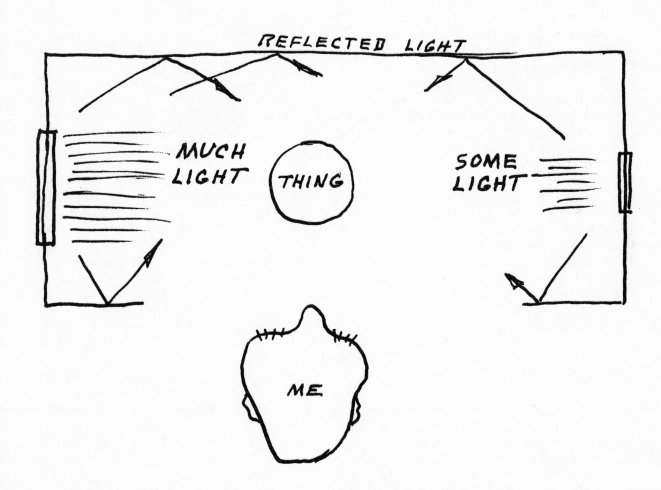

Here I have sketched a top view of a sort of seeing box, showing the top of my head as I look to see what that thing is sitting in the middle.

The thing may be a chair or a post or a pretty girl. In any case, I recognize it by its shape. Skipping the pretty girl for the moment, here is what a round post would look like under various conditions of lighting:

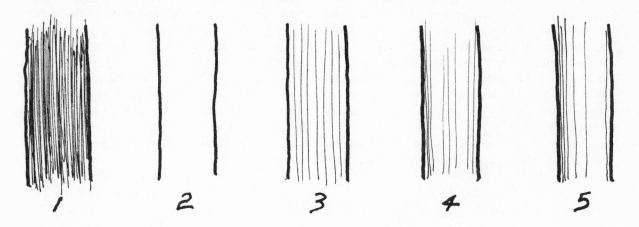

Number one shows all light from dead ahead, number two from straight behind me, and number three from directly above. In none of these is shape discernible. The thing could be square or round, and I wouldn't be able to tell the difference.

Numbers four and five are variations between some light from each side, in number four, and all light from one side, in five. In either case the thing will be visibly round. Number four permits the best vision. Number five is excessively contrasty, and leaves the shape of the dark side in doubt. The most pleasing as well as the most useful illumination provides much light from one side, with a little less from the other.

If in addition to looking, I am doing work with my hands, and am right-handed, I will prefer the major light source to be at my left and the minor source at my right. If I am left-handed, I will of course reverse the sources.

So far all of this is quite obvious to anyone with eyes in his head and the willingness to look. There is one important point in optical psychology which is not so obvious. A window, in addition to admitting light and letting you see out, also serves to rest your eyes. The eye in a state of rest is focused on distance. In order to focus on anything closer than let's say a hundred feet, the eye muscles have to work. They do this without being told. You can't keep them from working. The only way to rest your eyes from close work is to look at something far away.

The race has perversely worried its way into many bad habits about using light. The roller window shade which pulls down from the top is a striking example. First we build and pay for a window, then we buy a piece of opaque cloth on a roller and pull it down to cover the top half of the glass. If any part of the glass has to be covered, this is the wrong half. Light to see by should come from slightly above us, not slightly below. If the purpose of the roller shade is to achieve privacy, it should pull up from the bottom, keeping plenty of light, letting us see out when we want to, but keeping the other fellow from seeing in. I didn't invent this. Old-fashioned offices used to mount their roller shades this way.

The so-called glass curtain, a piece of translucent cloth which covers the entire window and keeps out three-quarters of the light, may be another attempt at privacy. You can stand in your bathrobe, pull the glass curtain aside, and peek out. I admit that such light as gets through a glass curtain has been pleasantly diffused, but there are more economical ways of achieving diffusion, without cutting off most of the light in the process.

Opaque curtains are important in both heat

and light control. To be effective such curtains must be installed so that they can cover the window completely, or be pulled clear of it completely. A common error is not to allow enough wall space to permit the curtains to be drawn back, so that you have paid for window, and paid for curtain, with the two overlapping. An extreme case concerns a woman I know who lives in a house which is all glass on the south side. She keeps the curtains closed all day long because she is afraid the sun will fade her furniture. It fades the curtains instead.

With sunlight from one side of the room only, we still can't see the shape of anything without reflected light, which provides our second or minor source. Much of our interior decoration seems designed to kill off light rather than spread it around. The best illumination is found where most, but not all, of the surface areas are fairly light in color and fairly well textured. That is to say, dark accents against light backgrounds produce good vision; light accents against dark backgrounds do not. Shiny, mirror-like surfaces work against seeing well, and textured surfaces improve it.

Another of our bad habits is to arrange a work area, whether it be writing desk, carpenter's bench, kitchen counter or sewing table, with the major light source coming from the wrong direction. To repeat the obvious rule; if you are right-handed and are doing work with your hands, keep the stronger light at your left. Simple indeed, yet I have seen whole factories which were laid out exactly wrong in this respect.

The last bad habit, and a very common one, is to arrange a work area so that you are staring into a wall. Your eyes are not allowed to rest by seeking out some distant object from time to time. A good arrangement is to have a window which your eyes can find by lifting or turning slightly. Best of all is one like this:

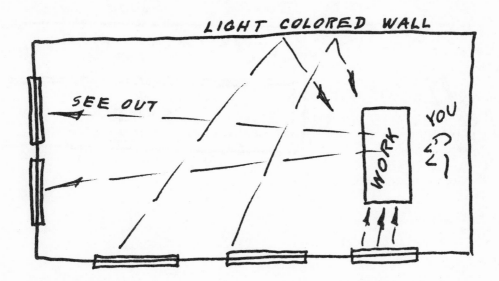

Here you are working with your back to the wall, facing across the room, and preferably looking toward a window on the other side. This way, night or day, your eyes will have plenty of chance to rest themselves as you go along.

Artificial light, though more expensive and perhaps less pleasant than natural light, is easier to control because we can turn it on and off, increase it or decrease it, rearrange it to suit ourselves. Potentially good, it can be destructively bad if we don't pay attention to what we're doing.

The principles we have already discussed still apply. The source of light must not be directly visible. There must be at least two sources, preferably somewhat above eye level, and oriented at right angles to our most important field of vision.

Here is a list of bad habits in our use of artificial light.

1. A visible light source overhead and in the center of the room. This is absolutely wrong on all counts.

2. A single light source where two are required. Example: many "de luxe" hotels continue to put one light above the bathroom mirror. It makes me feel like stealing their towels and sneaking out the back way.

3. The expensive "light fixture" selected for the alleged good looks of the fixture itself, not its usefulness in dispensing light. My feeling is that the ideal "light fixture" would not be visible at all. I believe that in the sense of illumination, light is to be used, not to be looked at.

4. The tendency to economize on the use of light, in the belief that light is expensive. I speak, of course, of electric light, which is the biggest domestic bargain going. You would be surprised what a small part of your electric bill goes directly for lighting.

5. Light fixtures buried in the ceiling. This type of installation is wrong on all counts except mood. Not only is it directly overhead, but the light has no chance to strike anything which will diffuse it.

The correct way to use artificial light—to see by, that is, not for mood or decoration—is what most people call "indirect," or more properly, "diffuse."

To achieve diffuse lighting, you can spend a lot of money if you fall into the clutches of a fixture salesman. Let me show you how simple it is to build.

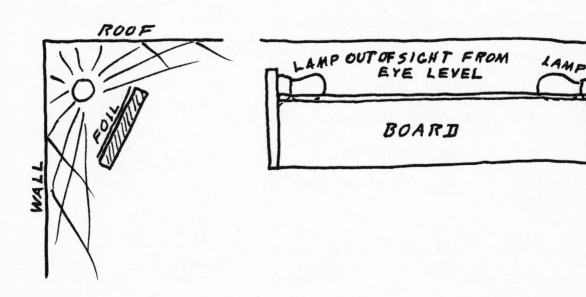

In the least expensive embodiment, we require one board, one strip of aluminum foil, two incandescent lamps with sockets, two wires and a switch.

The foil is stapled to the inside of the board, and the lamp sockets are mounted at each end.

The board is then located between roof and wall, in such manner that no person at any reasonable spot in the room, sitting or standing, is forced to look directly at either of the light sources.

All the requirements have been met. The

direct source can not be seen. The two lamps, separated by several feet, create the effect of a light source enlarged in area and thus lowered in brilliance per square inch. The usable light has been diffused from wall and roof, in such manner that the total source is slightly above eye level. The light source is roughly similar to daylight. Now put two of these on opposite sides of a room. Perfect. You did it all for about $3.75.

Naturally there are other arrangements that you can work out in terms of what you have and what you want. The principles remain the same. Many types of long tube lamps, either filament or gas-filled, will create the same effect. The gas lamps, as opposed to the incandescent or filament lamp, will give you more light for a dime, plus a choice of flattering colors as well. However, they all cost more to install and maintain.

The ultimate solution may be the glowing wall panel, which is being developed. When that is available, we will simply plug in the wall and get light. I don't yet know what the glowing panel will cost to install, run, and maintain.

I continue to lean toward the filament lamp, which is old-fashioned now and admittedly creates more heat and therefore less light than a fluorescent lamp for a dime's worth of electricity. But the filament lamp is cheap to install, easy to maintain, and can be bought anywhere.

The fluorescent lamp is next in usage. It is efficient, comes in a variety of colors, and has a low unit brilliance. The lower brilliance tempts some folks to expose the naked lamp, but I still won't budge. Rule number one is that we never expose the source of light. The lower fuel cost of the fluorescent lamp is also tempting, but many years of use are required to repay the greater installation cost. I'm not knocking the gas-filled lamp. I'm saying it's one of those things which, on a low building budget, you can get along without for now, then add later when you can afford it.

To summarize my ideas about achieving the best light: get yourself plenty of it, whether natural or artificial, but keep the sources multiple, spread out, and as low in area brilliance as possible. This is the best way I know of to keep those squint lines from forming between your eyebrows.

49. Notes on sound

Here is my favorite true story about noise.

In the process of adding a bedroom to Mrs. Nemo's house, I found that there was no economical way to avoid having the ceiling slope with the slope of the new roof, about an inch to the foot. Mrs. Nemo may have missed this on the plans, because when she saw the ceiling in place, she flew into a rage. In the hope of quieting her enough to get paid I pointed out first that the ceiling had to be that way, and second that it would make a wonderful improvement in the acoustics.

"Who," she cried, "ever heard of acoustics in a bedroom!"

In Section 11 I roughed out some acoustical principles. I said that when you are building from scratch, pleasant sound can be had for nothing—in fact, less than nothing. Most of the building methods which make for an irritatingly noisy house are expensive, while most of the methods which make for good acoustics are cheap. This represents the something for nothing bonanza of all time.

In order to understand why good sound comes cheap, we need first to throw out the idea of "acoustic treatment." This means a patch job on a building which was done wrong in the first place. Not only is acoustic treatment expensive, but it will probably result in only limited success.

Next I need to discuss the difference between absorbing noise and dissipating it. Absorption is the conversion of sound energy into heat. It takes place slowly within the air. To absorb sound energy quickly we have to use deeply yielding materials within which the energy can wander around and get lost. Sound energy which is either reflected by a surface or transmitted through it is not being absorbed.

Sound dissipation, however, is accomplished for nothing by the shape of the confined space. In Section 11 I discussed this principle. Most of the structural shapes and methods which have been suggested in this book are acoustically good. I feel so strongly about the importance of pleasant acoustics to physical and mental health, that if I knew a design to be acoustically bad, I would throw it out for that reason alone. Fortunately, noise reduction and pleasant aesthetics seem to go hand in hand.

We are assailed by many kinds of sound. I find it convenient to think of all this racket as being made up of speech, music, pleasant noise, and unpleasant noise. While the concert hall is designed for music and the lecture hall for speech, the home tries to deal with music, speech, and assorted noises all at once. Outdoors, barring an occasional echo, sound goes nowhere but away. Indoors, it keeps bouncing around. Some persistence is desirable, too much is not. How much is too much depends on the kind of sound, and whether it is pleasant or unpleasant.

Indoors, we can do two things with sound, absorb it or dissipate it. If sound is to be absorbed, we would need to devise a psychic-selective absorber capable of deciding which noises we thought pleasant and which unpleasant. Sound dissipation solves this problem for nothing. It creates an environment in which the desired sounds can be heard and understood, while the undesired sounds are made less irritating.

The ultimate acoustic horror is a square, plastered, hardwood-floored, flat-ceilinged room where someone has forgotten to turn off the radio, and within which twenty women are pretending to play bridge. Starting with this worst of all torture boxes, we can work upward toward acoustic comfort.

The intelligibility of speech is a function of its higher frequencies. If the highs are removed, speech can not be understood. At the other extreme, if the highs reverberate (bounce around the room) too long, conversation is not only cloudy and hard to understand but hard on the ulcers as well. If the highs don't linger at all, we have the padded cell effect of lifelessness.

The beauty, audibility, and clarity of the human voice and of music is a function of the range of frequencies which can be heard, plus a reverberation time which is neither too long nor too short, plus absence of reverberation patterns.

Short of noise at the level of actual pain, the irritating aspects of noise lie in the higher frequencies. The greater weight of noise lies in the low frequencies which because they are more difficult to absorb travel farther, reverberate longer, and penetrate physical barriers with less diminution.

The inexpensive way to solve the problem is to shorten reverberation time on the high frequencies and dissipate the low ones. Both can be done at no cost through proper room shape.

The worst possible acoustic shape for a room

is a perfect cube. The shape improves from there as we depart from cube dimensions and, more important, as we decrease the number of major right-angled or parallel surfaces. Practically, the throwing of one or two of the six major room surfaces out of square or parallel is a big improvement.

There are also some dimension ratios which help. If a room has to be rectangular in all three planes, the best compromise shape makes its width slightly over one and a half times its height; its length slightly over one and a half times its width. For example:

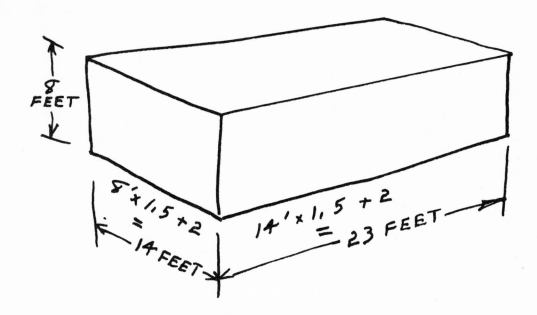

The dimensions eight by fourteen by twenty-three represent a recommended proportion, not a recommended size, but it would still be a good place to hold a bridge party.

If, fortunately, the room need not be rectangular in all three planes, the desired proportions sketched here still hold good, but become less critical. It would seem that pleasant acoustic shape also fits with many of our aesthetic notions.

If you insist that your room look rectangular in all three planes, you can still do a lot of good by building a couple of its walls and corners out of exact parallel and exact square. Two or three degrees departure from ninety, less than anyone can notice, is a big help. A famous university, cramped as usual for money and space, built the study cubicles in its acoustics laboratory like this:

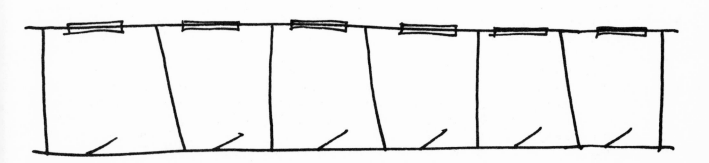

With shower-stall dimensions in exactly rectangular cubicles the students would have been frightened by the beating of their own hearts. One crooked wall quieted down two cubicles at once.

Back in Section 11 I observed that all irregularities, all departures from geometric precision, such as beams, arches, open doorways, angles, bookshelves, and unintentional structural deviations brought on by accident or time, contribute to noise reduction.

We now see why many people insist that an old house is more comfortable than a new one. They may not know it, but the comfort they refer to is largely acoustic comfort. The old house probably wasn't built square in the first place, and has become less so as time went by.

For about two generations master carpenters, convinced that houses should be built by the square instead of by eye, have been in all innocence committing acoustic atrocities. They pride themselves on the flatness of walls, the exact squareness of corners. Plasterers, using harder plaster than before, strive for dense, plane surfaces. More and more glass is used, and the people who haven't read this book still set it straight up and down. House areas have shrunk, and with prices tied to number of rooms rather than square footage, room areas have shrunk even more.

Since the old rules haven't changed, it is small wonder that in a bedroom ten by ten by eight with hardwood floor and geometrically perfect plastered walls and ceiling, the smallest belch, squeak, rumble or snore sounds like gunfire.

Hallways are a special acoustic atrocity, for different reasons, and deserve special attention. Draw two parallel lines:

whose length is several times that of the space between. You have drawn a hallway, you have drawn a tunnel, and with the same two lines you have drawn an organ pipe. Even with the ends open, our organ pipe (hallway) reverberates every sound therein. With the ends closed off square, it's worse.

Now imagine this hallway lined with bedrooms, as in some houses, all dormitories, and all hospitals. Or imagine it lined by offices filled with chattering typewriters and chatting executives, and traversed by pretty girls wearing high-heeled shoes. An organ pipe works fairly well no matter where the sound is begun, with the result that the entire hallway community shares, whether with glee, irritation, or embarrassment, the noises of every member.

The best solution is of course to arrange things so that no hallway exists. Short of that, there are many ways to mitigate the racket.

On the next page are suggestions—an offset, a change in width, walls out of parallel, ends out of square, and a series of corners.

Once your choice of architecture has stuck you with a slick, straight, organ-pipe hallway it will do you little good to put curtains on the walls or carpeting on the floor. The shape has done more damage than a change of materials can correct. Repairing some part of this damage comes under "acoustic treatment," and is always expensive.

Having looked at some ways in which a conventional house goes acoustically wrong, let's turn with glee to look at some ways in which the engineered house is acoustically right, without anyone having done a thing about it.

In the long list of acoustic advantages, the most important are: Open plan, with partitions replaced by counters and storage walls. Beamed, sloping ceiling. Walls which have been angled

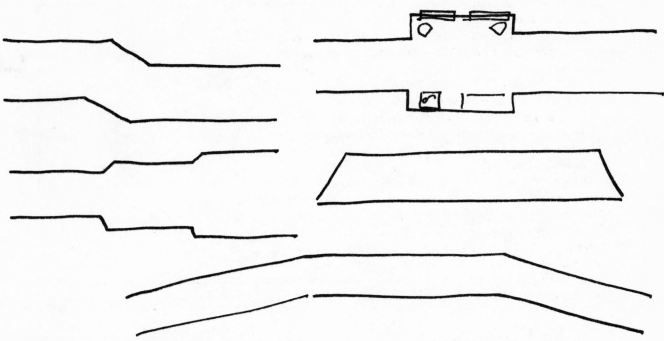

to fit site. Wall surfaces broken by revealed structure and slanted windows. Avoidance of hard surfaces in favor of textures. Single level design which puts distance between noise sources, and which avoids sound transmission through floors which are necessarily stiff and thus noisy.

Outdoor Noise. Up to now these notes have worried only about indoor noise. Although the great outdoors is more tolerant of acoustical error, our penchant for architectural squareness and symmetry still can lead us into some annoying mistakes.

We have all had fun shouting at a barn, like this:

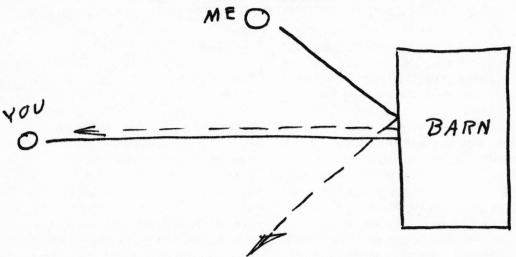

You say hello, and Little Sir Echo says hello right back to you, but not to me. I wouldn't deny you the fun of an occasional echo, if the echo remains occasional.

Now see what happens when you have two barns, or a barn and a house, sitting at right angles to each other.

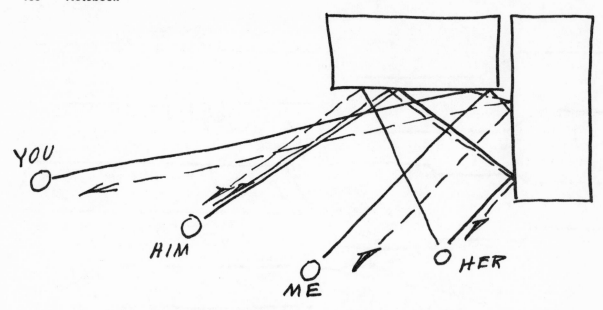

The ninety-degree inside angle will send an echo back to any place in the yard, where we are all running around playing touch football. In such a situation, not only does everyone get his own echo all the time, he gets everyone else's too. This sort of continuous playback quickly ceases to be fun.

Applying the same inside corner principle, here is a good and often used way to annoy the arriving guest:

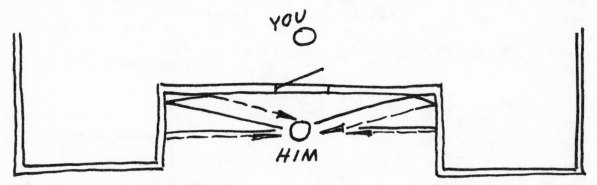

This is the first time I ever sketched a front door exactly centered between two ells, yet people build them that way all the time. When you open the door and say hello, he says hello, and in his own ears he hears himself saying hello-lo-lo-lo-lo-lo. This is a shattering experience, which wouldn't have happened had the door been located three feet off center.

Outdoors as well as in, the inside square corner is the acoustic menace to be shunned. Fortunately, it costs not one penny to avoid it. Even the city planners are beginning to realize that they can reduce urban noise by setting their towering skyscrapers a little bit off square. Geometric symmetry in structure is always noisy, especially inside square corners. There is noise enough without coming home to a room that has, not one square corner, but four.

Reproduced Sound. Canned sound in one form or another has become part of our lives. More of the noises we listen to come out of a box than out of people, and like it or not, the loudspeaker has become a member of the family. Since it is a constant presence, and a most vocal one at that, its location is worthy of at least as much architectural attention as where we sleep.

I have said that everything right about acoustics is inexpensive. This remains true for reproduced sound, whether we are discussing the housewife whose radio blats unheard commercials while she does the ironing, or the high fidelity buff who insists on religious calm while soaking himself in symphony.

Manufacturers of sound reproducers in the quality range like to encourage the idea that a noise box is also a piece of furniture. As a piece of furniture, it falls under the scrutiny of the housewife who decides how it should look and where it will be located.

Treatment of a noise box as a piece of furniture to be looked at rather than heard seems to me at least as silly as saying that a light fixture is to be looked at, rather than seen by. Ideally the light fixture shouldn't be seen at all and the noise equipment shouldn't be seen either. It should be built into the house as part of the machinery.

The situation is further complicated when the manufacturers, for their own reasons, locate the loudspeaker or speakers and the necessary amplifier and controls all in the same box. This is dead wrong and they know it, but they reason that it is easier to sell one piece of furniture than two.

In any given sound reproducer of any quality whatever the amplifier and control section is relatively small; the loudspeaker, to be of the same quality, is relatively large. Splendid developments have come along to reduce the size of loudspeakers of an equivalent quality, but the same designer will in any case produce a better speaker if he is given more room to work in. This is because air accepts sound reluctantly. The larger the area, the better.

Good loudspeakers are bulky contraptions, believed by non-speaker-lovers to be un-handsome. Many a music fan has had his sound apparatus banished from the front parlor because of its size. But hurray for our side. Now that a new house is being planned, hi-fi husband and furniture-polish wife can stay friendly, because the loudspeaker is going to be built in. (Stereo fans can read speakers for speaker, but that's a deep-dyed hi-fi argument that has nothing to do with architecture.)

Here are the simple rules for building in a speaker. The most efficient acoustic location for any speaker is in the extreme top or bottom of the corner of a room, with the upper corner being usually more convenient. The speaker should face diagonally across the area where you plan to do most of your attentive listening. The high frequencies should reach your favorite easy chair in a direct line. Remember that most speakers have a rather narrow cone of highs. Within this cone, you have "listening music." Outside of it, you have "dinner music."

For best results, the speaker corner should be acoustically "dead," with the opposite corner "live." Like this:

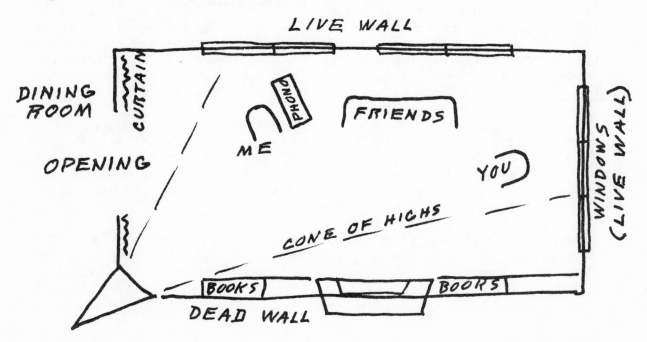

The idea behind this arrangement is to provide a short reverberation time on the highs, and a longer one on the low frequencies.

Mounting a cone speaker in the wall is an economical acoustic device that buys a lot of domestic harmony for nothing. Its variations are many. Here is a schematic diagram of how the trick works.

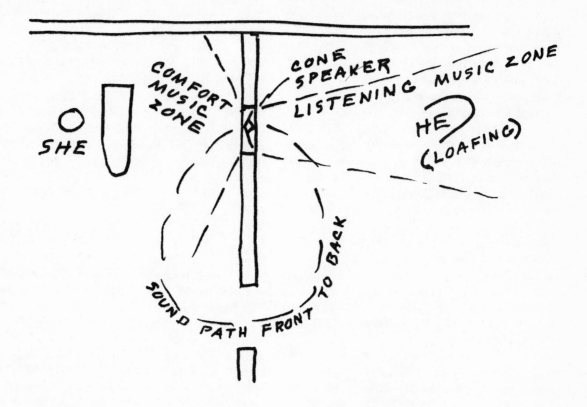

All you did was take a coaxial cone speaker and mount it in a hole in the wall. On the front side of the speaker you get listening music, and on the back, dinner or working music. Acoustically, the arrangement can be criticized, but still, keeping everyone happy with one noise box is quite a bargain.

If, by chance, you can arrange matters so that the air path from front to back of the speaker is between twenty and thirty feet, the bargain will be improved, because the speaker itself will have become almost twice as efficient as it was before.

Whether you choose my first suggestion, which approaches the ideal, or my second, which is bargain basement, satisfaction is guaranteed whether your favorite noise be speech, music, or advertising.

Happy listening.

50. Notes on materials

All other things being equal, the least expensive materials are those found in your own back yard. Contemporary architects discuss the use of "native" materials, an unfortunate phrase which seems to imply that the native stuff, though inferior, should be struggled along with somehow because it is aesthetically correct to do so. I suggest that "native" materials should be judged on their own merits. You may learn that they are as good or better than their brothers from a thousand miles away, and they are certainly cheaper.

It is a human failing to believe that "imported" is bound to be better than "local." Opera singers used to take Italian names, and everyone knows that the definition of an expert is another dumbbell but one who comes from out of town.

The range of materials multiplied by places where they are found is vast. You have to make your choices for yourself. I'll start off with an example. I happen to be sitting in New England, surrounded by northern white pine. In Colonial days, this wood was taken to England, where it was called the King's wood. Only master cabinet-makers were allowed to use it, because of its two great virtues, the first aesthetic, a lovely texture, and the second mechanical, its dimensional stability. Nothing has changed since. The wood is snapped up eagerly, but by non-New England buyers. Let a neighbor see what I am using for a dining table and he will say, "What's that made of? Oh! Just pine."

Therefore we find houses in Oregon sided with cypress from Florida, and houses in Florida sided with redwood from Oregon. We find houses in Mississippi floored with white pine from Maine, and houses in Maine floored with yellow pine from Mississippi.

Shipping lumber around is bad enough, but shipping rocks is worse. I have heard of marble from Italy which showed up in Vermont, and granite from Montpelier finding its way to Milan. All of which is not to deny that there are special things found in special places. My point is that once we get over the hump of regarding local, nearby, home-grown and provincial as derogatory words, the bulk of our building materials will be found close at hand.

We have discussed what various materials can do. Some materials are, shall we say, beneficent. They like to be used in a house. They are tolerant of our mistakes, doing some good no matter how badly we treat them. Other materials respond less gratefully. They fight back when maltreated.

Steel is strong, faithful, and he works cheap. The servant type, he looks after us to the limit of his strength, but prefers to remain below-stairs. His only serious fault is his excessive appetite for oxygen. He rusts.

Wood is the hero, the glamor boy of our little drama. He is everywhere, doing everything, both on and off stage. He accepts abuse quietly, but, like most glamor boys, is at his charming best when treated with respect and understanding.

Concrete is the heavy. He is the owner of the bank, firm, unyielding, without whom you could do little, but with whom it is advisable not to get too intimate. Assembled Masonry used to own the bank, but he is retired now, serving only as lobby sitter emeritus.

Aluminum is the maid-of-all-work who dashes in and out fluttering her skirts. Within her strength, she will do anything you ask, and you are never sorry to have her around.

Glass is the heroine, beautiful, weak, fragile, and hard to handle, but for whom no substitute has yet been devised. She has, by the way, some country cousins from the Plastics family, who will be very handy to have around when they grow up.

Waiting outside the door are several applicants who didn't get into my play at all. I feel sorry for the first one in line. They call him Brick, he's been around a long while, he's worked hard for everybody, but he never learned to do anything really well.

Also around for quite a while, though the police have been after him, is an ugly fellow called Tar Paper. This guy I would pay just to stay away. He does everything wrong. He attracts heat when I don't want it, and throws it away when I need it most. He works cheap, but badly. Mistress Aluminum does everything he can do, and does it right instead of wrong.

Pretending to ignore Tar Paper is another unemployed slicker called Plaster. He used to play butler parts back when people hired butlers. Plaster's a front man, all grin and no muscle, and he gives up when the going gets tough. Though a pretty boy, for my money he's priced himself out of the market.

The name of that handsome fellow in the harlequin suit is Paint. He's a good lad in the right role and maybe we can find a place for him later. The rest of the crowd are bit players, no great shakes at the box office, but useful when we need them.

The ones who really make the show click are wood and concrete, the hero and the heavy. Let's see what it takes to make them perform at their best.

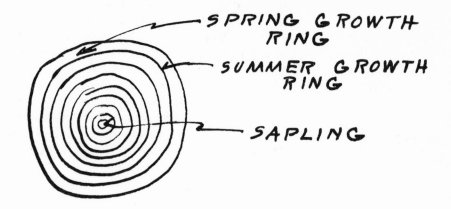

For simplicity, I have sketched only a few of   Here's what happens when the log is sawed.
the growth rings in this cross section of a tree.

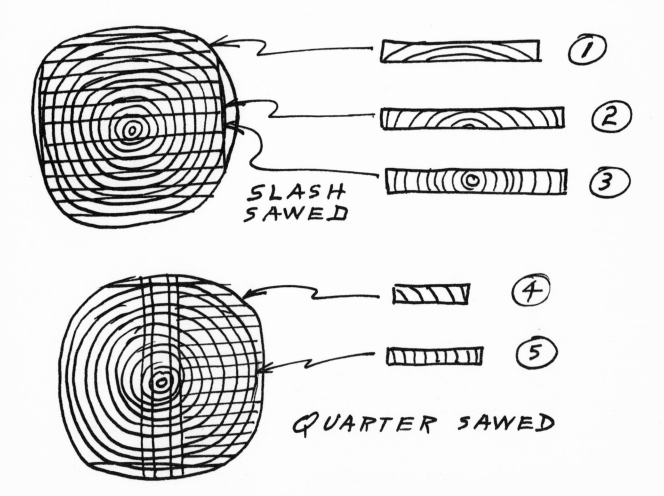

The methods shown here are sketched with apologies to all sawyers for oversimplifying their procedures.

Our first problem is that wood is many times as strong in one direction as in the other. I could break board number three up there with my bare hands, like this:

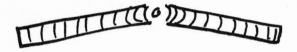

No strain. I broke it through the center of the tree, where the sapling remains. To break board number one would have required a sharp blow, but try to break either of these boards in the other direction and you've got yourself a job.

The second and more complicated problem is that wood changes its dimensions with changes in its moisture content, and not equally in all directions at that. Lengthwise of the grain (up and down the tree) the change is very slight and we can ignore it. To look at what happens across the grain, here is a blown-up sketch of board number one:

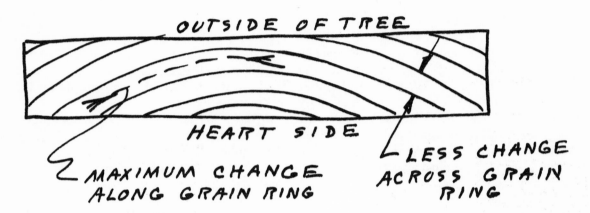

OUTSIDE OF TREE

HEART SIDE

MAXIMUM CHANGE ALONG GRAIN RING

LESS CHANGE ACROSS GRAIN RING

The dark, narrow, hard lines in any wood's grain are the summer growth. The lighter, softer, wider space in between two dark bands is the spring growth, during which time the tree made its annual spurt. Unfortunately, the dimensional change between wet and dry is greatest looking around the tree, that is, along the circle of spring growth. The change is a good deal less looking directly across the growth ring.

Now let's say that our board was flat, as sketched, at a moisture content of around 15 per cent. Along comes a dry spell, and its moisture drops to 10 per cent. The board will look like this:

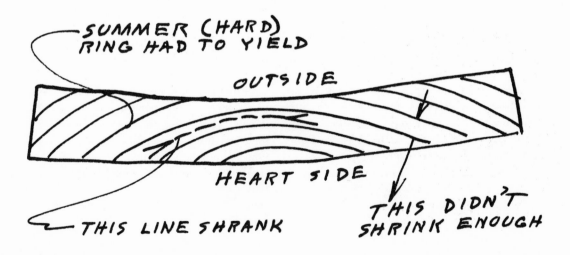

SUMMER (HARD) RING HAD TO YIELD

OUTSIDE

HEART SIDE

THIS LINE SHRANK

THIS DIDN'T SHRINK ENOUGH

In geometric terms, the shrinkage was greater along any circumference than along any radius.

The board had to go out of flat. It couldn't help itself.

Here is a blow-up of board number five:

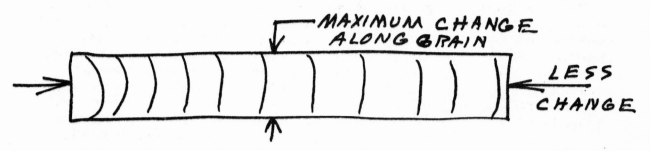

During the same dry spell, the greatest proportional shrinkage in this board was its thickness, but because it wasn't very thick in the first place, you didn't notice it. A proportionately lesser change occurred in its width. Since the board, being quarter-sawed, wasn't wide to begin with, you may not have noticed that either. Though the board shrank, it did not go out of flat, because there was no growth ring entering and leaving from the same side, therefore no string being pulled around a corner and no force exerted.

The phenomenon of going out of flat is known as "cupping." No slash-sawed board can avoid it. Cupping is not the same as "warp." A warped board was defective, usually because of internal stresses from a crooked tree. The warped board went out of straight, or twisted out of plane, or split itself down its own grain.

The only way to avoid normal cupping is quarter-sawing. Aesthetics now must be considered. When nine out of ten people talk about a beautiful wood grain, they refer to slash sawing, that is, board number one, which cups. Board number five, quarter-sawed, doesn't cup, but though it retains a flat surface, it has no grain beauty worth mentioning.

A partial solution to this dilemma is to use narrow boards, which may cup or not, but since they're narrow, it doesn't matter. Aesthetics gets into the argument again, with at least eighty out of a hundred people regarding a wide board as prettier than a narrow one.

Back we go to geometry. Different woods vary in the amount of their dimensional change. The cupping effect we have observed is greater, by and large, with hardwoods than with softwoods. A piece of maple cups several times as much as pine of the same width. Therefore we find hardwoods used in narrow strips, nailed side by side in a floor or glued together in a table. If we want wide boards to look at, they will almost inevitably be softwood.

Wood, the glamor boy of our materials group, requires understanding. Here are ways in which he is frequently misunderstood.

Trouble arises in the use of the words "wet" and "dry." After sawing, wood must be dried in the sense that, with time, most of the sap comes out. The rule-of-thumb time required used to be called one year per inch of thickness. Commercial haste has reduced this figure to three months, without specifying whether the three months be July through September or January through March. At any rate, this kind of "drying" proceeds rapidly on the first day after sawing, then slower on each succeeding day thereafter, until some time within the first "year per inch of thickness," when the wood is as dry, or free of sap, as it is ever going to get.

From then on the word "dry" refers to moisture content, which varies up and down with the weather and with ventilation. The most widespread and persistent fallacy concerning wood is the belief that the older it gets the drier it gets. This is not only wrong, but leads by implication into another fallacy, the idea that dryness is somehow a measure of quality.

A wood salesman, who should have known better, assured me that he had some "fine old boards, sawed thirty years ago and dry as a bone." The lumber turned out to be stacked in a tight pile on the floor at the north side of his cow barn. You could make the stuff squirt water by squeezing it.

A curious variation on this "old therefore dry therefore good" fallacy is the notion that "kiln drying" produces dryer therefore better wood. There are several reasons for kiln drying, all economic, such as the weight of loaded freight cars and the interest charges on operating capital. As far as the wood itself goes, the best you can hope for is that kiln drying, done carefully, does no damage.

Under no circumstances can kiln drying make the wood any better than it was when it was placed in the oven. One week after leaving the kiln, or somewhere around Kansas City in a shipment from Seattle to Baltimore, the wood isn't any drier, either. To repeat, the moisture content of a piece of wood depends on the weather and on ventilation, not time.

Still another variation on this fallacy is the notion that the moisture change problem can be eliminated by the use of wood finishes such as paint or varnish. It isn't so, but more on that subject in the next section. The chances are that by painting you will have rendered the wood less able to keep pace with moisture changes, therefore most of the time it will be undesirably wetter than its environment.

Which brings us to the circumstances under which wood rots. A piece of wood completely immersed in water does not rot. Neither does one completely surrounded by air. If ventilated, and allowed to dry out thoroughly after every wetting, a piece of wood of almost any kind will retain its strength over a period which, compared to my lifetime, amounts to forever.

Wood rots under conditions of wetting followed by imperfect drying. A good example is the stake which you drove into the loam of your garden and forgot to remove last fall. Pull it out, and you will find that it began to rot precisely at the surface of the ground. That part of the stake which was deeper in the ground has not yet begun to rot. Down there it got wet and stayed wet.

For the same reason, wood in direct contact with masonry will rot, because masonry is hydroscopic. It stays wet. The situation is different only in degree from driving a stake into loam. Absolutely the nastiest thing you can do to a wooden post is to set it in concrete. Yet people keep on doing it, and when the post breaks off exactly at the surface of the concrete they feel the post must have been defective. Question: then what should the posts be set in? Answer: coarse gravel, which drains and ventilates.

In order for the hero and the heavy to get along with each other, wood in direct contact with masonry must be chemically protected. There are many effective chemicals available. I recommend their use at all places where wood cannot be ventilated. I ask you to remember that rot-inhibiting chemicals are not to be confused with finishes.

With all this attention being paid to his foibles, it might seem that wood is a capricious beast. Not at all. We study wood in detail because it is the most versatile of all domestic building materials. Chief among wood's virtues is the ability to save us a lot of money if we learn to use it skillfully.

Here are some important notes on how to use wood right. Starting with a stack of "log run" lumber, you will find that most of your boards are slash sawed, looking like board number one or number two in the first sketch. With both sides equally ventilated, each and every one of these boards will cup away from the heart side, as shown in the next sketch. That is, the bulge will invariably occur toward what was the center of the tree. If one side is wetter than the other, the bulge will be toward the wet side.

From these facts comes a very important rule for using lumber. "Heart side up, heart side out!" Wherever a board may be used, its showing or working face should be the heart side of the tree, as sketched on the next page.

For clarity, these curvatures are shown in exaggerated fashion. I think you can see the point to the heart side out rule. To explain all the reasons would take a long while. They include continuity of surfaces, proportion of heartwood, correct ventilation to avoid excessive cupping, and security and size of knots. Footnote: Much to my surprise I find that many carpenters pay no attention to the heart side rule. Insist that your carpenters do.

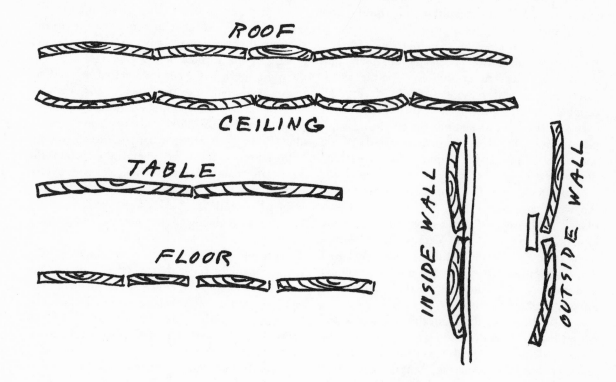

The subject of knots reminds us that a knot structurally is a defect, no matter how much press agentry may be expended on selling knotty boards. The price of lumber depends on its freedom from knots. Few of us could afford to build a house of wood which was entirely "clear." There is a lot of money to be saved by learning to use wood which is knotty and therefore cheap.

In the language of our structural engineering course, a knot is a defect when placed in tension, but not when placed in compression. A knot is only a minor defect, structurally, when it occurs in or near the center of a board or timber, but a major defect, both structurally and aesthetically, when it reaches the edge of a board or timber.

Starting with the assumption that we want to use knotty wood because it is cheap, here are some ways to use it wrong.

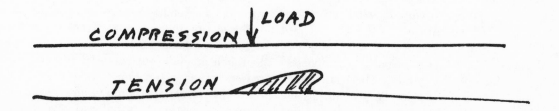

This beam was put up by an alleged carpenter who should be in some other line of work. The beam was junk to begin with, but if he had turned it over, putting the knot on the compression side, no harm would have been done.

No. 1 shows a timber which should never have been used as a load-carrying post at all. A bad knot cuts it half in two at the point of greatest buckling stress.

No. 2 is a timber with knots in the center, which makes a fine post. The buckling stress goes down the outside, where there are no knots. Sketch 3 is board number three from our first sketch of a sawed log. At worst, this board is firewood. At best, it can be used on the roof, but keep it out of sight.

No. 4 is what the saw may have found a couple of boards away. With knots running into the edge, it may be used for roof, but with caution. Knots in the edge of a board don't behave well, whether the board be stress-loaded or not. No. 5 sketch is a board you can use anywhere, without fear of structural failure. It is both aesthetically pleasing and structurally sound, which is not surprising, because much of our aesthetic sense is based on good structure. This board is

worth many times as much as the horrible examples, yet if we bought unselected or "log run" lumber, we got all three for the same price, or less than half the price of "selected" lumber.

Because all three boards came out of the same tree, once more we see why wood is a glamor

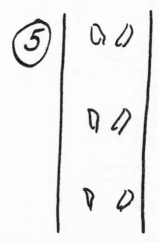

boy, who does many things well but insists on being treated right. In the sense that wood is a natural, ever-varying material, it demands the services of a good carpenter who will think even as he acts. Out of one tree such a carpenter can get posts, beams, roof, floor, walls, trim, and furniture.

Our ancestors did it that way. We now find it convenient to use several different trees, but in the use of wood, the carpenter's thought processes remain the essential ingredient.

The second member of our domestic materials team is concrete. He is a solid soul, and though not as versatile as wood, is able to perform indispensable tasks when properly put to work. Concrete is a manufactured material, far simpler than wood. Its proper care and feeding can be described in much less time.

Concrete is a mixture of cement, sand, and some sort of aggregate or filler. Its strength is established by the bond between grains of sand and particles of cement. The cement particle is hundreds of times smaller in diameter than the grain of sand. When mixed together dry, each grain of sand becomes coated with thousands of particles of cement. With the addition of water, the cement undergoes a chemical change, gets sticky, and holds the whole mass together in whatever shape we have pushed, poured, smoothed, formed or sprayed it in the meantime.

Properly mixed, then allowed to dry slowly and for a long while, concrete is astonishingly strong. Under the best of care, its weakness remains in tension. To concrete which is going to be stressed we always add reinforcement on at least the tension side, like this:

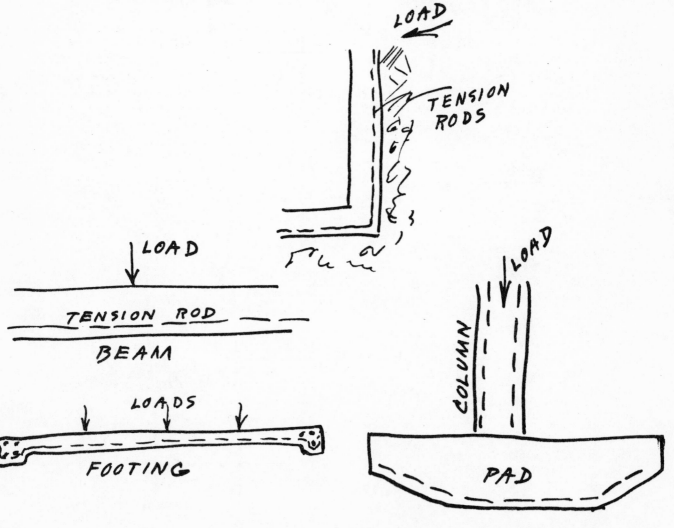

Because concrete can be formed around anything, we are allowed to locate tensile reinforcing steel where we want it. This is the best thing about concrete. We wish we could do the same with all building materials. All, without exception, are to some extent weaker in tension than in compression.

The tensile strength of concrete is greatest when it has been mixed very dry. All vendors of mixed concrete, when they are not being governed by engineered specifications, mix it much too wet. They do this in order to make the concrete mix quickly, pour easily, and go into the forms without much work. Given adequate tensile reinforcing, this is the most economical procedure, but it doesn't produce the best concrete.

Each grain of sand has been coated with thousands of grains of cement. Add a little bit of water, the correct figure being perhaps fifty pounds of water to a hundred pounds of cement, and the whole mass becomes sticky. Add a lot more water, and the cement particles wash off of the grains of sand. Under the action of puddling and finishing, many of the cement particles are driven to the top. The finished concrete now has its best tensile strength at the top, where it normally isn't necessary, its lowest strength at the bottom, where strength is most needed.

For the best result, concrete should not be "poured," it should be pushed. Where pushing involves excessive labor, some compromise is required. Insofar as concrete can be mixed and formed close to the proper dryness, less concrete is required for a given structure. The exact compromise depends on the situation, and each one is different. All I can do here is alert you to the fact that concrete is generally mixed too wet.

My second word of warning is that most builders, under pressure to get a job done quickly, load their concrete structures too soon. The strength of concrete increases strikingly during its first month of existence. Provide a month of curing time if you can arrange it.

My last warning is to remind you that concrete absorbs moisture. Polyethylene film is now available to minimize the difficulty. This wonderful plastic enjoys the property of excluding moisture while admitting air. Crazy, but it works. Nurserymen wrap their plants in it for shipment. The plants can breathe, and still stay moist. All concrete in contact with the ground should have a polyethylene moisture barrier under it.

In summary, concrete, reinforced on the tension side, mixed dry, allowed to cure, and protected from moisture, is a magnificent building material.

The amount of space devoted in these notes to the basic domestic building materials, wood and concrete, is roughly in proportion to the amount of money you will spend for them. Other materials, though helpful, take smaller parts of your well-spent dollar.

In cutting up the dollar I include the array of materials which are manufactured from wood and from concrete. To list all of them would require as much space as this entire book. Take plywood, for instance, a family of products numerous and widely used. There may by now be people who have never seen a board.

Plywood is a fine and useful material, in its place. Cement and its family of aggregate building blocks is also a fine and useful material. Composite materials, with stiff skins of wood or metal bonded to insultative interiors, become constantly more numerous. There are so many kinds of manufactured materials that to review them with any honesty would keep us up all next year.

Boards and concrete, I repeat, remain the basic materials. The purpose of composite materials is to save labor. They themselves are more expensive per unit of strength. Boards and concrete, in the hands of the well-adjusted carpenter, will still give you the most structure for your money.

51. Notes on finishes

The word finish has many meanings. In a building, it means either to complete or to cover up. In making a machine, the word finish means degree of smoothness. In protecting a material, it means a chemical change or addition to that material's surface. In decorating a material, the word means to add a layer of some different material.

To reduce confusion, I will stick to building materials, dividing finishes into two classes, chemical and cosmetic. Cosmetic finishes generally have no ability to protect, except that they wear away and are renewed.

Steel rusts in the presence of oxygen. We paint it, and because the exclusion of oxygen is less than perfect, we paint it some more. The paint, being an added surface which effected no chemical change in the steel, didn't stop the oxidizing process, it just slowed it down. Some metals, such as aluminum, can be oxide stabilized, which is a chemical resurfacing.

Wood, our hero from the previous chapter, can be treated chemically to slow down rot. Chemicals can also be distasteful to insects, who go somewhere else and chew up somebody else's wood.

In the building business, when most people talk about finishes, they are discussing paint. Mostly, they are talking about putting paint on wood. They have been led to believe that wood requires "preservation," and that paint will do it.

There is the customary grain of truth in all this nonsense. Paint does offer mechanical protection against erosion. In four or five hundred years the action of wind, rain, sleet and hail can erode an inch board to half its original thickness. Or so they tell me. If you keep painting a board, what erodes away is the paint, and then you put on some more paint.

I have no objection to paint, used for cosmetic purposes. I do object to paint salesmen who tell me that paint is a preservative for wood. It isn't. It is not a chemical treatment, it's a decoration. If you want a board to be white, paint it white.

That is the only reason I know of for painting it at all.

Hold the paintbrush while I make one more point. Painting is like getting married; easier to do than undo. Once having painted, you and your progeny keep on painting forever. I have tried to make it clear that your house will not fall apart tomorrow if it isn't painted. Good enough. Now if you still want to paint, pick up your brush, and let's see how to do it right.

Essentially, paint is a mixture of oil and pigment. In the old days, linseed oil and white lead were the only ingredients, plus a little color if you didn't like white. Oil "wets" wood, so the mixture went on and stayed a while. A house painter, not being pressed to produce color in a twinkling, began with a first coat of plain oil, without pigment. His next coat included white lead and the whole thing stuck together. If you're going to paint at all, do a good job. The first coat should not include pigment.

Stain, another cosmetic treatment, is not as versatile as paint. It can change brilliance in only one direction; darker. You can change your mind and scrape paint off if you want to work hard enough. Stain is there to stay. Depending on how you feel about it, this can be a virtue or a fault. Once you have painted something, repainting is just around the corner, but you don't have to keep re-staining.

The subject of cosmetic finishes becomes clearer if we distinguish between sub-surface finish and re-surface finish.

Every finish has to be based on some kind of liquid carrier. If we begin by using nothing but that carrier, so much the better. For simplicity, let's call the carrier "oil." In this sketch, every bit of the oil soaked in a little way, with virtually

nothing remaining outside the original surface of the wood. Perhaps a second application will also soak in. It depends on what oil, and what wood.

The ability of any wood to accept any penetrant except water is limited. Somewhere around the third coat of oil part or most of it remains outside. If in the meantime we have begun to add pigment, with luck a little of that will pene trate along with the carrier. Most remains on the outside. As we move on toward a paint, which contains ground up solids, or a varnish, which is made of resins, we completely cover the original surface of the wood, establishing a new, or re-surface.

NEW SURFACE LAYER, INCLUDING PIGMENT

PENETRATED LAYER, MOSTLY CARRIER

BOARD

The wood purist contends, and I agree, that it is a mistake to create any finish outside of the wood itself. He argues, and I'm with him, that the re-surface is likely to be more susceptible to mechanical, chemical, or thermal damage than the original wood.

To make his point, the purist seizes upon varnish as a horrible example, pointing to your dining room table which has been varnished "to protect the wood." The varnish protects the wood all right, in the sense that a scratch is now a scratch in the varnish, not in the wood, and when a hot coffee cup or a cold beer can leaves a ring, the ring is not in the wood, but in the varnish. Varnish is much more susceptible to thermal and mechanical damage than wood. When the varnish has been damaged, you either buy a new table or remove the varnish and start over.

This is the same idea as our layer of paint, which protects the wood from erosion by itself becoming the thing which erodes.

The clearest argument against adding a new surface to wood is "Why bother?" Why not just go ahead and wear out the wood? It started out in life with a more tolerant surface than anything you can put on it.

To many people wood finishing becomes a game, a hobby, an end in itself. From the pipe smoker who rubs pipe on nose in order to coat the pipe with nose oil, to the furniture buff who has his own formulae for how many coats in be-tween what grades of garnet paper and when to switch from linseed to tung oil, each of the hobbyists derives his pleasure not so much from the results as from the work involved.

With the finish hobbyist I have no quarrel. There is a sensual pleasure in spreading paint, if you think so, or in sandpapering shellac, if you think so. Each hobbyists thinks his method is the best, and if he enjoys it, it is.

I seek only to ease the hobbyist's struggles by asking him to remember the difference between sub-surface, or penetrating finish, and re-surface, or coating finish. He will find life easier if he makes up his mind which he seeks. I ask him to be skeptical about any finish whose advertisers claim that it both penetrates and coats in one application. The chances are it doesn't do either particularly well.

I am, of course, a hobbyist myself. My hobby is not to spend money unnecessarily. On the sub-ject of finishes, my hobby expresses itself in eliminating as many finishes as possible. I carry it right down to none at all. It could be that my no-finish-at-all hobby will wind up saving you more money than any other single idea in this book.

Happily, I have been able to cross off all wood finishes whose advertised purpose is to "pre-serve."

With no hesitation I cross off all finishes ap-plied either to wood or metal for the purpose of increasing durability.

I am left with cosmetic finishes, simply making something a different color from what it was before, and therefore presumably more beautiful. This leaves us with purely aesthetic considerations, which are not debatable.

I have never been able to see anything wrong with the original color of maple, mahogany, walnut, pine, spruce, or oak. These colors, by the way, bear no resemblance to the stains for which their names have been borrowed by the finishing materials industry. It is my opinion that in every case where a wood's name has been borrowed to describe a color, the result has been not only different from, but less beautiful than the original.

All of these ill-named finishes prepared by the professional aestheticians have two things in common; they are all darker than their name-fathers, and they are all in some shade of brown; light brown, dark brown, yellow-brown, red-brown, gray-brown, or some-brown. In this respect the aestheticians are only imitating nature.

Wood does this all by itself. When left alone, any kind of wood goes toward a darker shade of brown, of some hue or another, depending on the kind of wood. Sunlight accelerates the process. Rain turns the color toward gray. A piece of wood left in alternating sunlight and rain will go through brown into gray, some kind of gray. The same piece exposed to sunlight but protected from rain will eventually turn a deep brown.

Here are three different house walls.

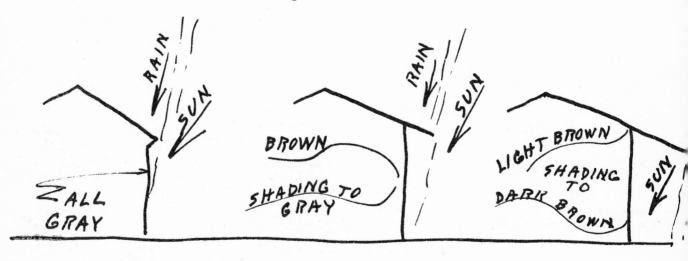

Sun and rain, gray. All sun, brown. A vertical board in the middle sketch would turn out like this—with brown at the top shading down to gray at the bottom. In the house sketch where the overhang has been moved out two feet farther, no rain to speak of falls on the siding. The resulting color is all brown, shading from light down to dark because of the difference in the amount of sun.

Inside the house, the same kind of coloring takes place, but in gentler fashion because there is less sun. My wife has cupboard doors which show the effect clearly. They are light tan at the top, shading smoothly to deeper tan at the bottom, that being the way the sun falls. The effect

of this gradation is pleasing; I wouldn't know how to duplicate it with paint.

Aesthetically, inside or outside, I think natural coloration has a mellowness and a textured beauty which no applied finish can achieve. On sight, ten out of ten visitors agree, except that five out of ten ask for the secret formula, refusing to believe that such beautiful colors just happened. Anything that handsome, say the skeptics, couldn't possibly have been had for nothing.

There happens to be a catch. The catch is that although these wonderful colors came for nothing, they did not arrive overnight. It takes two or three years, during which time one or the other of you may have decided to go live with mother.

This is where compliance comes in. Con yourselves into becoming hobbyists too. Go intellectual. Remember that "patina" is a synonym for well-mixed dirt. Ignore the guy who defines patina as dirt well-mixed by someone who lived a hundred years ago.

Start yourselves off with a coffee table or a kitchen counter which has no finish whatever. Explain to the neighbors that you are conducting an experiment in patina production. For the first few months you won't be happy, but stick with it. I guarantee that a year later you will be proud of your patina. The experiment will have consisted of an oversupply of spilled milk, gravy, cheese crumbs, cigarette burns, pipe ashes, goose liver, cream and sugar, numerous swipes from a soapy sponge, and the well-greased fingerprints of presumably laughing little children.

52. Notes on people

Some people I know were attracted by a site, then managed to persuade their chosen architect, a man of good reputation, to approve its purchase. Why he did this I don't know, because, squeezed between the site, his clients' notions, and his own desire not to lose the business, he wound up with the following impossible arrangement:

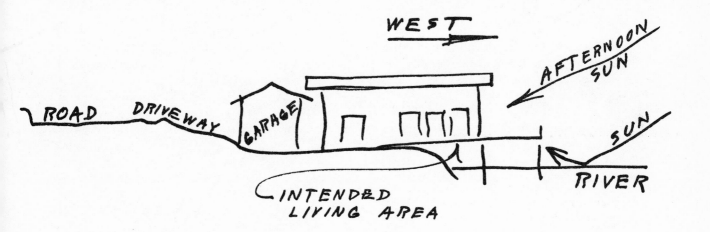

In summer, the afternoon sun, its impact almost doubled by reflection from the river, turns the all-glassed, west-facing end of the house into a furnace. In winter, the wind, whooping unimpeded down-river, makes it an icebox. The driveway runs from sun into perpetual winter shade cast by garage and house. Snow melts in the sun then re-freezes in the shade, creating an impassable glacier.

The moral of this story is not what you expect. Our protagonists just love their house. They have nothing but praise for the architect, who breathes a sigh of relief. When the living room gets too hot, well, what can you expect in summer so let's go out back for a breath of air. When it gets too cold, shucks, these modern houses do seem chilly but then everyone knows the winters are severe around here. As for the glaciated driveway, the garage is now happily converted to a playroom, and the family cars are parked down the road in a neighbor's barn.

There's nothing so wonderful as people. We can put up with anything. We can even put up with the consequences of our own folly, and in time come to believe that we intended things to be that way.

Man is the most adaptable creature on earth. He survives in swamp, jungle and mountain, tropic and arctic, desert, prairie and heath. He eats more different things than any other animal, and can keep going in greater extremes of temperature. He can live alone or with others. He can sleep or do without. Given a dinosaur to kill, he can kill it, and, given time enough, he can run down and capture a wild horse. Man, and this is not intended as a joke, can even survive on Madison Avenue.

The thing which makes man so adaptable is not his strength, which is puny, nor his digestive apparatus, which is defective, nor his physical armor, which is non-existent. His adaptability springs largely from his vast determination.

From the viewpoint of many technical disciplines, the vastness of this determination is unfortunate. To the architect, the unfortunate effect of determination is that it dulls awareness.

Place a dog and a man together on the side of a hill. The dog will know more than the man about how hot it is, where it would be cooler, whether the sun is shining, where the birds, bugs and field mice are and what they are doing, what branches are scraping together, where to find a drink of water, and which path leads toward home.

The dog's world teems with input data; sight, sound, odor and feeling. The man is much less aware of his immediate environment. While he enjoys a walk in the woods, his mind, larger than the dog's, is preoccupied with his larger world, which includes memories, hopes, predictions, and the constant need for decision.

What's the use, says the architect, in designing houses which are warm, dry, light, and quiet, if the people who are to live in them don't know the difference?

Man's ability to understand his environment depends largely upon five skills: he can see, hear, smell, feel, and think. Lack of skill in any one of these departments makes him less aware of environment. Some will say the heck with environment. Man would be happier not to know about it. I don't happen to agree.

Let's begin with our eyes, for most of us the greatest source of input data. We abuse our eyes by putting up with unnecessarily poor conditions. We give them too little light, or too much. We put up with glare. We arrange our work in shadow, then try to rest our eyes by looking into light.

The fellow I would like to help is the one who doesn't seem to be aware that his eyes are being maltreated. He has headaches, lines between his eyebrows, gets tired too quickly and can't do as much work as he would like. He thinks that a man's man should be able to put up with almost anything. He is determined to use the light he's got without making a fuss.

Next come our ears. Some of us are ear-skilled, receiving even more input data from our ears than from our eyes. We have no "ear-lids," and there is no rest for the weary ear. I can't but wonder if people realize how much of their fatigue comes either from excessively loud or excessively irritating sounds.

I have stood in an echoing hallway, the din in my ears almost intolerable, and said to the man next to me, "We must do something about the noise in this place." "What noise?" he says. I know that his ears are as good as mine, but his determined mind refuses to pay attention. "Listen," I say, and snap my fingers. "Good heavens," he cries, his attention captured. "That's awful!" Suddenly he is aware of the noise and consciously disturbed by it.

Have I done him a favor or not? Was he happier in his determination, or will he be happier in his awareness? I prefer to believe the latter, because once aware, he can avoid fatigue by doing something about it.

The absence of irritating noise is more difficult to demonstrate. First you have to show your neighbor what it is he doesn't like, then you take him into a different environment and ask him to appreciate that what he didn't like isn't there any more. One problem of the acoustical engineer is that the absence of noise is more difficult to recognize than its presence.

The human sense of smell, at best imperfect

and almost vestigial, supplies us with information about our environment which we interpret in an entirely subjective manner. Smell provides almost all of the information which we call taste. Taste is popularly supposed to warn us of food which is not good to eat. It doesn't do so at all. Taste is entirely a personal matter between us and what foods we have learned to enjoy.

Smell is also popularly supposed to warn us of dangerous breathing conditions. It doesn't do that either. Many lethal gases have no odor, including the very dangerous carbon monoxide produced by your automobile. Some dangerous, odorless gases have an artificial scent added to warn people of their presence.

Apart from danger, good smells and bad smells are a matter of personal preference, whether we are discussing salt air drifting in over the clam flats, an ounce of brandy swirled in a snifter, a drop more or less of perfume behind my lady's ears, or the odor of burnt steak—depending of course on whether it got burnt indoors or outdoors.

Furthermore, smell is commonly supposed to warn us of inadequate ventilation. Though my nose may tell me if the man in the next seat had a slice of onion on his hamburger, it will not tell me the oxygen content of the air I am breathing. Above minimum requirements, ventilation is extremely subjective. Some like the wind blowing in their faces, others can't stand even an imagined draft. Many insist on sleeping with the window open, a practice which our grandparents firmly believed to be unhealthy.

Below minimum ventilation requirements, the nose gives no warning. All you do is get sleepy. This is not a reliable indicator. Many other things, such as having been out too late the night before, may also make you sleepy. Fortunately, most houses are pretty leaky and not until the crowd begins to gather do we need to be concerned.

Aside from lack of sleep, the most common cause of getting sleepy is to feel warm, but the sense of feeling is impossible to define. We feel local pain, indigestion, headache, hangnails, and sometimes we just don't feel good. Our fingertips can feel the difference between a dime and a nickel, and in a handshake my hand can feel whether your hand is wet or dry. Sometimes I don't feel like going out tonight, but if I go I feel that I ought to wear my new jacket.

Architecturally speaking, let us narrow this welter of assorted kinds of feeling down to feeling warm and feeling cold. I doubt that the working architect has any greater problem. Many people simply don't know whether they are warm or cold. Of a winter day I have seen two men on my sundeck, one stripped and sweating so hard he had to give up and look for protection from the heat. The other, wearing sweater, jacket, and overcoat, shivered and waited for the moment he would be allowed to go inside to breathe some warmed air. Which was right? I have to admit that both were right, and am forced to the reluctant conclusion that many people "feel" by the calendar and not by the nerve endings in their skin.

It has to do, I guess, with the mind, which is man's last but overriding sense. Unlike the dog and the cat, who know without being told which corner is warm and which is cold, man has a mind so determined that it can inhibit or distort his senses.

Though he controls his sources of light, he can remain determined to do without.

Knowing how to manipulate sound, he can allow himself to remain assailed by noise.

Possessed of the means for making and controlling heat, he can persuade himself to tolerate thermal discomfort.

Man's social habits have led him to accept his self-imposed discomforts. Many people think environment should not be mentioned in polite society. It is at home, where much of our time is spent, that we can freely admit whether we are comfortable or not.

Birds build nests in chosen places, with no two exactly alike. I wonder if they are not seeking for themselves and their children something a little better than the neighbors possess.

Our architecture is the attempt to express in stone, wood, and metal what we, the people, think we are. I am convinced that if we ourselves can once decide what we are, and what we want, the design of our houses will express these decisions.

What we are seeking is more than the perfect house. It is ourselves.

SUMMARY

I have tried to answer these questions:

WHAT is your engineered house?

Your house is a place for your family to meet, love, work, play, wash, dress, greet, eat, and sleep.

To perform these tasks comfortably, your house needs to be warm, dry, light, quiet, clean, useful, spacious, pleasant, and paid for.

Your house is a structure which shelters you, and a machine which works for you. In your lifetime, you will spend more effort and money on your house than on anything else. What you get for this expenditure depends on you, on your ability to decide what you do and do not need.

WHERE shall it be?

If your house is to please you, its location is the most important decision you will have to make. It is a large world. Your house should have plenty of room around it. How much room it takes to make you feel comfortable in your house depends on your tastes and attitudes.

WHEN shall it be built?

Within the time of your life, build early rather than late. Then build again if you are so minded. It helps, but is not necessary, to have a settled job location, and it helps to have some cash in hand. You need time, a year or two, for site selection and for planning. You will benefit by choosing an off-peak time of year for building.

HOW will it be built?

The habit of building a house in a certain way is not proof that the habit should be continued. There are no building habits that cannot be improved. Many of our present building methods are wrong, expensively wrong. I have tried to suggest building techniques which are inexpensively right.

WHY will you build it?

Because only by building your house can it be uniquely yours. Because only by building it can you seize at least the opportunity of saving a lot of money.

WHO are you?

You are a person who wants your house to be the visible expression of yourself. You want your house to tell the world who you are.

These ambitions can be realized with economy. In building your own house, you will question style, you will profit by technology, you will spend your effort for what you want rather than what you think the neighbors want you to have, or what the advertisers say you should have.

You know by experience that most houses are uncomfortable, too small, too expensive. These are not for you.

You can build a comfortable house by learning the technology of heat, light, sound, and movement. This is called human engineering, the human in this case being you.

You can build an inexpensive house by surrounding yourself with handsome structure rather than applied decoration. Avoiding non-structural decoration will cut the cost of your house, however big it may be, in half.

You can build a large house by remembering that some areas in a house are costly, some are not. You will establish your minimum requirements for expensive areas, then create living space in the less expensive rooms out back.

You will engineer your own house. The purpose of engineering is to arrive at an improved result. The method of engineering is to ask why. Why is it the way it is? Why can't it be done better?

While you engineer your house, keep asking why. Why do I need this? Why not spend my money for something I want?

"Why do I want a house?" This is the most important question of all. I hope, when your house is built, that my suggestions will have helped you answer it.

Planbook

A Village House

Many people, for many reasons of their own, want to live in town. If that is your pleasure, here are some of the considerations which will influence your planning.

You do not regard architectural conformity as a prime essential in your living plan, but neither do you wish to startle or offend. If conformity can be had at a reasonable price, you prefer it. Since you are to live in close proximity to your neighbors, you want to play, as far as your convenience will permit, by your neighborhood's aesthetic rules.

The area available to you will be small, and surrounded by firmly established families. They will welcome you as a newcomer, junior grade.

In the usual property line, or "lot" plan, the depth of your property as measured away from the street will be somewhat greater than its frontage. The neighboring houses will be closer to yours along the sides of the property than at the back.

Street and property lines once were laid out to include a handy convention called the "alley," which was in effect a back door street between two front door streets. The alley permitted a house to have a back and a front. With the passing of the alley, the "back of the house" has vanished. Everything is now presented to the street side of the house, including gas, water, electricity, sewage facilities, parcel delivery trucks, repair men, garbage men, bill collectors, trash collectors, milk men, mail men, grocery men, asphalt driveway salesmen, and, stumbling through this welter, the community association arriving for its afternoon meeting. Your village house has four sides. but one side, still sometimes called the front, usually is asked to do all the work.

Much of your work and play will be indoors. Your house in a village setting will have to be larger for a given amount of family activity than it would have been in a more secluded spot. For outdoor loafing areas, you will want a reasonable though not unfriendly amount of screening.

Loafing is a lost cause if too many people watch you do it.

If at all possible, you will want to avoid the conventional driveway aimed straight at your garage door. Courtesy to your guests requires off-street parking, but without the necessity of moving two cars to get a third one out. In snow country, the snowplow certainly must not dead-end at the garage.

Ideal orientation of your house to the sun's movements may be difficult because of space limitations, zoning rules, set-back and boundary line clearance. If so, your interior plan, which is controlled by no regulations, can be arranged to adjust the family's movements to the sun.

All of these considerations will cause you to pack a lot of functions into a relatively small land area. This is not as difficult as it may sound. Most of the questions suggest their own answers.

If the question is conformity, from the street your house will not appear much different from those on either side. There probably won't be any "front" door. A drive-in area will lead eye, auto, and foot to a "middle" door, observable from the kitchen window, which is the center of the whole plan.

Since the street side has all the utilities, the "barn" functions will be there. Social functions will be mid-way, just beyond the drive-in area, and private functions will be far away. Outdoor functions will remain somewhat formal, related generally to indoor facilities. For example, the dedicated gardener will find it pleasant to spend more of his time in a greenhouse, from which the outdoors is available at his convenience.

It is all fairly simple. If you will lay aside your previous conceptions of how a street-fronted house should be arranged on the inside, your village house will practically design itself. Here is a sample. Though it is only a sample, it may serve to indicate how you can achieve an extremely useful house on something less than half an acre.

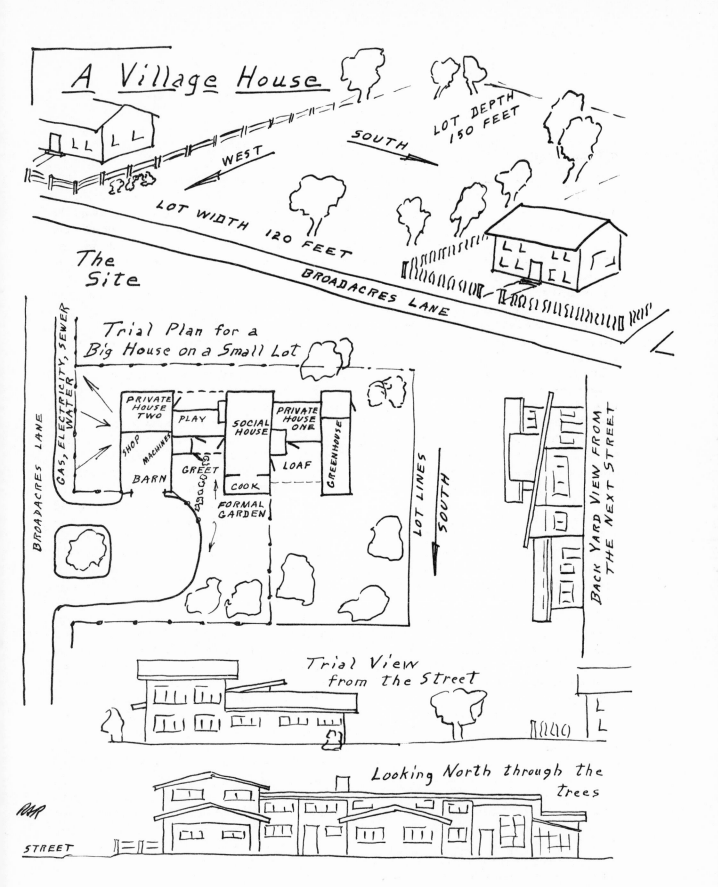

A Village House

The Site

LOT DEPTH 150 FEET

SOUTH

WEST

LOT WIDTH 120 FEET

BROADACRES LANE

Trial Plan for a
Big House on a Small Lot

BROADACRES LANE

GAS, ELECTRICITY, SEWER WATER

PRIVATE HOUSE TWO

PLAY

SOCIAL HOUSE

PRIVATE HOUSE ONE

GREENHOUSE

SHOP

MACHINES

BARN

GREET

LOAF

COOK

FORMAL GARDEN

LOT LINES SOUTH

Back Yard View from the Next Street

Trial View from the Street

Looking North through the Trees

STREET

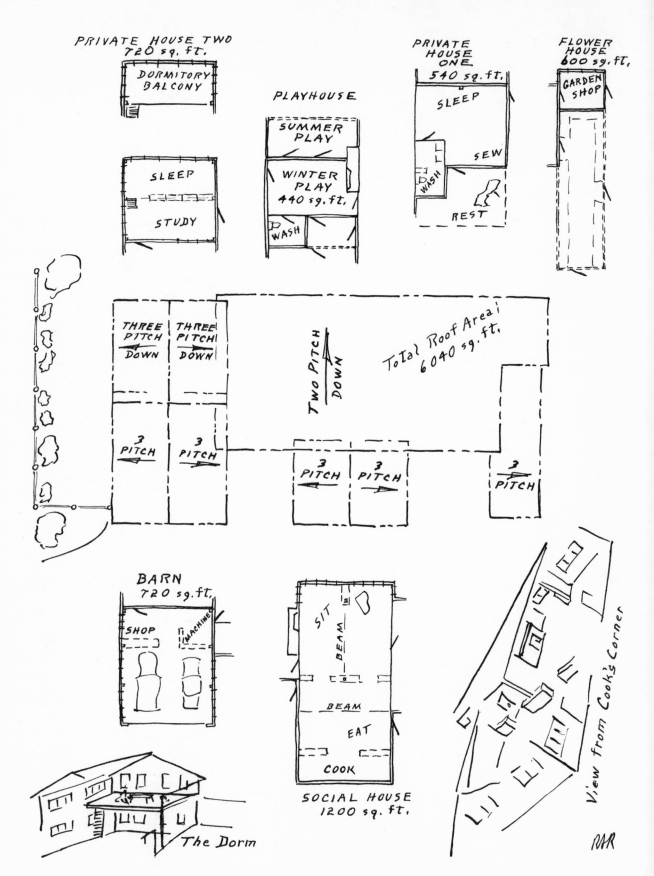

PRIVATE HOUSE TWO
720 sq. ft.

DORMITORY BALCONY

SLEEP

STUDY

PLAYHOUSE

SUMMER PLAY

WINTER PLAY
440 sq. ft.

WASH

PRIVATE HOUSE ONE
540 sq. ft.

SLEEP

SEW

WASH

REST

FLOWER HOUSE
600 sq. ft.

GARDEN SHOP

THREE PITCH DOWN

THREE PITCH DOWN

TWO PITCH DOWN

Total Roof Area
6040 sq. ft.

3 PITCH

3 PITCH

3 PITCH

3 PITCH

3 PITCH

BARN
720 sq. ft.

SHOP

MACHINE

SIT

BEAM

BEAM

EAT

COOK

SOCIAL HOUSE
1200 sq. ft.

The Dorm

View from Cook's Corner

RAR

212

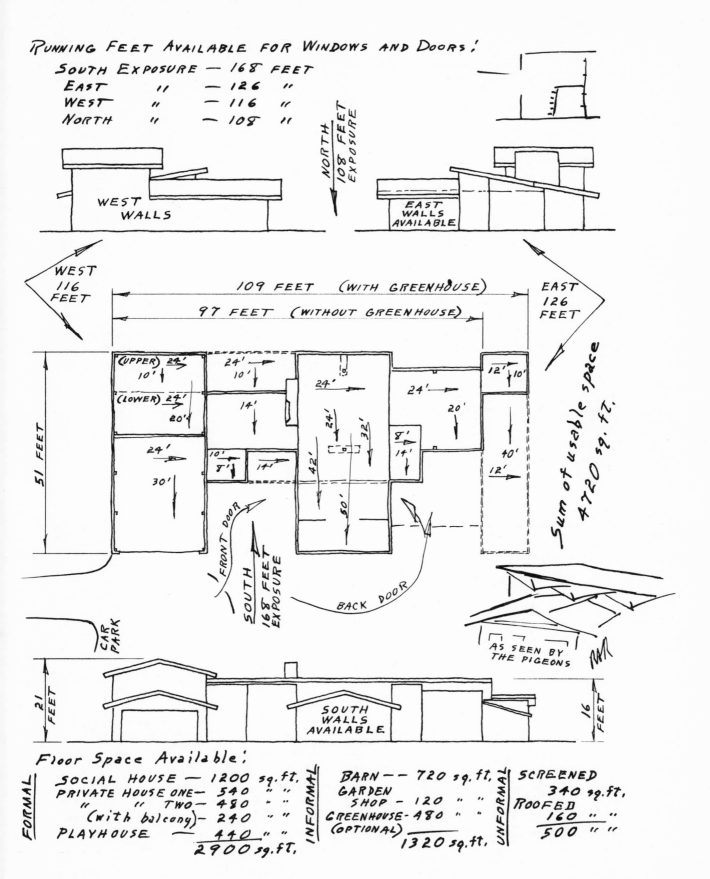

Running Feet Available for Windows and Doors:

South Exposure — 168 Feet
East   "   — 126 "
West   "   — 116 "
North   "   — 108 "

WEST WALLS

EAST WALLS AVAILABLE

NORTH 108 FEET EXPOSURE

WEST 116 FEET

109 FEET (WITH GREENHOUSE)
97 FEET (WITHOUT GREENHOUSE)

EAST 126 FEET

Sum of usable space 4720 sq. ft.

(UPPER) 24' 10'
(LOWER) 24' 20'
24' 10'
14'
24'
42' 50' 32'
24'
8' 14'
24' 20'
12' 10'
40' 12'
24' 30'
10' 8' 14'

51 FEET

FRONT DOOR

SOUTH 168 FEET EXPOSURE

BACK DOOR

AS SEEN BY THE PIGEONS

CAR PARK

21 FEET

SOUTH WALLS AVAILABLE.

16 FEET

Floor Space Available:

FORMAL
SOCIAL HOUSE — 1200 sq. ft.
PRIVATE HOUSE ONE — 540 " "
   "   "   TWO — 480 " "
   (with balcony) — 240 " "
PLAYHOUSE — 440 " "
            2900 sq. ft.

INFORMAL
BARN — — 720 sq. ft.
GARDEN
  SHOP - 120 " "
GREENHOUSE- 480 " "
(OPTIONAL)
            1320 sq. ft.

UNFORMAL
SCREENED
     340 sq. ft.
ROOFED
     160 " "
     500 " "

A Valleyside House

Every year good house sites are harder to come by. Still, the chances are that right in Briggsville there are many excellent spots which have been overlooked. Some of them are only a mile from the center of town.

You remember that in order to find something you want at a reasonable price, you will look for what other people aren't looking for. Most people believe that a house site above the road is preferable to one below the road. Therefore, if you want to find a site close to town, you will look below the road. The garages will be at road level in either case. In both cases, you will want to present a reasonably conventional facade to the street. What you do as the valleyside drops away and becomes the intervale is your business. Privacy in which to indulge your personal whimsies is easier to find below the road than above it.

Another virtue of the valleyside house is that water seldom flows over the tops of hills. It always finds its way into the valleys, having made them in the first place. The chances are there will be some water, either visible or available, in the vale below your valleyside house.

Here are some of the things to be considered.

As you approach the bottom of a valley, the climate gets more severe. Cold nights are colder, and hot days are hotter. Never put a house in the extreme bottom of a valley if you can avoid it. A moderate amount of air drainage makes for a moderate climate.

Consider the possibility of flooding, and stay above the flood line. That is not hard to determine. If the area being drained through your valley is only a few square miles, you have no problem. If it is a million square miles, go somewhere else.

We all like water, and lush meadows, and so do mosquitoes. In the early evening at the valleyside house you will live on your screened porch.

From the road, your house will not look imposing. The passerby will not get the full treatment at a glance. Many people, including me, regard this as a virtue rather than a fault.

Compass orientation of a valleyside house is extremely important, because possible barriers to sun slope and air flow are to be avoided. A valleyside facing south or southeast is much the best; east retains many virtues; west or southwest valley slopes are tricky but can be fine if your interior arrangement takes account of the problems; north is—well, nothing is impossible, but for the same amount of ingenuity and effort I think you will be happier elsewhere.

Here is a trial design in which I suggest essentially two separate houses, a little one on the road and a big one facing the vale. My sketch suggests that in the roadside house you could have a workshop or run a business, undisturbed by the presence of your family some fifty feet away. You will notice that what I have called the office need not be built at all. Starting from the garage you reach the valleyside through a screened path. The length, direction, and elevation levels of this path are determined by what you want and how the land lies.

The valleyside house components can be built as and when you like, undisturbed by passersby or immediate neighbors. I have suggested that the two-level section be put up first. It is very expensive to add height to an existing building. As your family or your income grows, add single-level extensions at each end. Increasing length can be achieved any time, with no dollar penalty, if you have laid your plans for this extension in advance.

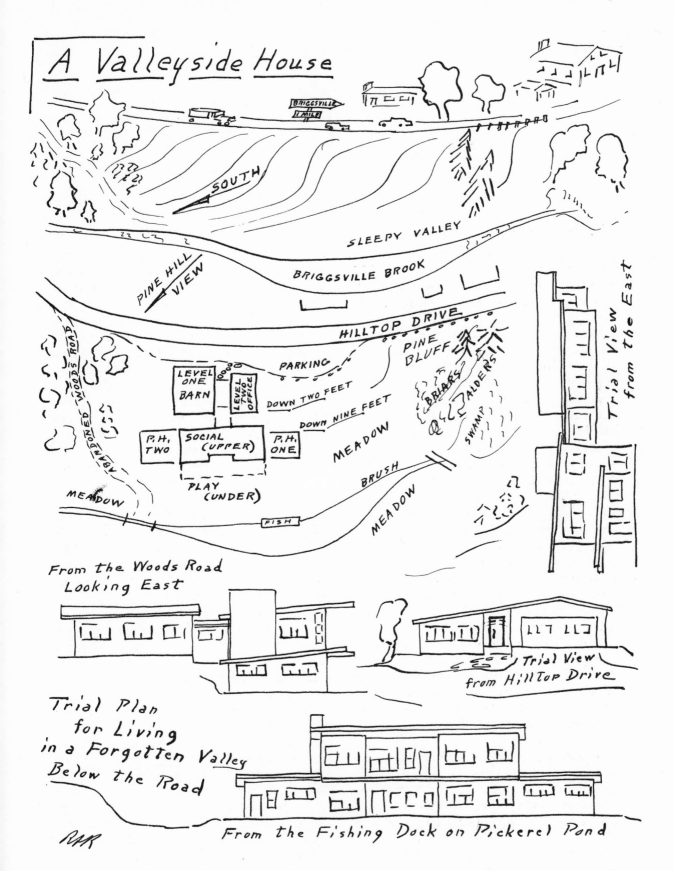

A Valleyside House

BRIGGSVILLE 1 MILE

SOUTH

SLEEPY VALLEY

BRIGGSVILLE BROOK

PINE HILL VIEW

HILLTOP DRIVE

Trial View from the East

PARKING

LEVEL ONE BARN

LEVEL TWO OFFICE

DOWN TWO FEET

DOWN NINE FEET

PINE BLUFF

BRIARS

ALDERS

SWAMP

MEADOW

P.H. TWO

SOCIAL (UPPER)

P.H. ONE

MEADOW

BRUSH

PLAY (UNDER)

MEADOW

FISH

MEADOW

ABANDONED WOODS ROAD

From the Woods Road Looking East

Trial View from Hilltop Drive

Trial Plan for Living in a Forgotten Valley Below the Road

From the Fishing Dock on Pickerel Pond

RAK

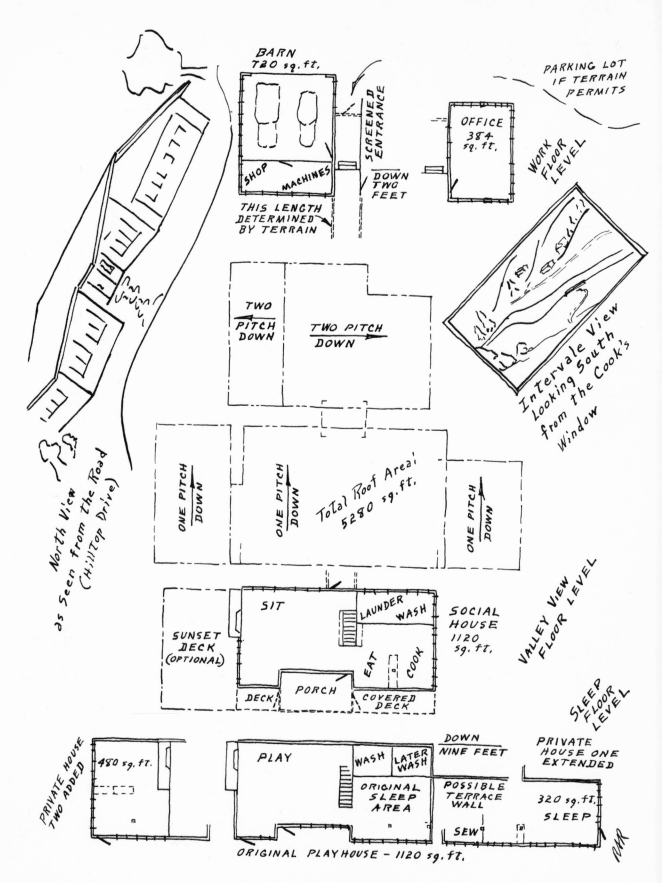

BARN
720 sq.ft.

PARKING LOT
IF TERRAIN
PERMITS

SHOP

MACHINES

SCREENED
ENTRANCE

DOWN
TWO
FEET

THIS LENGTH
DETERMINED
BY TERRAIN

OFFICE
384
sq.ft.

WORK
FLOOR
LEVEL

North View
as Seen from the Road
(Hilltop Drive)

TWO
PITCH
DOWN

TWO PITCH
DOWN

Intervale View
Looking South
from the Cook's
Window

ONE PITCH
DOWN

ONE PITCH
DOWN

Total Roof Area
5280 sq.ft.

ONE PITCH
DOWN

SIT

LAUNDER

WASH

SOCIAL
HOUSE
1120
sq.ft.

VALLEY VIEW
FLOOR LEVEL

SUNSET
DECK
(OPTIONAL)

EAT

COOK

DECK

PORCH

COVERED
DECK

SLEEP
FLOOR
LEVEL

PRIVATE HOUSE
TWO ADDED

480 sq.ft.

PLAY

WASH

LATER
WASH

DOWN
NINE FEET

PRIVATE
HOUSE ONE
EXTENDED

ORIGINAL
SLEEP
AREA

POSSIBLE
TERRACE
WALL

320 sq.ft.
SLEEP

SEW

ORIGINAL PLAYHOUSE - 1120 sq.ft.

216

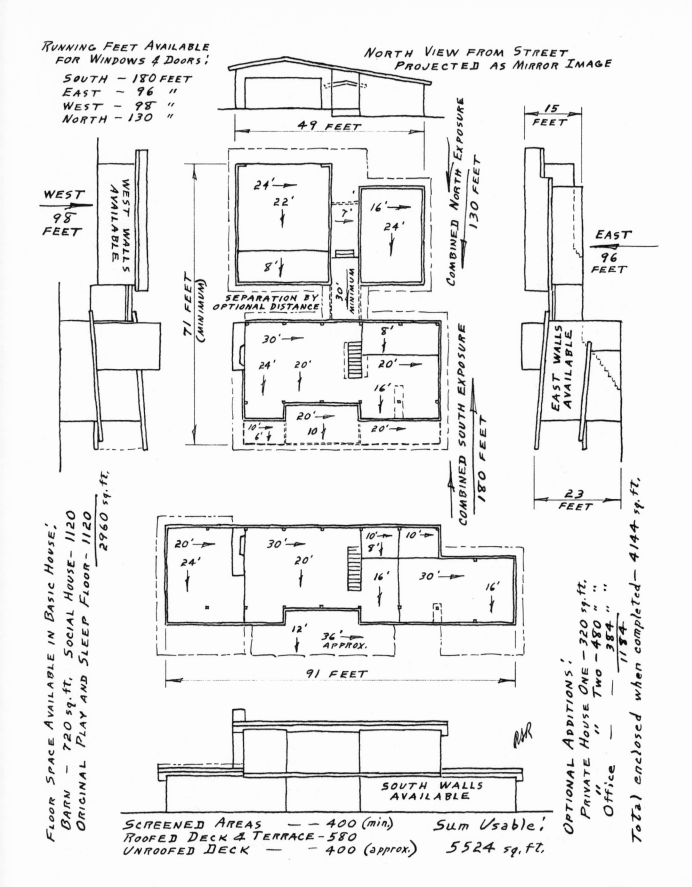

RUNNING FEET AVAILABLE
FOR WINDOWS & DOORS:

SOUTH — 180 FEET
EAST — 96 "
WEST — 98 "
NORTH — 130 "

NORTH VIEW FROM STREET
PROJECTED AS MIRROR IMAGE

49 FEET

15 FEET

WEST
98
FEET

WEST WALLS AVAILABLE

24'
22'
8'

16'
24'

7'

COMBINED NORTH EXPOSURE 130 FEET

30' MINIMUM

SEPARATION BY OPTIONAL DISTANCE

71 FEET (MINIMUM)

EAST
96
FEET

EAST WALLS AVAILABLE

30'
24' 20'
20'
16'
10' 6' 10'
20' 10' 20'
8'

COMBINED SOUTH EXPOSURE 180 FEET

23 FEET

FLOOR SPACE AVAILABLE IN BASIC HOUSE:
BARN — 720 sq. ft. SOCIAL HOUSE— 1120
ORIGINAL PLAY AND SLEEP FLOOR— 1120
2960 sq. ft.

20'
24'
30'
20'
10' 8'
10'
16'
30'
16'
12'
36' APPROX.

91 FEET

SOUTH WALLS AVAILABLE

SCREENED AREAS — — 400 (min.)
ROOFED DECK & TERRACE — 580
UNROOFED DECK — — 400 (approx.)

SUM USABLE:
5524 sq. ft.

OPTIONAL ADDITIONS:
PRIVATE HOUSE ONE — 320 sq. ft.
" " TWO —480 " "
" Office — 384 " "
1184

Total enclosed when completed — 4144 sq. ft.

217

A Hillside House

This sketch of a hillside house is offered with the firm reminder that it is only one of a million possible arrangements. Nowhere are there any two hillsides with the same aspect, slope, road location, wind, rain, and sun slant, or the same near, middle, and long view scenery. Nor are there any two hillsides with the same zoning regulations, tax assessors, neighbors with or without horses, school bus stops, ground or piped water, proximity to the fire station, or reliability of electric power line maintenance.

One thing about hillside building is that it is impossible, sensibly, to make any two houses alike. It is expensive to remodel a hillside. It saves money to do your remodeling with pencil and paper, that is, re-plan your house and leave the inexorably unique hillside alone.

Hillsides can be exploited architecturally in many different ways. Given any slope—westward, for instance—you can go up or across, advance toward the road or retreat from it, put the entrance where you please, the lawn where you want it, locate the sunset to suit you, build the house on one level or let it climb the slope, and find the view from wherever you have decided to put yourself in order to look at it.

If you have an east or south slope, read the same remarks and fill your sketchbook with possible orientations, all beginning with the direction of slope. Given a north slope, continue to read the same remarks but reduce your expectations. A good house can be built on a north slope, but because your orientation options have diminished your ingenuity has to increase.

Here are some points to consider about a hillside house. Most of them are in one way or another involved with our tendency to make too much of a good thing.

A little way up the hill you will find plenty of air drainage and a moderate climate. At the very top of the hill, as at the bottom, the climate gets severe. There is too much wind, too much rain, and too much work to get there.

It is difficult to choose the right location on a hillside. When you stand with your feet in the grass, remember that your line of sight is many feet lower than it will be when you stand inside your completed house. A few vertical feet make a big difference in what you see. Please bring a stepladder. Then you won't site your house much farther up the hill than it need be.

Vertical distance is costly in leg work, especially if you're carrying groceries. It also reduces water availability. If you're buying water from a pipe, every vertical foot costs you half a pound per square inch in water pressure at the faucet.

That man who mows the grass will know that a moderate slope of moderate length is easy to work on and easy to maintain. A steep slope, or a long one, once disturbed, will give you no end of erosion trouble.

Your hillside house may require two driveways and two parking areas, the upper for convenience and the lower for weather emergencies.

If you live in snow country, remember that a hillside house (above the road) is harder to reach than a valleyside house (below the road), because a snowplow coming to clear your driveway prefers to make its first pass downhill.

In this sketch, I have used five ground floor levels. For its size, this house achieves a maximum of south wall. It also achieves maximum privacy at a minimum of exterior surface. Four of the five levels are connected by what I call the communication porch. Though it may take you a while to get used to this idea, it has many virtues. Stairways, which chew up expensive inside footage to achieve nothing but going up and down, are here located in a sort of quasi-outside.

Whatever we call this design, it's cheaper than many. It permits the entering guest to get under cover quickly, then take his choice of which door he wants to enter. Also it's the only way I know to eliminate the fire danger of sleeping on an "upper" floor.

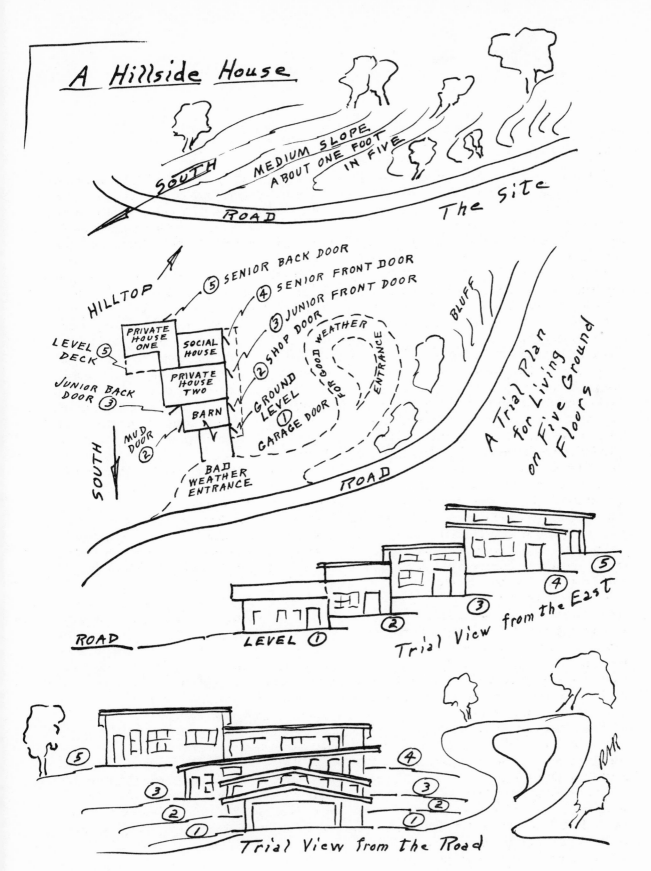

A Hillside House

SOUTH MEDIUM SLOPE. ABOUT ONE FOOT IN FIVE

ROAD

The Site

HILLTOP

⑤ SENIOR BACK DOOR

④ SENIOR FRONT DOOR

③ JUNIOR FRONT DOOR

② SHOP DOOR

PRIVATE HOUSE ONE

SOCIAL HOUSE

LEVEL DECK ⑤

PRIVATE HOUSE TWO

JUNIOR BACK DOOR ③

BARN

SOUTH

MUD DOOR ②

GROUND LEVEL ①

GARAGE DOOR FOR GOOD WEATHER

ENTRANCE

BLUFF

BAD WEATHER ENTRANCE

ROAD

A Trial Plan for Living on Five Ground Floors

ROAD   LEVEL ①   ② ③ ④ ⑤

Trial View from the East

⑤ ④ ③ ② ①

Trial View from the Road

RMR

219

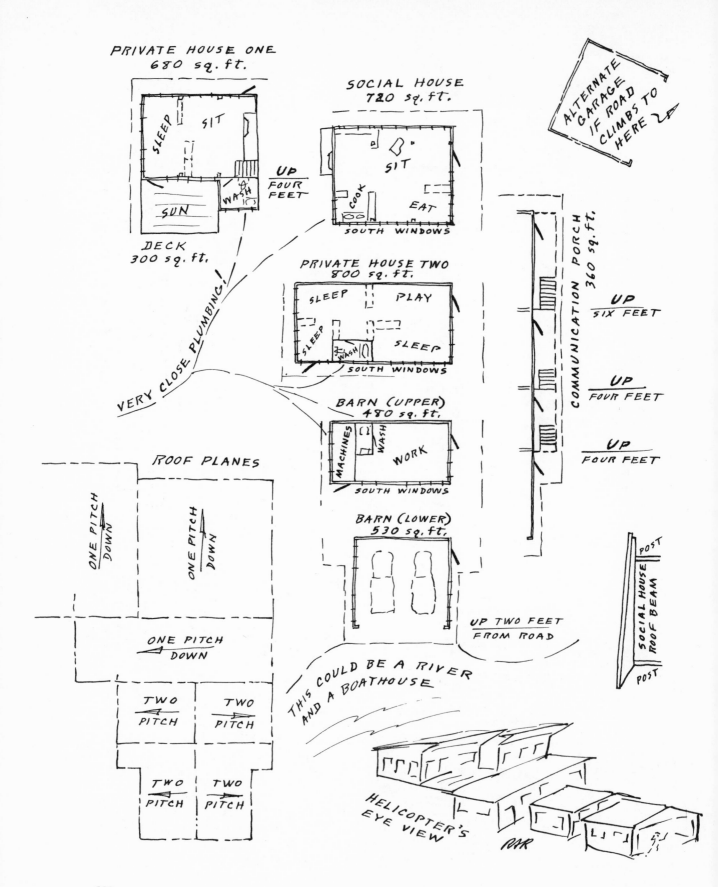

PRIVATE HOUSE ONE
680 sq. ft.

SLEEP   SIT

WASH

SUN

UP
FOUR
FEET

DECK
300 sq. ft.

SOCIAL HOUSE
720 sq. ft.

SIT

COOK   EAT

SOUTH WINDOWS

ALTERNATE GARAGE IF ROAD CLIMBS TO HERE

VERY CLOSE PLUMBING!

PRIVATE HOUSE TWO
800 sq. ft.

SLEEP   PLAY

SLEEP   WASH   SLEEP

SOUTH WINDOWS

BARN (UPPER)
480 sq. ft.

MACHINES   WASH   WORK

SOUTH WINDOWS

BARN (LOWER)
530 sq. ft.

UP TWO FEET
FROM ROAD

COMMUNICATION PORCH
360 sq. ft.

UP
SIX FEET

UP
FOUR FEET

UP
FOUR FEET

ROOF PLANES

ONE PITCH DOWN   ONE PITCH DOWN

ONE PITCH DOWN

TWO PITCH   TWO PITCH

TWO PITCH   TWO PITCH

THIS COULD BE A RIVER AND A BOATHOUSE

SOCIAL HOUSE ROOF BEAM
POST
POST

HELICOPTER'S EYE VIEW

RPR

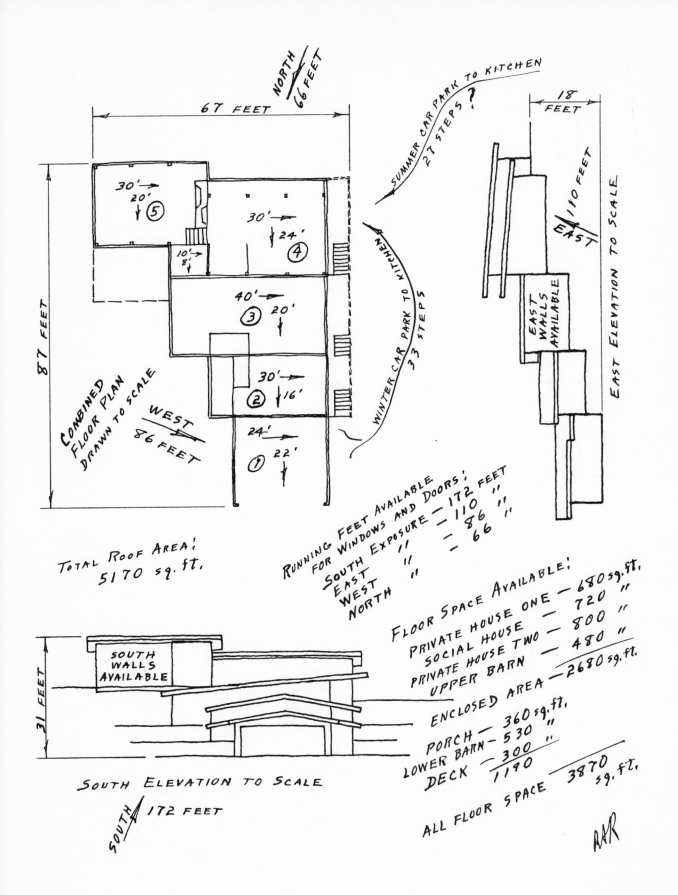

NORTH
66 FEET

67 FEET

87 FEET

SUMMER CAR PARK TO KITCHEN
27 STEPS ?

18 FEET

110 FEET

EAST

EAST ELEVATION TO SCALE

EAST WALLS AVAILABLE

30' →
20' ↓
⑤

30' →
24' ↓
④

10' →
8' ↓

40' →
20' ↓
③

30' →
16' ↓
②

24' →
22' ↓
①

WINTER CAR PARK TO KITCHEN
33 STEPS

COMBINED FLOOR PLAN DRAWN TO SCALE

WEST
86 FEET

TOTAL ROOF AREA:
5170 sq. ft.

RUNNING FEET AVAILABLE
FOR WINDOWS AND DOORS:
SOUTH EXPOSURE — 172 FEET
EAST   "   — 110 "
WEST   "   — 86   "
NORTH   "   — 66   "

FLOOR SPACE AVAILABLE:
PRIVATE HOUSE ONE — 680 sq. ft.
SOCIAL HOUSE   — 720   "
PRIVATE HOUSE TWO — 800   "
UPPER BARN   — 480   "
ENCLOSED AREA — 2680 sq. ft.

PORCH — 360 sq. ft.
LOWER BARN — 530   "
DECK — 300   "
1190

ALL FLOOR SPACE 3870 sq. ft.

SOUTH WALLS AVAILABLE

31 FEET

SOUTH ELEVATION TO SCALE
SOUTH 172 FEET

AAR

A Waterside House

Out of a hundred people who came to me wanting to buy land, ninety-nine of them insisted that they wanted to be on water of some kind, the only difference between them being in the amount of water they had in mind. Their understandably atavistic desires, ranging all the way from a bird bath to an ocean, have been expressed in the way our populations have always arranged themselves in some fashion between land and water.

Water is fluid-soft, flowing, buoyant, beautiful, and dangerous. No wonder we love it. Fluid water, our stuff of life, having apparently no will of its own, is able to fit comfortably into any container until it gets excited. No wonder we admire it. We like to look at it from far and near, listen to it, swim in it, float on it for work or pleasure in everything from kayak to liner. Man has always been willing to risk its dangers to gain its bounty.

The dedicated watersider can't get close enough to the water to suit him. His numbers are growing rapidly. There doesn't seem to be enough waterside to go around, so the buyer must travel farther to find water room. Oceansides near population centers have become marine apartment houses. The first trick in finding waterside may be to leave the ocean to its lovers and look for inland water instead. In terms of water frontage, there's a lot more of it.

The next trick may be to find a piece of waterside that didn't look too good to the rest of the folks. This is where your imagination becomes important. The more obviously good sites will already be occupied. You will look for the good ones which aren't so obvious.

Almost everything you will have to consider in a waterside house will originate in one way or another with the water itself. For one thing, the waterside may be crowded, yet to enjoy the water you will need to design your house for reasonable privacy. I would rather have the only house on a small pond than one of hundreds on a big one. How you may feel about it is another matter.

Some of your water neighbors, if there are any, will be addicted to thunderously high powered outboard engines. They present a problem to those in search of acoustic repose. If you yourself find your repose in the making of a loud noise, no criticism from me, but also no comment.

If the body of water is large, you will be buffeted by wind, but favored with moderate extremes of temperature, the water itself being a thermal reservoir. If your water is at the bottom of a narrow valley, your winds will be less violent, but the high-low temperature variation will be greater.

Your most serious consideration will be water level. I know of no body of water that maintains an exactly constant level. In most cases there will be discernible flood marks. You must, of course, stay above these. Possible low water may then be inconveniently far down. The most dependable water level is found in a good sized pond with controlled outlet and not much drainage area above it. One of the least dependable situations is on a large river. The house sketched here is not suggested for such a setting. It is also not suggested for those oceanside areas which have extreme tidal range. These special problems can be solved comfortably enough, but in other ways.

One nice thing about my trial sketch is that car park and boat are separated by three jumps of a teen-ager. Another goal I pursued in sketching was relative family privacy from the neighbors, yet the opportunity for family members to be relatively private from each other when they wish.

You will notice that private house two can contain either boat stalls or bedrooms or any combination thereof, as you wish. In fact, you don't have to build that part of the house at all until you get around to it. Structurally, it's a completely separate entity.

A Waterside House

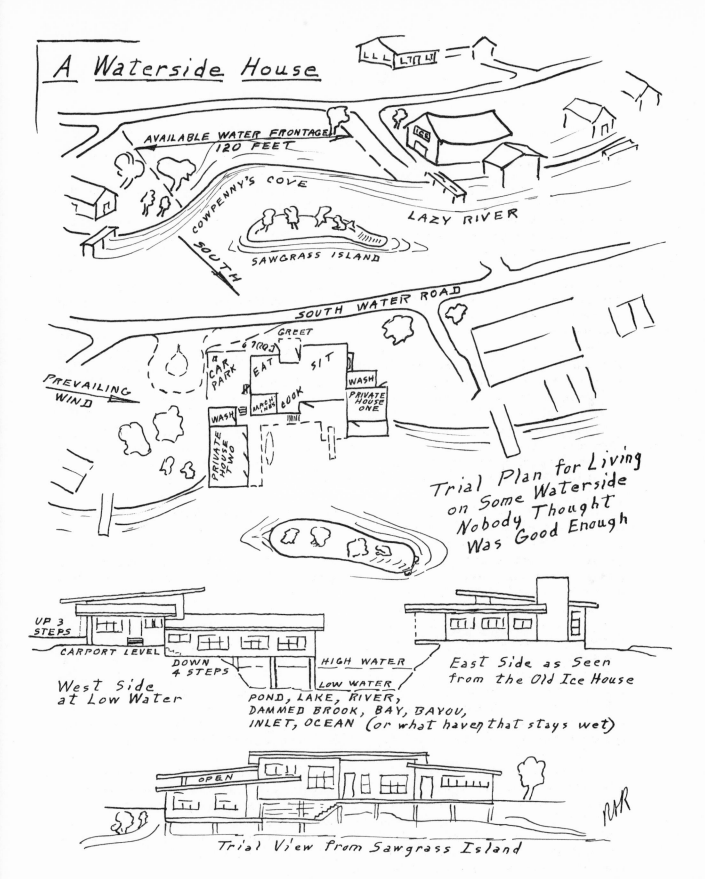

AVAILABLE WATER FRONTAGE 120 FEET

COWPENNY'S COVE

LAZY RIVER

SOUTH

SAWGRASS ISLAND

SOUTH WATER ROAD

PREVAILING WIND

GREET

CAR PARK

EAT

SIT

COOK

MACHINES

WASH

WASH

PRIVATE HOUSE ONE

PRIVATE HOUSE TWO

Trial Plan for Living on Some Waterside Nobody Thought Was Good Enough

UP 3 STEPS

CARPORT LEVEL

DOWN 4 STEPS

HIGH WATER

LOW WATER

West Side at Low Water

East Side as Seen from the Old Ice House

POND, LAKE, RIVER, DAMMED BROOK, BAY, BAYOU, INLET, OCEAN (or what have you that stays wet)

OPEN

Trial View from Sawgrass Island

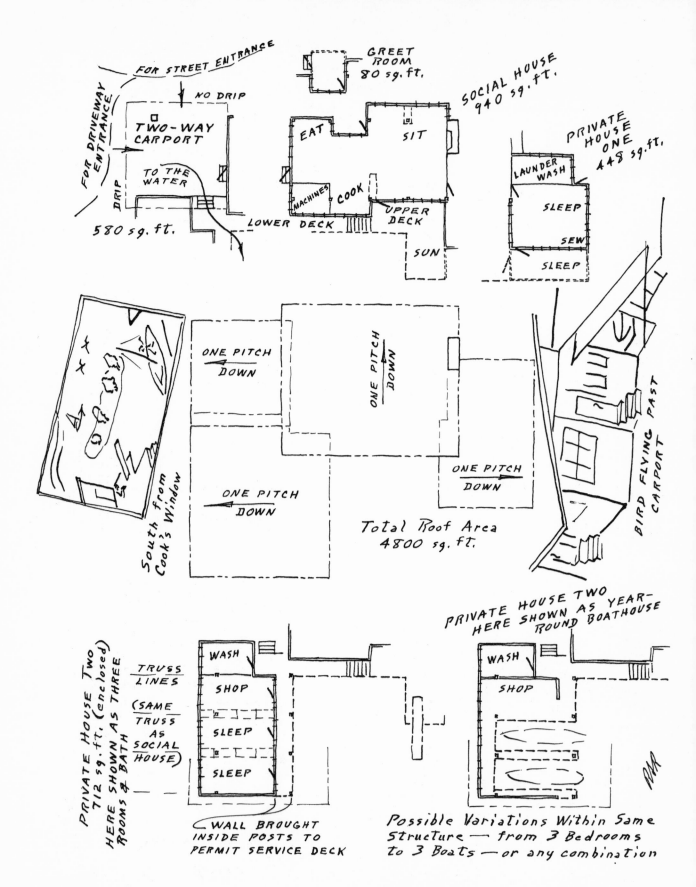

FOR STREET ENTRANCE

FOR DRIVEWAY ENTRANCE

NO DRIP

DRIP

GREET ROOM 80 sq. ft.

TWO-WAY CARPORT

TO THE WATER

580 sq. ft.

SOCIAL HOUSE 940 sq. ft.

EAT

SIT

MACHINES COOK

LOWER DECK

UPPER DECK

SUN

PRIVATE HOUSE ONE 448 sq. ft.

LAUNDER WASH

SLEEP

SEW

SLEEP

South from Cook's Window

ONE PITCH DOWN

ONE PITCH DOWN

ONE PITCH DOWN

ONE PITCH DOWN

Total Roof Area 4800 sq. ft.

BIRD FLYING PAST CARPORT

PRIVATE HOUSE TWO 712 sq. ft. (enclosed) HERE SHOWN AS THREE ROOMS & BATH

TRUSS LINES (SAME TRUSS AS SOCIAL HOUSE)

WASH

SHOP

SLEEP

SLEEP

WALL BROUGHT INSIDE POSTS TO PERMIT SERVICE DECK

PRIVATE HOUSE TWO — HERE SHOWN AS YEAR-ROUND BOATHOUSE

WASH

SHOP

Possible Variations Within Same Structure — from 3 Bedrooms to 3 Boats — or any combination

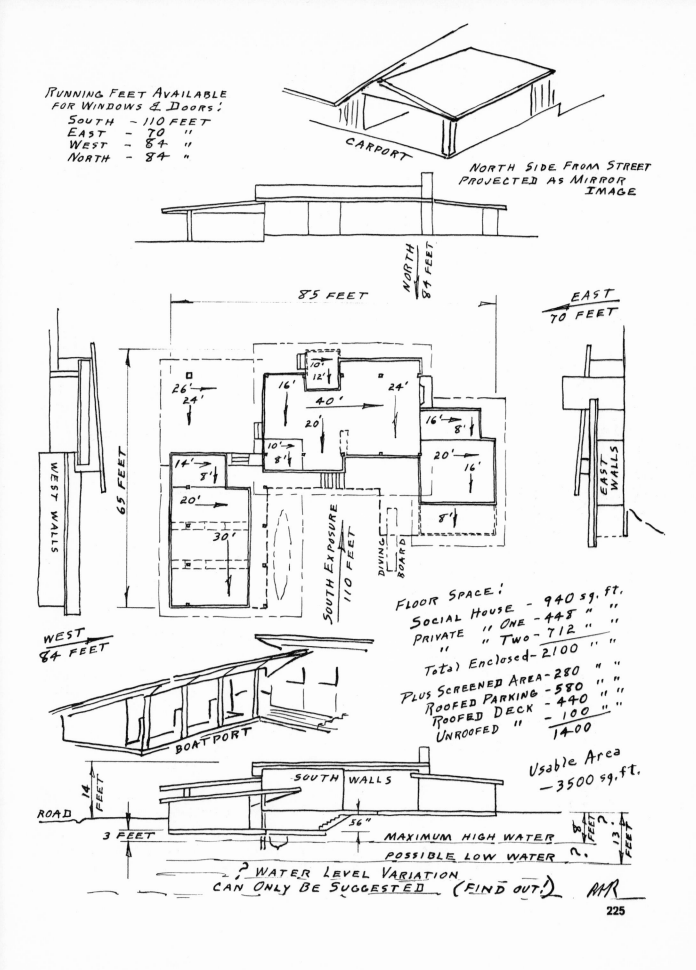

RUNNING FEET AVAILABLE
FOR WINDOWS & DOORS:
SOUTH - 110 FEET
EAST - 70 "
WEST - 84 "
NORTH - 84 "

CARPORT

NORTH SIDE FROM STREET
PROJECTED AS MIRROR
IMAGE

85 FEET

NORTH 84 FEET

EAST 70 FEET

65 FEET

WEST WALLS

EAST WALLS

26' 24'
16'
10'
12'
40'
24'
20'
16' 8'
10'
8'
20'
16'
14'
8'
20'
30'
8'

SOUTH EXPOSURE 110 FEET

DIVING BOARD

WEST 84 FEET

FLOOR SPACE:
SOCIAL HOUSE - 940 sq. ft.
PRIVATE " ONE - 448 " "
" " TWO - 712 " "
TOTAL ENCLOSED - 2100 " "
PLUS SCREENED AREA - 280 " "
ROOFED PARKING - 580 " "
ROOFED DECK - 440 " "
UNROOFED " - 100 " "
1400

USABLE AREA
- 3500 sq. ft.

BOATPORT

14 FEET

ROAD

SOUTH WALLS

3 FEET

56"

MAXIMUM HIGH WATER
POSSIBLE LOW WATER

8 FEET ?
13 FEET ?

? WATER LEVEL VARIATION
CAN ONLY BE SUGGESTED (FIND OUT!)

RMR

A Lost House

"Getting away from it all" ranges, architecturally, all the way from providing for an occasional week-end to taking care of full time living. Because of the variety of demands included in the concept of getting away from it all, the boards, stones, and machines must be competent for all occasions, but adaptable to your mood.

Most people have something of a problem in deciding what they really want the lost house to do. They start out by saying, well, let's toss up a little shack in the woods where we can get away from it all for a couple of weeks in the summer. Having begun this way, they're hooked. They want to get away from it all for a spring week-end, then for a couple of winter week-ends, and then of course there's that trip to look at the fall foliage. Soon their sturdy friends discover the place and want to borrow it for a winter week of skiing. All of a sudden the little shack in the woods is neither large enough nor warm enough.

In the not-very-extreme case, the owners of the little shack in the woods find that with changes in family, occupation, and finance, they want to live there all the time. They regret that the money they've been putting into the place still hasn't made it suitable for full-time survival.

Even if this point is never reached in your case, the uses of your retreat house will inevitably increase. Its value to you will increase in inverse ratio to the time spent getting there. The closer it is, the more you will use it. Four hours' drive up-country may once have been fun, but the five hours getting back never was. Don't put your lost house too far away, and keep some part of it equipped and ready to receive you. The water system should be functioning and some part of the house simmering along at low heat.

Once you possess a lost house, the number of friends who are willing to share it with you seems to keep growing. This delights you, and your house should be capable of sheltering, in some fashion, about four Eff people, or four times the members of your own family.

Since the house was intended to be lost, you will not find it convenient to fix and tend and mend. Your house must take care of itself most of the time, then on demand offer a warm heart of refuge in cold weather and an expandable spread when the thermometer is smiling.

I'll tell you about one serious problem rather than let you find it out later. A full-time house, known to be full-time, can be left the year round with its doors unlocked. Thieves know better than to open an unlocked door. Sad to relate, however, your part-time house, known to be part-time and known to be unobserved (because that's the way you wanted it), becomes a target for every easy-going pilferer who can find his way to Tumble Creek Road. Your lost house requires a come-back-later room where the negotiable valuables can be left in some degree of security.

Don't, please, fall for the notion that you can lose yourself happily at the end of a long, climbing driveway. Come adversity, you won't be able to get there at all. My advice is to lose yourself, if possible, with your entrance driveway at road level. In this particular sketch—again only one of a million possibles—I have suggested that a bench on the side of a mountain, granted level access to the road, makes for getting lost the easy way.

The house can be built in sections, as you get around to it. When you first start to get lost, everything seems easy. In this sketch I have hinted that the stairway to the balcony will be part of the second section. In the hard core beginning, you climb a ladder to your balcony. Some few years later, the children borrow the same ladder to reach their own balcony, while you are entertaining the guests.

The important thing in a lost house is to avoid the little shack beginning. Instead, establish a core of usefulness which is itself adequate for all occasions and all temperatures. From this beginning, you will never have to retreat.

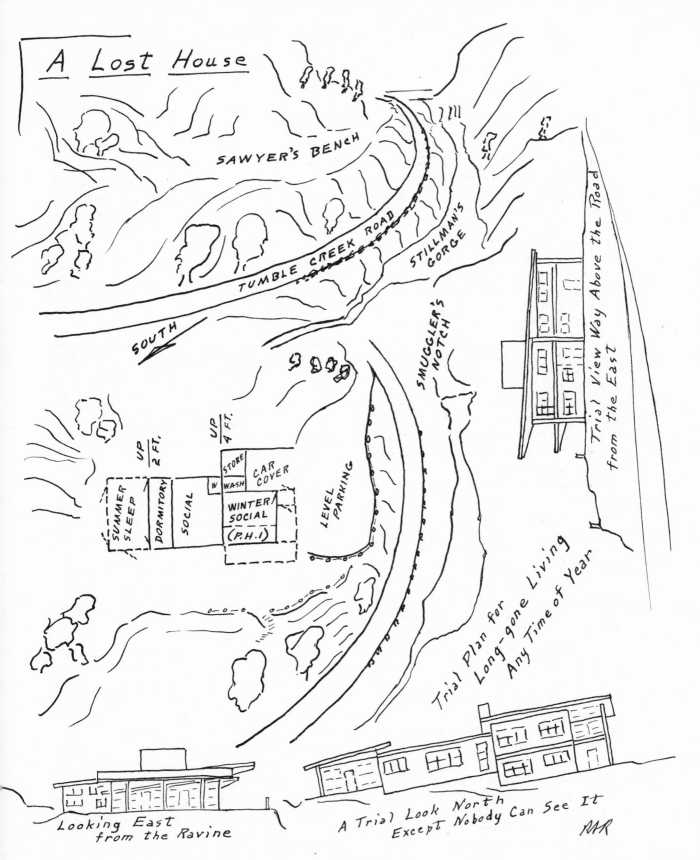

A Lost House

SAWYER'S BENCH

TUMBLE CREEK ROAD

SOUTH

STILLMAN'S GORGE

SMUGGLER'S NOTCH

Trial View Way Above the Road from the East

UP 2 FT.

UP 4 FT.

SUMMER SLEEP

DORMITORY

SOCIAL

STORE

W WASH

CAR COVER

WINTER SOCIAL (P.H.1)

LEVEL PARKING

Trial Plan for Living Long-gone Any Time of Year

Looking East from the Ravine

A Trial Look North Except Nobody Can See It

RAR

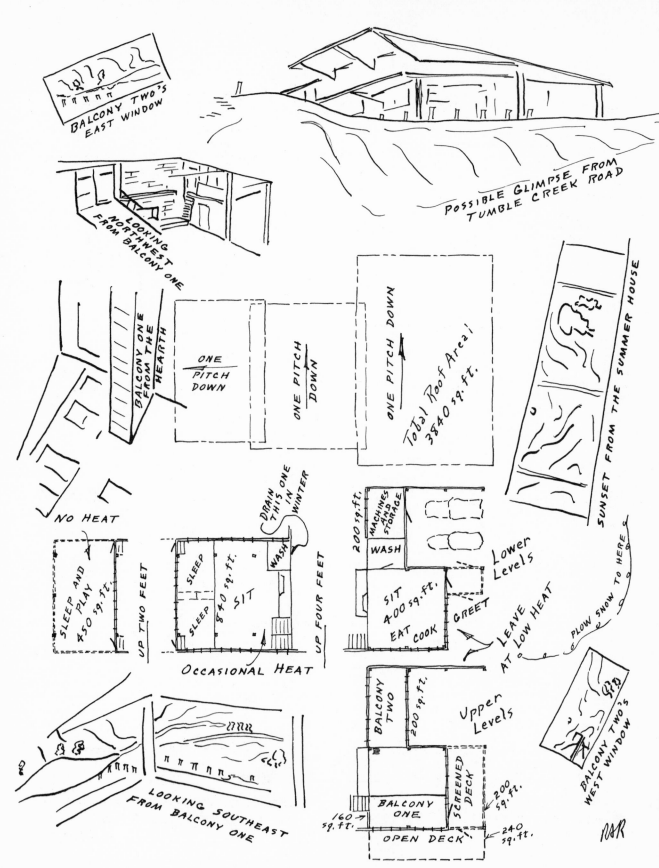

BALCONY TWO'S EAST WINDOW

LOOKING NORTHWEST FROM BALCONY ONE

POSSIBLE GLIMPSE FROM TUMBLE CREEK ROAD

SUNSET FROM THE SUMMER HOUSE

BALCONY ONE FROM THE HEARTH

ONE PITCH DOWN

ONE PITCH DOWN

ONE PITCH DOWN

Total Roof Area: 3840 sq.ft.

NO HEAT

DRAIN THIS ONE IN WINTER

200 sq.ft.

MACHINES AND STORAGE

WASH

Lower Levels

LEAVE AT LOW HEAT

PLOW SNOW TO HERE

SLEEP AND PLAY 450 sq.ft.

UP TWO FEET

SLEEP

SLEEP

840 sq.ft. SIT

WASH

UP FOUR FEET

SIT 400 sq.ft. EAT COOK

GREET

OCCASIONAL HEAT

LOOKING SOUTHEAST FROM BALCONY ONE

BALCONY TWO 200 sq.ft.

Upper Levels

BALCONY TWO'S WEST WINDOW

BALCONY ONE

SCREENED DECK 200 sq.ft.

160 sq.ft.

240 sq.ft.

OPEN DECK

RSR

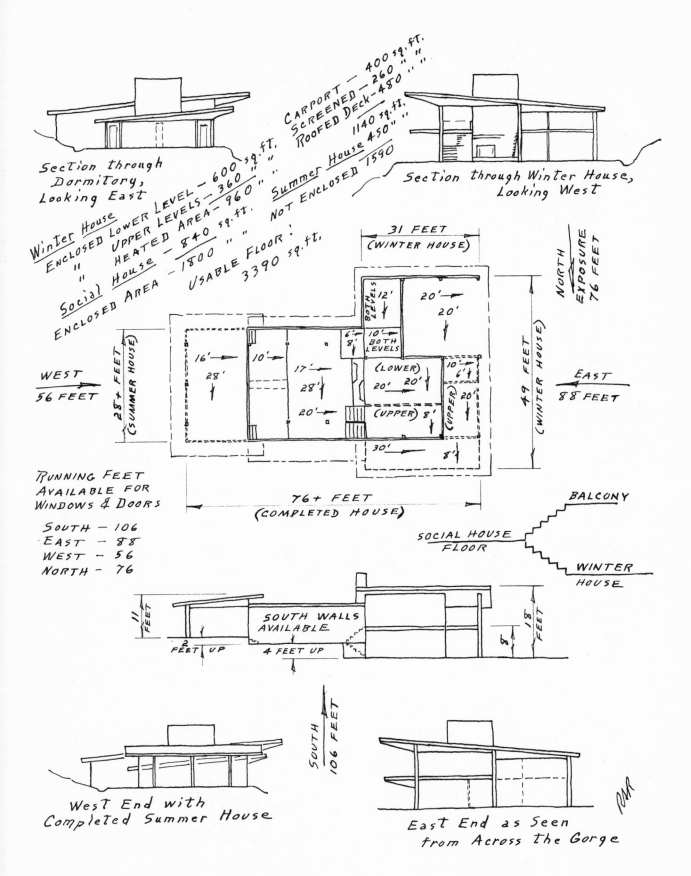

Section through
Dormitory,
Looking East

Winter House
Enclosed Lower Level — 600 sq. ft.   Carport — 400 sq. ft.
"   Upper Levels — 360 " "   Screened — 260 " "
"   Heated Area — 960 " "   Roofed Deck — 480 " "
Social House — 840 sq. ft.   Summer House 450 " "
Enclosed Area — 1800 " "   Not Enclosed 1590   1140 sq. ft.
Usable Floor :
3390 sq. ft.

Section through Winter House,
Looking West

31 FEET
(WINTER HOUSE)

NORTH
EXPOSURE
76 FEET

12'

20'
20'

6'   10'
8'   BOTH
     LEVELS

49 FEET
(WINTER HOUSE)

EAST
88 FEET

16'
28'

10'

17'
28'

20'

(LOWER)
20' 20'

(UPPER)
8'

10'
6'
(UPPER)
20'

WEST
56 FEET

28+ FEET
(SUMMER HOUSE)

30'
8'

RUNNING FEET
AVAILABLE FOR
WINDOWS & DOORS

SOUTH — 106
EAST — 88
WEST — 56
NORTH — 76

76+ FEET
(COMPLETED HOUSE)

BALCONY

SOCIAL HOUSE
FLOOR

WINTER
HOUSE

11
FEET

SOUTH WALLS
AVAILABLE

2
FEET UP

4 FEET UP

8'

18
FEET

SOUTH
106 FEET

West End with
Completed Summer House

East End as Seen
from Across the Gorge

229

INDEX